Forging Arizona

LATINIDAD

Transnational Cultures in the United States

This series publishes books that deepen and expand our understanding of Latina/o populations, especially in the context of their transnational relationships within the Americas. Focusing on borders and boundary crossings, broadly conceived, the series is committed to publishing scholarship in history, film and media, literary and cultural studies, public policy, economics, sociology, and anthropology. Inspired by interdisciplinary approaches, methods, and theories developed out of the study of transborder lives, cultures, and experiences, these titles enrich our understanding of transnational dynamics.

Matt Garcia, Series Editor, Professor of Latin American, Latino, and Caribbean Studies and History, Dartmouth College

For a list of titles in the series, see the last page of the book.

Forging Arizona

A History of the Peralta Land Grant and Racial Identity in the West

Anita Huizar-Hernández

RUTGERS UNIVERSITY PRESS

NEW BRUNSWICK, CAMDEN, AND NEWARK,
NEW JERSEY, AND LONDON

Library of Congress Cataloging-in-Publication Data

Names: Huizar-Hernández, Anita, author.
Title: Forging Arizona : a history of the Peralta land grant and racial identity
in the West / Anita Huizar-Hernández.
Description: New Brunswick : Rutgers University Press, 2019. | Series: Latinidad:
Transnational Cultures in the United States | Includes bibliographical references and
index.
Identifiers: LCCN 2018028958 | ISBN 9780813598826 (cloth) | ISBN 9780813598819 (pbk.)
Subjects: LCSH: Reavis, James Addison, 1843-1914—Claims vs. United States. | Land
grants—Law and legislation—Arizona. | Land tenure—Law and legislation—Arizona. |
Fraud—Arizona—History. | Swindlers and swindling—West (U.S.) | West
(U.S.)—Race relations—History. | Arizona—History—To 1912. | United States.
Court of Private Land Claims.
Classification: LCC KFA2855.5.R43 H85 2019 | DDC 343.791/0253—dc23
LC record available at https://lccn.loc.gov/2018028958

A British Cataloging-in-Publication record for this book is available from the
British Library.

www.rutgersuniversitypress.org

Manufactured in the United States of America

*For Sofia Peralta-Reavis and the many other women of color
whose stories we only glimpse in the archives*

Contents

Forging Arizona

Introduction

In the late nineteenth century, an ex-Confederate soldier from Missouri named James Addison Reavis planned what was going to be the largest swindle in U.S. history: he was going to steal the better part of Arizona. His plan hinged on the treaty that ended the U.S.-Mexican War, the 1848 Treaty of Guadalupe Hidalgo, and its promise to honor Spanish and Mexican land grants in the newly acquired territories so long as their title could be validated in a U.S. court. With these provisions in mind, Reavis decided to fabricate and then present to the U.S. Court of Private Land Claims a fake land grant that stretched for twelve million acres across most of central Arizona and a small part of western New Mexico and included the southern route of the transcontinental railroad, the growing metropolis of Phoenix, and valuable mining and agricultural land (figure 1).[1]

Reavis's counterfeit depended on his ability to prove two things: first, that his invented Peralta Land Grant was a real, verifiable Spanish land grant, and second, that he could claim a right to its title. Both required extensive documentation, so Reavis began a twenty-year mission to forge archival documents around the globe that would prove not only the existence of his spurious claim but also his right to its ownership. To invent the claim, he traveled to Spain and forged colonial archives in order to create a man, Don Miguel Peralta, whose service to the Crown was so distinguished that the king awarded him a tract of land, what would become the Peralta Land Grant, also known as the Barony of Arizona. To invent his right to ownership of said claim, Reavis then forged archives throughout Spain, Mexico, and the southwestern United States to create a chain of inheritance that led to a woman of uncertain parentage named Sofia Treadway, who Reavis affirmed was the long-lost Sofia Peralta, the only living heir to the Peralta Land Grant. Reavis claimed to have met the woman in a chance encounter on a train to Sacramento, during which time he supposedly asked her questions about her family and her childhood that revealed her distinguished

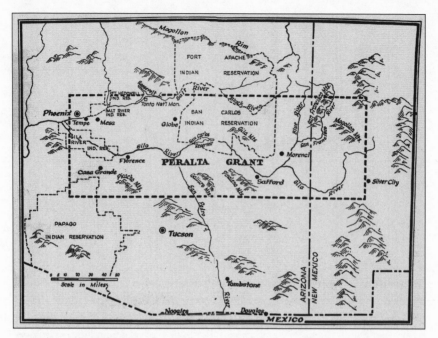

Figure 1. A map of the boundaries of the Peralta Land Grant. Image courtesy of
Special Collections, the University of Arizona Libraries.

lineage. His final step was to connect himself with her fabricated claim, and so
he married her and subsequently presented his invented Peralta Land Grant to
the U.S. Court of Private Land Claims on behalf of his now wife, Doña Sofia
Loreto Peralta-Reavis.

Though today the Peralta Land Grant is all but forgotten, the case garnered
national attention when it came to trial in 1895. From small towns to big cities,
people across the country closely followed the court proceedings in the pages of
their local newspapers. After the case concluded with the dramatic revelation
that Reavis was a con artist and the Peralta Land Grant was a fraud, Reavis's
scheme went from front-page news to fiction, becoming the subject of novels and
films for decades to come. By the second half of the twentieth century, however,
the case began to fade from both popular culture and history books. Now, the
story that once gripped a nation rarely warrants more than a footnote within
the history of Arizona and the settlement of the U.S. West.

COUNTERFEIT NARRATIVES AND WESTWARD EXPANSION

Though the sensational details of the Peralta Land Grant case make it an undoubtedly exciting recovery project, in *Forging Arizona* I argue that the creation,

collapse, and commemoration of Reavis's plot represents much more than an amusing bit of trivia about the Old West. Instead, it is a window into the conditions that produced U.S. westward expansion and the short- and long-term consequences of that expansion. Two earlier book-length studies, both from the 1960s, recover the details of Reavis's elaborate scheme, though without the larger frame I propose here. In *The Peralta Grant* (1960), University of Arizona librarian Donald Powell offers a carefully researched history of the Peralta Land Grant, from Reavis's early plotting to his eventual conviction and imprisonment.[2] In the more narrative-driven *Baron of Arizona* (1967), author E. H. Cockridge builds on Powell's study to create a hybrid text that is part novel, part historical recovery.[3] Cockridge imagines and inserts dialogue into Powell's recovery, but both follow closely the details of the case as they were presented in newspaper clippings, archival documents, and the transcript of the 1895 Court of Private Land Claims trial.

In *Forging Arizona*, I revive the subject of these half-century-old studies with new questions about what the history of the Peralta Land Grant reveals about the relationship between crafting narratives and shifting borders. Though it was not the only contentious land grant case to arise in the years following the U.S.-Mexican War, the Peralta Land Grant is unique in that it was based on falsehood instead of fact, providing a distinct vantage point from which to examine the dynamic relationship between forming narratives and forging borders.[4] The forgeries and fictions on which Reavis based his case form what I call a *counterfeit narrative*, mimicking the logic of the dominant narratives about U.S. westward expansion that erased the Native American, Spanish, and Mexican history of the territory and marginalized its non-Anglo inhabitants.[5] Studying how Reavis attempted to mask his counterfeit narrative as true exposes the inner workings of the dominant narratives he imitated, ultimately revealing how they themselves were fabrications. Certainly, dominant narratives are dominant not because they are true but rather because the people who create and disseminate them are powerful. The fact that Reavis's counterfeit narrative was *almost* believable reveals the precarious nature of historical memory, as well as the perilous power of those who shape it.

By foregrounding counterfeit narratives as a new approach to understanding and contesting the logic of dominant narratives, I add to the large body of ethnic and cultural studies scholarship that has traditionally used counternarratives to dispute the validity of dominant narratives about the history and culture of the United States. The institutionalization of ethnic studies as an academic discipline in the United States grew out of the civil rights movements of the 1960s and 1970s. Since that time, scholars working in Chicanx/Latinx, Native American, African American, and Asian American studies have turned to archives, oral histories, autoethnography, and fiction in order to preserve and present the marginalization of these communities, as well as their strategies and practices of resistance. In the U.S. West and Southwest,[6] these studies have brought to light long histories of displacement and discrimination, as well as struggles to demand just treatment.[7]

I propose that examining the history of the Peralta Land Grant, from the creation and collapse of Reavis's counterfeit narrative to its subsequent fictionalization and eventual disappearance from the national imaginary, provides a related yet unique window into the conditions and consequences of U.S. westward expansion. The uncertainty westward expansion created surrounding land titles allowed Reavis to convince everyone from homesteaders to powerful business leaders that his obviously fraudulent Peralta Land Grant was real. Likewise, the instability that westward expansion provoked with regard to race, citizenship, and national identity allowed Reavis to convince those same people that his wife was not a mixed-race orphan named Sofia Treadway but rather a landholding Spanish baroness named Doña Sofia Loreto Peralta-Reavis. The robust recovery of the Peralta Land Grant case and Peralta-Reavis's role within it therefore challenges what Latinx studies scholar Rodrigo Lazo describes as "a tendency in U.S. society to exclude or forget certain cultural and political resonances, particularly those that emerge from immigrant communities whose populations are not easily integrated into an Anglo or a black/white conception of the nation."[8] These forgotten cultural and political resonances include the hemispheric collisions brought about by the U.S.-Mexican War, which unsettled the temporal and spatial borders of the U.S. Southwest, and how that unsettlement impacted the people living there.[9] Retracing the elaboration, repudiation, fictionalization, and eventual forgetting of Reavis's counterfeit narrative about the Peralta Land Grant and its purported owner exposes how the racial, gender, and class ideologies that underpinned westward expansion have shaped the borders of the United States since the nineteenth century and continue to frame the limits of national identity today.

LATINX HISTORY AND THE ARCHIVE(S)

The archives are at the center of Reavis's counterfeit narrative and, consequently, my analysis here. In this regard, *Forging Arizona* joins a large body of scholarship emerging from Latinx studies that engages the archives to recover the understudied history of Latinx people in the United States. The Recovering the U.S. Hispanic Literary Heritage Project is one of the most successful examples of this type of coordinated effort "to locate, preserve and disseminate" the textual traces of this geographically, linguistically, and ethnically diverse community. The now considerable collection of recovered documents has fundamentally altered scholarship on the history of Latinx people in the United States, particularly during the nineteenth and early twentieth centuries, profoundly shifting how we understand this foundational period of U.S. history and undermining ahistorical claims that Latinx people are new arrivals.[10]

My framing the history of the Peralta Land Grant in terms of what archives can reveal about Latinx history may seem unconventional for two reasons. First, there are no Latinx people actually involved in the case. Sofia Peralta-Reavis in all likelihood had no claim to either Spanish or Mexican ancestry. Second, the archive that is at the center of the Peralta Land Grant story is a fictional one. Reavis fraudulently altered Spanish, Mexican, and U.S. archival records to weave his counterfeit narrative about Miguel Peralta, the Peralta Land Grant, and Sofia Peralta. Nevertheless, in *Forging Arizona* I argue that it is precisely because of these inventions that the Peralta Land Grant is a valuable case study for scholars, taking the fabricated nature of both racial categories and the archives that define them to their (il)logical extremes.

Reavis exploited the archives in order to create a record of a history that never happened, in the process exposing the slippage between the past and its archival traces. Challenging the gap between history and its record has been a key concern for scholars participating in the so-called archival turn within the humanities and social sciences.[11] The "move from archive-as-source to archive-as-subject," as Ann Laura Stoler describes it, is most notably associated with French theorist Jacques Derrida's influential *Archive Fever: A Freudian Impression* (1996) and has prompted an interdisciplinary interrogation of how what is included and excluded from archives shapes historical narratives and power relations.[12] As archival studies scholar Michelle Caswell has noted, however, this archival turn in the humanities and social sciences has largely failed to connect with parallel conversations happening within the archival sciences, creating a disconnect between "critiquing 'the archive'" and engaging "archives—emphasis on the 's'"—as "collections of records, material and immaterial, analog and digital . . . the institutions that steward them, the places where they are physically located, and the processes that designated them 'archival.'"[13] Despite this disconnect, many critiques emerging from the archival sciences are similarly invested in rethinking how to approach the archives, including how to account for its many gaps, silences, and omissions.[14]

In *Forging Arizona*, I endeavor to bridge the divide of scholars engaging the metaphorical and material archive(s) in the falsified archive of the Peralta Land Grant. Though a fake archive may seem like an odd place from which to consider actual archives, the fraudulent nature of the Peralta Land Grant archive invites a critical examination of both the archive as abstraction and the archives as physical collections. With regard to the archive as abstraction, I build on the work of postcolonial, feminist, and queer studies scholars who have theorized how to approach the archive's gaps and omissions, from Stoler's appeal to read "along the archival grain" to expose the inner workings of colonial regimes and their logics to the calls of Chicana feminist historians Emma Pérez and Maylei Blackwell to work against the archive by engaging a "decolonial imaginary" and activating a "retrofitted memory," respectively.[15] Drawing from these scholars,

I propose counterfeit narratives as an analytic that takes seriously not only the omissions but also the outright fictions that are *always* inherent within the archive because of its very nature as a constructed representation of the past. By grounding this discussion in a concrete consideration of how archives are actually constructed, I connect my critique with the recent reformulations proposed by scholars in the archival sciences regarding the fundamental principles of and approaches to the archives. In particular, I draw from postmodern theorists who question both the evidentiary value of archives and the neutral role of the archivist.[16]

In addition to building on these interdisciplinary conversations about how to account for the limits of the archive(s), my analysis of the Peralta Land Grant also joins the work of scholars who have recently used the archives as a catalyst for imagination and speculation. In particular, I draw from literary scholars Anna Brickhouse and Raúl Coronado, whose work engages the archives in order to reimagine the trajectory of the conquest and formation of the Americas. Following Brickhouse's *Unsettlement of America: Translation, Interpretation, and the Story of Don Luis de Velasco, 1560–1945* (2014), in which she proposes *unsettlement* as a term that "signals not merely the contingency and noninevitability but also the glaring incompleteness of the history of the New World as we currently know and write it," I argue that the Peralta Land Grant unsettles the history of the U.S. Southwest, revealing not only the incompleteness but also utter inaccuracy of how that history has been and continues to be told.[17] In this way, my recovery of Reavis's plan to forge archives to invent and claim a fake Spanish land grant responds to Coronado's proposal in *A World Not to Come: A History of Latino Writing and Print Culture* (2013) that we can "learn from the history of unrealized aspirations," as Reavis's near success prompts a reconsideration not only of what is true but also what is false about our understanding of southwestern settlement.[18]

RACIAL IDENTITY AND MANIFEST DESTINY

Reavis's counterfeit Peralta Land Grant narrative exploited the wide gap that separated the myths from the realities of U.S. westward expansion. The doctrine of Manifest Destiny justified and normalized the rapid expansion of the United States from thirteen small colonies clustered along the Eastern Seaboard to a large collection of states and territories that stretched across the North American continent and extended overseas to islands in the Pacific and Atlantic Oceans. Grounded in religious and racial ideologies, Manifest Destiny contended that as an Anglo, Christian nation, the United States was destined to expand and extend its superior form of government beyond its current borders. Aside from the obvious prejudice that is inherent in such an assertion, the doctrine of Manifest Destiny justified U.S. expansion through a variety of contradictory claims.

On the one hand, it characterized the land that lay to the west as a *terra nullius* that was free for the taking, unhampered by other people and pasts. On the other hand, it also justified U.S. expansion by affirming that it would civilize inferior communities and forms of government, implying that the land the United States planned to take over was not in fact unoccupied.[19]

Reavis depended on the ignorance that each of these contradictory claims bred in order to convince people that his falsified history of the Peralta Land Grant was true. Using these broad misconceptions about the land and people of the West to conceal his counterfeit, Reavis set out to abuse the terms of the 1848 Treaty of Guadalupe Hidalgo, the treaty that ended the war between the United States and Mexico and resulted in the United States' acquisition of nearly half of Mexico's territory.[20] Reavis's power of persuasion hinged on the cognitive dissonance and outright confusion that the U.S.-Mexican War created regarding how to incorporate not only new land but also new people within a U.S. national identity that was built on linguistic, cultural, and racial exclusion. As U.S. settlers quickly learned, the formerly Mexican land was not a *terra nullius* but rather filled with complex multiethnic communities. The Treaty of Guadalupe Hidalgo offered some members of these communities access to citizenship and its accordant rights, including the right to property.[21] The treaty further stipulated that the United States would respect all Spanish and Mexican land claims, so long as they could be verified. As a result, the dominant narrative that emerged from the U.S.-Mexican War was that the United States respected the rights of Mexicans (though, importantly, not Native Americans living in the acquired territories) and made them equal citizens of their new nation.[22]

However, scholars have turned to counternarratives to demonstrate how Mexicans' supposedly guaranteed rights were undermined in the aftermath of the war. Richard Griswold del Castillo's groundbreaking study *The Treaty of Guadalupe Hidalgo: A Legacy of Conflict* (1990) carefully traces the disenfranchisement of Mexicans in the aftermath of the war. He reveals the legal processes through which landowners lost their holdings, detailing how their land claims languished in legal limbo for years and forced many to mortgage and eventually lose their land to finance complex and expensive litigation.[23] Building on Griswold del Castillo's work, in *Telling Identities: The Californio Testimonios* (1995), Rosaura Sánchez turns to the archives to analyze counternarratives of westward expansion offered by thirty Spanish-speaking Californios in the years following the U.S.-Mexican War. Sánchez's analysis shows how the *testimonios* document and resist the dispossession and marginalization of Mexicans under U.S. control.[24] Since the publication of *Telling Identities*, many scholars have mined the archives in order to recover the diversity of experiences of men and women living in the ceded Mexican territory, producing works such as Deena J. González's *Refusing the Favor: The Spanish-Mexican Women of Santa Fe 1820–1880* (1999), Miroslava Chávez-García's *Negotiating Conquest: Gender and Power in*

California, 1770s to 1880s (2004), María Raquél Casas's *Married to a Daughter of the Land: Spanish-Mexican Women and Interethnic Marriage in California, 1820–1880* (2007), Raúl A. Ramos's *Beyond the Alamo: Forging Mexican Ethnicity in San Antonio, 1821–1861* (2008), Anthony Mora's *Border Dilemmas: Racial and National Uncertainties in New Mexico, 1848–1912* (2011), Omar S. Valerio-Jiménez's *River of Hope: Forging Identity and Nation in the Rio Grande Borderlands* (2013), and Karen R. Roybal's *Archives of Dispossession: Recovering the Testimonios of Mexican American Herederas, 1848–1960* (2017).

My examination of Reavis's counterfeit land claim complements these studies by shifting the focus from U.S. treatment of the conquered peoples living in the ceded territory to the internal discordance of U.S. expansionist policies and ideology. Reavis's counterfeit narrative was only possible because of the contradictions inherent within the dominant narrative of Manifest Destiny that justified the war. Because Reavis's victims were under the impression that the land was a *terra nullius*, they were ignorant of its transnational history.[25] When confronted with an elaborate story about a Spanish baron who was given the land, which was then supplemented by mounds of official-looking archival documents, they lacked sufficient knowledge of Spanish and Mexican history to determine that the story was forged.

What is more, their ignorance of the Spanish and then Mexican communities that had lived in the land for centuries and the Native Americans that had lived there for thousands of years made Reavis's victims unable to evaluate the genealogy Reavis forged for his wife, Sofia Peralta-Reavis, the supposed heiress. Though Reavis was the architect of the Peralta Land Grant plot, Peralta-Reavis was its cornerstone, and it is through her that the impact of westward expansion on not only the physical but also the cultural borders of the United States comes into sharp relief. At the Peralta Land Grant trial and in the newspaper coverage and subsequent fictionalizations of the case, Peralta-Reavis's racial identity is simultaneously the linchpin of the plot and the only aspect of the case that was never fully resolved. While the archival records Reavis forged were thoroughly discredited at the trial, Peralta-Reavis's true identity remained a mystery. Though the court determined that she was not the heiress to the Peralta Land Grant (because it never existed), it refused to rule on the validity of the government attorney's assertion that Peralta-Reavis was the illegitimate daughter of an Anglo settler and a Native American woman. That is to say, it was clear who Peralta-Reavis was not, but not who she was. Tracking the evolution of the debates surrounding who Peralta-Reavis was over the course of the century that separates the trial from the present day reveals the shifting trajectories of U.S. racial regimes and their relationship to constructions of citizenship and belonging, especially in the Southwest.

The contemporaneous documentation that emerged as the case unfolded in the 1890s shows how in the immediate aftermath of the U.S.-Mexican War, despite the legal guarantees of the Treaty of Guadalupe Hidalgo, the citizenship status and rights of the former Mexicans were precarious thanks to their ambiguous racialization. The uncertainty surrounding Peralta-Reavis's racial identity in both the trial transcript and the newspaper coverage demonstrates that although Mexicans were legally considered white, their everyday racialization was in fact vague. Laura E. Gómez describes their racialization as "off-white," meaning that the recognition of their rights as citizens was uneven.[26] This confusion was partially the result of the collision between U.S. and Spanish racial regimes in the West. The United States used a binary system that classified people as either black or white, categorizing anyone with even one drop of nonwhite blood as wholly not white.[27] This U.S. model contrasted sharply with the Spanish system, which recognized a complex assortment of identities that were classified according to various permutations of specific racial mixtures.[28] The result of these colliding paradigms was a legal and cultural gray area that fomented discrimination against Mexican people.

This discrimination stemmed from Mexicans' connection to indigeneity. As Natalia Molina explains, "After the U.S. War with Mexico . . . Mexicans entered the United States linked to two competing racial scripts: indigeneity and whiteness. The war and the ideology of Manifest Destiny that justified it highlighted Mexicans' inferior racial position due to their indigenous roots. But in the aftermath of the war, under the Treaty of Guadalupe Hidalgo, Mexicans residing in the acquired territories were offered U.S. citizenship, a privilege extended only to whites at the time. These conflicting scripts that simultaneously marked them as legally white but socially and culturally 'other' and inferior would serve to complicate their status for generations to come."[29] In response, some Mexican Americans chose to associate themselves solely with Spanish ancestry, denying any connection to indigenous roots.

Peralta-Reavis was thus not the only person to appeal to a Spanish heritage in order to avoid racial discrimination by distancing herself from an indigenous heritage. Mexicans throughout the Southwest strategically emphasized their Spanish ancestry, what Carey McWilliams calls the "fantasy heritage" and Raymund Paredes the "hacienda syndrome."[30] This racial reframing was a survival mechanism, as Martha Menchaca explains: "Given the nature of the U.S. racial system and its laws, the conquered Mexican population learned that it was politically expedient to assert their Spanish ancestry."[31] These racial politics were clear at the Peralta Land Grant trial, as much of the debate regarding the legitimacy of the land claim had less to do with the validity of the grant itself and more to do with the validity of Peralta-Reavis's Spanish heritage—that is to say, her racial identity.

As time went on, the uncertainty that characterized the initial reaction to Peralta-Reavis's racial identity in the late nineteenth century faded. In the later fictional adaptations of the Peralta Land Grant saga, she is unequivocally

portrayed as someone with "Indian blood." As historians Katherine Benton-
Cohen and Eric V. Meeks have shown, over the course of the twentieth century,
in Arizona the borders that divided Anglo, Mexican, and Native American racial
identity hardened.[32] At the same time, the racialized myths that underpinned
the doctrine of Manifest Destiny became enshrined as fact, and the history of
the settlement of the West transformed into a dominant narrative of Anglo
superiority.[33] These hardening racial boundaries and hierarchies are evident
in the changing depiction of Peralta-Reavis's racial identity. Whereas discus-
sions of her racial identity are nuanced in the late nineteenth-century trial transcript and newspaper coverage, by the mid-twentieth century, she is portrayed
in fictional adaptations as a stereotypically tragic "mixed blood."

Eventually, Peralta-Reavis's racial identity, and the history of the Peralta Land
Grant in general, faded from memory altogether. Though this could be interpreted as a natural result of the passage of time, I argue that the broader implications of Reavis's counterfeit narrative ensure that the history of the Peralta
Land Grant is not simply forgotten; it *cannot* be remembered precisely because
it points to the instability and inaccuracy of dominant narratives about race,
citizenship, and U.S. expansion. Reavis's counterfeit narrative unsettles those
dominant narratives that are foundational to U.S. national identity, plainly demonstrating how borders, both physical and cultural, are only as stable as the
narratives that define them.

RACE, STATEHOOD, AND CITIZENSHIP IN ARIZONA

In *Forging Arizona*, as the title suggests, I foreground Arizona's role in the development of these dominant narratives about U.S. expansion and national identity.
The forgetting of the Peralta Land Grant saga is in many ways a metaphor for the
erasure of the history of the state in which it took place. This erasure has been
performed by groups across the political spectrum, from white supremacists who
seek to suppress Arizona's multiethnic heritage to academics who have over-
looked the state as an important site for study. Just as I argue that the forgetting of
the Peralta Land Grant suggests an unwillingness to engage with the racialized
underpinnings of westward expansion, I contend that the forgetting of Arizona
history suggests an unwillingness to engage with the state's long-standing role as
a flashpoint for national debates about citizenship and belonging.

Arizona has been at the center of disputes over the physical and cultural borders of the nation since its incorporation into the United States at the end of the
U.S.-Mexican War. While gold-rich California was granted statehood shortly
after the war's end, Arizona and New Mexico both languished in territorial status from 1848 to 1912. During these sixty-four years, territorial leaders from
both political parties actively and repeatedly lobbied federal lawmakers in order
to convince them that the Arizona Territory was fit for statehood.[34] Time and

again these national legislators rejected the territorial leaders' requests, citing concerns regarding territorial Arizona's demographics—namely, its large non-Anglo population.[35]

In response to this hesitation, Arizona's territorial leaders elaborated their own counterfeit narrative. They quantitatively and qualitatively minimized the state's non-Anglo, primarily Mexican and Native American, population, arguing that they were too insignificant to pose a threat to the racialized borders of U.S. national identity. Their counterfeit narrative of Arizona as a *terra nullius* discovered and developed by Anglo pioneers became the foundational fiction of the state,[36] "built into the very identity of Arizona from its inception," as Meeks affirms.[37] Territorial leaders minimized, negated, and even erased Arizona's multiethnic history, replacing it with a counterfeit history that featured U.S. Anglo pioneers at its center.[38] It was this counterfeit history that enabled Reavis's near success, as widespread ignorance of the history of the territory and its people prevented his victims from identifying the many unbelievable aspects of his story.

In recent decades, the ugly consequences of this counterfeit history were made plain in the passage of two controversial pieces of legislation: Arizona Senate Bill 1070 and Arizona House Bill 2281. On April 23, 2010, Arizona governor Jan Brewer signed the Support Our Law Enforcement and Safe Neighborhoods Act, otherwise known as Senate Bill 1070, which was meant to bolster the enforcement of federal immigration law within Arizona by "mak[ing] attrition through enforcement the public policy of all state and local government agencies in Arizona."[39] According to the governor and her supporters, the federal government had failed to address the "crisis caused by illegal immigration and Arizona's porous border," forcing the state to take matters into its own hands to secure its border.[40] The law made it a misdemeanor crime to be in Arizona without proper documentation, required law enforcement officers to inquire about a person's status if there was "reasonable suspicion" that he or she was in the state illegally, and penalized those who prevented in any way the full enforcement of federal immigration law.[41] SB 1070 reified the counterfeit narrative of Arizona history, mandating the policing of the borders that its whitewashed history established.

Immediately, supporters and opponents of the law sprang up across the country, voicing their opinions in newspapers, on television, and in the streets. Supporters applauded Arizona's determination to enforce federal immigration policy and take a stand against undocumented immigration. Opponents, on the other hand, rallied and railed against what they deemed the "show me your papers" law, marching in protest and calling for a boycott of the state. Many of the protests and calls for boycotts focused on section 2B of the law, which required law enforcement officials and agencies within the state to make "a reasonable attempt . . . when practicable, to determine the immigration status" of any person with whom they had lawful contact when there was "reasonable suspicion that the person [could be] an alien who is unlawfully present in the United States."[42] Though Governor Brewer and fellow supporters of the law argued that this clause did not authorize racial profiling, opponents contended that race was the law's implicit metric for determining reasonable suspicion of a person's legal status.

Less than a month later, on May 11, 2010, Brewer signed House Bill 2281. While SB 1070 targeted immigration, HB 2281 targeted education, prohibiting the teaching of ethnic studies in Arizona's public schools. The law, written by school superintendent Tom Horne and carried out by his successor John Huppenthal, was meant to target Tucson's Mexican American studies program. The program was found to be in violation of HB 2281, which prohibited any courses that "promote the overthrow of the United States government, promote resentment toward a race or class of people, are designed primarily for pupils of a particular ethnic group, [and] advocate ethnic solidarity instead of the treatment of pupils as individuals."[43] HB 2281 also stipulated that the state would withhold up to 10 percent of the monthly funding of any district found to be in violation of the law. Not willing to lose such a significant portion of an already reduced budget, the Tucson Unified School District eliminated the Mexican American studies program from its curriculum.

Students and teachers denied that the Tucson Mexican American studies program violated HB 2281, maintaining that the program had a positive, not negative, impact on students. An audit commissioned by Huppenthal and carried out by the Cambium Learning Group supported their position; the auditors found "no observable evidence . . . to suggest that any classroom within the Tucson Unified School District is in direct violation of the law."[44] Seven years later, a federal judge found "that the state showed discriminatory intent" when it targeted the program, affirming that "both enactment and enforcement were motivated by racial animus."[45] Again, the acceptance of the counterfeit narrative about the state's past was what allowed politicians like Horne and Huppenthal to assert that the curriculum of the Mexican American studies program was antithetical, as opposed to integral, to Arizona's educational priorities.

Although people across the country expressed their support or opposition to SB 1070 and HB 2281, few asked, Why Arizona? In the aftermath of the controversial passing and implementation of both laws, Arizona became synonymous with civil rights abuses, discrimination, and racism. Late-night comedians made the state the butt of their jokes, and some opponents even suggested Arizona secede from the union. However, the demonization and dismissal of Arizona also facilitated a denial of the state's complex history and its relationship to the rest of the country. In the years since the passage of SB 1070 and HB 2281, growing xenophobia and white supremacist rhetoric on a national level have proved that Arizona is not the exception to but rather the epitome of national(ist) ideologies that have always exceeded the state's borders.

Still, I argue that Arizona was a fertile proving ground for these racist ide-ologies precisely because of the widespread ignorance of the state's history. In comparison with its neighboring southwestern states, Arizona has long been neglected in the fields of literature, history, Chicanx/Latinx, and American studies. My recovery of the Peralta Land Grant case joins the growing body of scholarship that seeks to fill these gaps by tracing a genealogy of Arizona's politi-cal, economic, and cultural formation, including Meeks's *Border Citizens: The Making of Indians, Mexicans, and Anglos in Arizona* (2007), Benton-Cohen's *Borderline Americans: Racial Division and Labor War in the Arizona Border-lands* (2009), and Geraldo L. Cadava's *Standing on Common Ground: The Mak-ing of a Sunbelt Borderland* (2013). In *Forging Arizona*, I add an important dimension to these critical histories by emphasizing and analyzing cultural production. The focus of this book is not on specific events but rather on the narrative telling and retelling of particular stories—both real and imagined—in the archives, in the press, in fiction, and in film. *Forging Arizona* is therefore a close examination of how narratives are formed and disseminated and the concrete consequences they produce.

INVENTING, REMEMBERING, AND FORGETTING
THE PERALTA LAND GRANT

The remainder of this book is organized into two parts. Part I, Inventing the Per-alta Land Grant, follows the late nineteenth-century story of the falsified claim, from Reavis's archival forgeries to the trial at the U.S. Court of Private Land Claims and eventual exposure of Reavis's fraud. Chapter 1 examines the archi-val evidence Reavis forged to prove the validity of his claim, arguing that its pre-sumed authenticity points less to Reavis's skills as a forger, which were both limited and flawed, and more to the striking ignorance of would-be investors and homesteaders about where the Peralta Land Grant was located. The chapter begins with the 1890 *Adverse Report of the Surveyor General of Arizona, Royal A. Johnson, upon the Alleged "Peralta Grant": A Complete Expose of Its Fraudulent Character*, which carefully rehearses the many irregularities and inconsistencies that plagued the Peralta Land Grant papers and, in Johnson's estimation, defin-itively discredited Reavis's claim.[46] Johnson's *Adverse Report* did not, however, deter Reavis, nor did it discourage the powerful investors who supported him.

To account for the temporary success of Reavis's counterfeit narrative despite its obvious flaws, I investigate the assumptions about archives and westward expansion on which it depended. The contrast between Johnson's unequivocal repudiation of the archival evidence Reavis presented and the public's initial acceptance of the Peralta papers' validity points to a fundamental distinction in how archives are understood, either as object or as source. Johnson's interrogation of the Peralta Land Grant papers shows that archives are objects that are formed, not in all cases by a con artist but certainly always by those who establish their records and curate their content. At the same time, the public's assumption that the Peralta Land Grant papers were valid simply because they resided in archives reveals an understanding of archives not as object but rather as the source of information. Examining the varied strategies Reavis employed to alter the archival record demonstrates how archives are not static sources but instead malleable objects whose content is always to a certain extent an invention. The credibility of the content of Reavis's forgeries equally relied on another invention, that of the United States' manifest destiny to expand westward into a virgin land. The doctrine of Manifest Destiny erased the history of pre-Anglo settlement in the Southwest, preventing Reavis's victims from recognizing the palpably forged nature of his counterfeit narrative about a Spanish land grant that was inexplicably large, perfectly rectangular, and unfamiliar to everyone. By placing Reavis's forgeries in this broader context, I trace their importance to the settlement of the West and its ramifications for both archives and the historical narratives they produce.

Chapter 2 shifts focus from the documents Reavis forged to the identity he invented for his wife and supposed heiress to the Peralta Land Grant, Sofia Peralta-Reavis. Because of the central role her identity played in her husband's con, the 1895 trial to confirm Reavis's counterfeit land claim transformed into a hotly contested debate over Peralta-Reavis's claim that she was the Spanish heiress to the vast and valuable grant. This chapter uses the trial transcript to recover the woman at the center of the scandal, arguing that Peralta-Reavis's fraudulent embodiment of a wealthy Spanish baroness unmasks the fluidity and fragility of racial categories, gender, and authenticity in the late nineteenth-century Southwest. Though the government did eventually prove that Peralta-Reavis was not in any sense who she claimed to be, the conversations surrounding her identity reveal lingering anxieties about how the U.S.-Mexican War altered not only the physical but also the cultural borders of the United States, and what the lasting consequences of those shifted borders would be. Read in this way, the Peralta Land Grant trial transcript archives not only a historical land fraud but also the fault lines of the late nineteenth-century U.S. racial imaginary.

The final chapter of part I traces the evolution of the public reaction to the Peralta Land Grant by turning to its coverage in newspapers. Before, during, and after the 1895 trial, people evaluated the legitimacy of Reavis's counterfeit narrative by following the developments of the case in their local newspapers. Though today the Peralta Land Grant case is all but forgotten, it dominated newspaper headlines in financial centers like New York and San Francisco and seemingly every city in between for the better part of two decades, from the mid-1880s to the early 1900s. Just as people today are entranced by fake news, people across the political spectrum were fascinated by the false story that Reavis invented about his wife the baroness and her claim to a Spanish land grant. When Reavis's story turned out not to be true, newspapers embellished the actual history of what happened with their own accounts of how Reavis and particularly his wife, Peralta-Reavis, had nearly won and then lost a fortune. The coverage developed its own counterfeit narrative that was not accountable to facts, instead underlining the desirability of upholding national fictions about race, gender, and class and foreshadowing how the Peralta Land Grant would evolve from legal debate to legend.

Part II, (Re)membering the Peralta Land Grant, transitions from immediate to retrospective reactions to Reavis's infamous fraud. While part I examined the historical import and impact of the Peralta Land Grant plot by closely reading Reavis's forgeries, the trial transcript, and newspaper coverage, part II reads later fictionalizations of Reavis's scheme as markers of how racialized narratives about U.S. empire evolved in the years following the official closure of the frontier and the commencement of U.S. formal and informal expansion overseas. Chapter 4 considers how William Atherton DuPuy's 1940 novel *The Baron of the Colorados* uses the Peralta Land Grant story to consolidate a nativist nostalgia about the settlement of the U.S. West. In the novel, DuPuy deploys what I call a counterfeit nostalgia about the settlement of Arizona in particular and U.S. continental and overseas expansion in general that remembers expansion as inevitable and unobstructed in the past in order to legitimize continued Anglo hegemony in the present and future. In his own twentieth-century moment of change, DuPuy returns to the late nineteenth-century period to ground his Peralta Land Grant story in a familiar narrative of Anglo superiority, celebrating not only the triumphs of Arizona's (Anglo) past but also the promises of its (Anglo) future. In his fictionalized retelling, DuPuy demonstrates how counterfeit nostalgia is central to the enduring logic of Manifest Destiny and its political, economic, and cultural consequences on the continent and around the globe.

Chapter 5 moves from the page to the screen, examining how Samuel Fuller's 1950 B movie *The Baron of Arizona* charts the long-term instability not only of Reavis's counterfeit Peralta Land Grant narrative but also of the contradictions inherent within the dominant narratives about U.S. westward expansion on which it relied. Though *The Baron of Arizona* has never garnered significant critical attention, its complex, confusing, and even contradictory presentation of key aspects of the Peralta Land Grant saga importantly reflects how the story lived on as legend long after the actual court case concluded. The film's presentation of Peralta-Reavis's contested identity, the settlers' hostility toward Reavis and Peralta-Reavis and their Peralta Land Grant, and Peralta-Reavis and Reavis's unorthodox romance dramatizes the afterlives of late nineteenth-century ideologies about Manifest Destiny, race, and the western frontier. By exploring all of these themes without offering a clear message about any of them, *The Baron of Arizona* reveals the continued irresolvability of questions about race, gender, and land rights that remain at the center not only of the case but also of the settlement of the West in general, and Arizona in particular.

Finally, in the epilogue I consider the forgetting of the Peralta Land Grant in the context of the erasure of the multiethnic history of the region in which it was supposedly located. As each of the chapters demonstrates, questions regarding the relationship between race and place were at the heart not only of the Peralta Land Grant saga but also of the evolving mythology of the settlement of the western frontier. The shifting narratives describing the Peralta Land Grant, from the original counterfeit narrative Reavis enshrined in the archives to the way that counterfeit narrative was presented at the trial and in the pages of newspapers to how it was fictionalized in DuPuy's novel and Fuller's film, parallel the shifting cultural and physical boundaries of the nation. As the U.S.-Mexican War and the changes it provoked grew distant, the mythology surrounding U.S. expansion quelled the contradictions inherent within the incorporation of new lands and people, first through distortion and then through outright erasure. The creation, alteration, and ultimate forgetting of the Peralta Land Grant provide a window into the inner workings of the myths of westward expansion and expose how they continue to reverberate in debates defining the borders of the United States today.

PART I

INVENTING THE
PERALTA LAND GRANT

CHAPTER 1

Counterfeit Narratives

THE PERALTA LAND GRANT ARCHIVES
AND THE FORGING OF THE WEST

On March 27, 1883, armed with facsimiles of forged maps, wills, codicils, and baptismal records that he had fraudulently inserted into archives around the world, James Addison Reavis presented his claim to the Peralta Land Grant to the U.S. government for confirmation.[1] Reavis had spent over a decade traveling to archives throughout Spain, Mexico, and the U.S. Southwest, physically altering official government records in order to create the fictitious Peralta Land Grant, which covered nearly all of central Arizona and part of western New Mexico Territory. When he presented his claim to the grant for confirmation, the mountains of evidence he provided to prove both the existence of the Peralta Land Grant and his ownership of it were then turned over to the surveyor general of Arizona's office, which was charged with investigating the legitimacy of the documents and the land grant they described.[2] Surveyor General Joseph W. Robbins began the investigation but soon died of tuberculosis, at which point his clerk, a man named Royal A. Johnson, took over the office and the high-profile Peralta Land Grant case.[3] Johnson was an attorney from the East Coast who had worked in Washington, traveled in South America, and eventually settled in the territory of Arizona.[4] He was known for his methodical work, and his time-consuming investigation of the Peralta Land Grant frustrated both Reavis and the anxious Arizona homesteaders he threatened to displace should his title be confirmed.[5] After six long years and several interruptions,[6] Johnson finally published his carefully researched and long-awaited findings in his 1890 *Adverse Report of the Surveyor General of Arizona, Royal A. Johnson, upon the Alleged "Peralta Grant": A Complete Expose of Its Fraudulent Character.*[7]

In his revealingly titled *Adverse Report*, Johnson eviscerates the archival evidence Reavis presented to substantiate his claim to the Peralta Land Grant. The 107-page report covers in painstaking detail the many issues and inconsistencies that marked the documents that Reavis submitted to the court. Though

Reavis was able to convince the casual observer, Johnson's laborious investigation revealed that the Peralta Land Grant papers included forged passages and additional pages that were written or inserted into government records, employed anachronistic writing instruments and styles, and did not comply with Spanish colonial grammatical norms or record-keeping practices. After completing his six-year study, Johnson found that the evidence discrediting the Peralta Land Grant was remarkable. Anyone with even a basic familiarity with Spanish land grants who could read the documents Reavis presented would immediately dismiss them as obvious forgeries and the Peralta Land Grant as a sham.

And yet, many people believed Reavis's preposterous story. Before his scheme was exposed, Reavis made as much as half a million dollars by conning victims to pay him for the right to settle or conduct business within the boundaries of his imaginary grant.[8] As librarian Donald M. Powell explains, "Reavis, papers in hand, went straight to the top. His acquaintances in California had given him introductions to financiers in New York. They listened to his ready flow of talk of his bright visions for irrigation works to bring thousands of acres of desert into green vigor, to his plans to induce settlers to take up lands, to the prospects of great mining development; and *knowing nothing of Arizona at firsthand*, they were impressed. They examined the photographs of ancient documents he carried; and *knowing equally little about Spanish manuscripts and grant procedures*, they were convinced."[9] Reavis's ability to profit so handsomely off a claim that was so clearly false was only possible because of the extreme historical myopia of his victims, who, as Powell establishes, "kn[ew] nothing of Arizona at firsthand" and "kn[ew] equally little about Spanish manuscripts and grant procedures." By the time Johnson's condemning report was published, Reavis's forged documents had already convinced everyone from individual homesteaders who purchased quitclaim deeds to protect their property to powerful corporations like the Southern Pacific Railroad and investors in New York and San Francisco, who all paid Reavis for the right to operate on what they believed was his land.[10] The Peralta Land Grant was ultimately discredited thanks to the work of Johnson and other government experts, but Reavis's stunning temporary success points less to his own skills as a forger, which were both limited and flawed, and more to the striking ignorance of would-be investors and homesteaders about the transnational history of the Southwest in general, and Arizona in particular.

COUNTERFEIT NARRATIVES

The elaborate false history that Reavis wove together through the many archival materials he forged exemplifies what I theorize as a *counterfeit narrative*—that is, an invented narrative that masquerades as true in order to consolidate political, cultural, or economic power. The political uncertainty, cultural

Figure 2. A map of the boundaries of the Peralta Land Grant. Image courtesy of
Special Collections, the University of Arizona Libraries.

ambiguity, and economic instability of the late nineteenth-century U.S. Southwest made fertile ground for counterfeit narratives, which thrive when power is in
flux and more easily co-opted. Fifty years after the United States acquired what
became the Southwest, nowhere was power more precarious than in the territories of Arizona and New Mexico, where Reavis's Peralta Land Grant was situated (figure 2). Neither territory had been granted statehood due to concerns
regarding their large non-Anglo populations, which, some argued, were too culturally distant from the rest of the population to allow for their full incorporation within the nation.[11] Though racism against Mexican and Native American
communities underpinned this argument, it also underscored how the people
and places of the Southwest were in fact different from their eastern and northern
neighbors. The legacy of Native American sovereignty, Spanish colonialism,
and Mexican independence in the region was palpable but not well understood,
creating the perfect conditions for a counterfeit narrative that exploited this
complex heritage to pass as true.

Accounting for *why* Reavis's counterfeit narrative was believable, at least for
a time, moves the Peralta Land Grant case from an interesting historical footnote to a central part of the story of westward expansion. While Reavis's counterfeit narrative was extreme in its overt fabrication of an invented reality, it was
not the only strategic falsification of the history of the region. The doctrine of
Manifest Destiny and its accompanying portrayal of the West as devoid of people
and a past was much the work of fantasy as Reavis's outlandish Peralta Land
Grant story. Recovering how Reavis, on a small scale, fabricated a past that would
legitimize his own claim to the land points to the mechanisms by which the dominant narratives he imitated relied on partial truths, exaggerations, and outright

fabrications in order to legitimize the large-scale expansion and settlement of the United States in the West. Though Reavis's con was ultimately exposed, first by Johnson in his 1890 report and then five years later in a highly anticipated trial at the U.S. Court of Land Claims, his momentary success underscores that in his day, the borders that divided true from false, old from new, and north from south were as fragile—and fictional—as they were foundational.

The archives were the ideal repository for Reavis to cultivate his counterfeit narrative, lending credibility to his forgeries despite their obvious fraudulence. Here too Reavis's case is extreme but instructive, as his falsified archive was not the only one to curate a limited or even deceptive record of the past. Even as Reavis was modifying records to legitimize his land claim, other entities, such as corporations, government offices, and pioneer historical societies, were also carefully curating a limited vision of the past that legitimized their own ability to operate within the same land. In this way, Reavis's alter archive is not an exception to but rather an amplification of the always illusory nature of archival authority and objectivity. All archives are shaped by those who create, keep, and curate the records they contain, making the distinction between Reavis's alter archive, with its more obvious modifications, and the larger archives that he altered neither clear nor stable. No archive, whether obviously forged or not, is unmediated or uncompromised.

Ultimately both the content of Reavis's counterfeit narrative (his invented history of the West) and the context in which he created it (his alter archive) undermine easy distinctions between true and false, real and genuine. In this light, the recovery of Reavis's counterfeit narrative unsettles the history of the southwestern territories in which it was supposedly located and the archives on which that history is built. Unsettlement, as used by scholars working within early American studies, contests the inevitability and extensiveness of U.S. settlement within the borders of what today forms the nation.[12] Reading the counterfeit narrative that created the Peralta Land Grant as an archive of unsettlement underscores the instability inherent within the larger fictions that plague the history of the western United States. Far from an amusing detour, the counterfeit narrative Reavis developed epitomizes, in the words of Anna Brickhouse, "not merely the contingency and noninevitability but the glaring incompleteness of the history of the New World as we currently know and write it,"[13] exposing how many questions remain unanswered about that history's content and continued impact on the present and future of the region.

UNSETTLING THE ARCHIVE(S)

Surveyor General Johnson's *Adverse Report* carefully retraces the mechanisms by which Reavis altered Spanish colonial records and inscribed his counterfeit narrative into the halls of history. Johnson dedicates the majority of his analysis to one part of Reavis's alter archive: the supposed title papers of the Peralta Land Grant. He writes that the papers are "bound together in pamphlet form by a cotton cloth back, and consist of a title page and six other pages of printed and written matter, all in the Spanish language."[14] Johnson notes that the title page curiously does not list the name Peralta or include any reference to the grant, instead indicating that the contents of the book relate to the Spanish Inquisition.[15] The only reference to the grant is, as Johnson explains, "in the back of this front or title page," where the phrase, "In relation to the concession to the Señor Don Miguel de Peralta, Baron of the Colorados," appears as an afterthought or later addition.[16] Upon careful inspection, Johnson found that the phrase was in fact "added to the back of this page within a few years," as it appears to have been "written with a steel pen, hair lines being apparent throughout the entire writing."[17] The document, supposedly written on January 3, 1748, could not possibly have been written on that date, as steel pens did not exist until 1803.[18]

Johnson notes that on the first page after the frontispiece, "'Yo el Rey' is printed at the bottom of the printed matter" and that "a seal printed on the paper also appears."[19] Nevertheless, this seal "is not impressed on the paper, and has no special significance," prompting Johnson to infer that "it would be comparatively easy to obtain and would not be difficult to duplicate."[20] Johnson observes that on the final page included within the title documents, the accompanying "seal is not impressed on the page proper, but is on a separate piece of parchment paper pasted on the page."[21] As Johnson was himself able to obtain an exact copy of such a seal by writing "to the proper Mexican authorities," he concludes "that the impress was readily obtainable and thereafter could be utilized for the fabrication of papers."[22] This particular seal also appears to be "brown[,] . . . looking as though it might have been scorched by being heated over a flame for detachment from its original resting place, or in placing it in its present position. In further proof it is cracked as though scorched."[23]

In addition to these highly suspicious irregularities, the form and content of the text of the title papers do not match other contemporaneous documents. Johnson maintains that "while the papers filed by Reavis invariably show a fine cut shapely modern S, whether the letters appear in the middle or at the end of the word; the documents issued by the Inquisition used both the old-fashioned and modern S according to their position in the word, and the modern S is not the shapely S used in the Peralta papers."[24] In addition to the shape of the letters, Johnson also notes the suspicious nature of the words included among the Peralta Land Grant papers. He cites a "brief submitted by the Hon. Clark Churchill" that details "many variations in spelling etc." found within the documents and decries "the class of Spanish used" as "not at all times of the high order that was used in the Castilian court of the last century."[25] It would seem that whoever wrote the Peralta papers was not a member of the court, and perhaps not even a native speaker of Spanish.

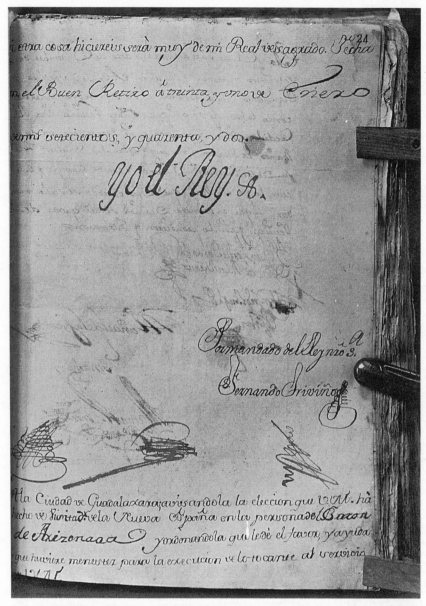

Figure 3. An example of one of James Addison Reavis's forgeries. A proclamation to the citizens of Guadalajara that Reavis altered to show the "Baron de Arizonaca" had been appointed royal inspector. Image courtesy of Special Collections, the University of Arizona Libraries.

Finally, Johnson remarks on the title papers' odd placement within the archival records not of the governmental administration of the Indies, as would be expected, but rather of the Inquisition. He insists that the contents not only do not match the frontispiece but in fact appear "much out of place," wondering aloud "by what propriety an original grant, or a copy of such a grant, by a Viceroy should leave its natural channel in the governmental archives to become part and parcel of the ecclesiastical records," for it would be "folly to talk about land grant records from the archives of the Inquisition as the law existed."[26] For Johnson, the evidence discrediting the Peralta Land Grant title papers was simply overwhelming. It was clear to him that Reavis invented and then inscribed within the archives the history of Don Miguel Peralta and his eponymous grant for Reavis's own personal enrichment.

The contrast between Johnson's unequivocal repudiation of the archival evidence Reavis presented and the public's initial acceptance of the Peralta papers' validity points to a fundamental distinction in how archives are understood, either as object or as source. Johnson's interrogation of the Peralta Land Grant papers shows that archives are objects that are formed, not in all cases by a con artist but certainly always by those who establish their records and curate their content. Though Reavis's alteration of the Spanish colonial records was fraudulent, his actions nevertheless underscore that the content and format of all records are the result of choices made by the people who create, collect, organize, and preserve them. At the same time, the public's assumption that the Peralta Land Grant papers were valid simply because they resided in archives reveals an understanding of archives not as object but rather as the source of information. This static assessment obscures the mediated nature of archives by ignoring the dynamic history of each record.

Because the Peralta Land Grant papers were *forged*, they provide a unique vantage point from which to compare the ramifications of these two different understandings of archives. Many of the questions deconstructing the archive as source that have preoccupied humanities scholars engaging in the "archival turn" within their respective disciplines are central to Reavis's case, which draws attention to both the mediated nature of the archive and its broad power to shape historical narratives and the power dynamics they produce.[27] Reavis's fraudulent alterations to the records, however, also push beyond these macro-level queries into the halls of actual archives where he took on (or over) the role of the record creator, prompting an interrogation of how archives are created, stored, and used. In the more than a century that separates Reavis's forgeries from the contemporary moment, theorization of the archives as an object has evolved from the modernist elaboration of fundamental archival principles to postmodern critiques of how the application of these principles produces historical narratives and shapes collective consciousness. The difference in scale of these metaphorical and applied lines of inquiry highlights the gap between two strains of archival

Figure 4. Another of James Addison Reavis's forgeries. A forged decree granting land to Miguel Peralta. Image courtesy of Special Collections, the University of Arizona Libraries.

criticism, one coming principally from scholars situated in the humanities and the other coming from scholars in archival studies.[28] Ironically, it is in Reavis's falsified archive that these two conversations come together, as his forgeries simultaneously invoke questions not only about the archive as abstraction but also about how archives are objects with a history of their own.

In *Archive Fever*, French theorist Jacques Derrida infamously declared, "Nothing is less reliable, nothing is less clear today than the word 'archive.'"[29] In this sense, Reavis's alter archive is not unique, exemplifying the unreliability and ambiguity that is always intrinsic to the archive. This ambiguity has only increased since the publication of Derrida's influential text in 1996. As Rodrigo Lazo notes, "The word *archive* is deployed currently in reference to sites of research as well as to the process of keeping and retrieving texts and information, sometimes even in the subjective sense of 'my archive.'"[30] This abundance of usages has sparked debates not only about how to define the archive but also about "how knowledge is constituted and delimited and how [the archive] fails to account for its failures."[31] By exploiting the archive's knowledge-producing capacity in order to create false information, Reavis's alter archive does account for the archive's failures, in particular its failure to act as an objective source of historical fact.

In addition to accounting for the failures of the archive as abstraction, Reavis's alter archive also accounts for the limitations of actual archives and the principles and practices that undergird them. A few years after Reavis's Peralta Land Grant scheme was exposed, three Dutch archivists wrote the influential *Manual for the Arrangement and Description of Archives*, also known as the *Dutch Manual* (1898),[32] which, as Jamie A. Lee explains, was "the first internationally accepted articulation of the codification, standardization, and professionalization of archival practices."[33] Lee affirms that since its publication, "many in the archival field have been taught to see archives as neutral and unwavering institutions of evidence," an attitude that was absolutely fundamental to Reavis's success.[34]

The modernist assumption that underpins the *Dutch Manual*'s rule—that is, that records have an innate integrity and are impartial evidence of what they describe—was what prevented Reavis's victims from seeing the obvious fraudulence of the evidence he provided to prove the existence of the Peralta Land Grant. Twenty-four years after the *Dutch Manual* was published, Hilary Jenkinson expanded on the principles the manual introduced, focusing in particular on the evidentiary value of records.[35] Jenkinson, who was impacted by the positivist thinking of his time, believed that if records were preserved exactly as they were created, with no interference from archivists, they could be regarded as accurate evidence. Jenkinson would have pointed to Reavis's forgeries as illustrative of his point. Clearly, in altering the records, Reavis undermined their evidentiary value.

However, Reavis's forged documents are not an exception to but rather an intensification of the questionable evidentiary value of records. Jenkinson's positivist approach to archives has now been thoroughly critiqued and revealed to be inadequate. In Jenkinson's model, those who have complete control over the creation and collection of their own records could shape the evidence of events in such a way that the records would not necessarily reflect the reality of the events as they occurred. As Terry Cook remarks, "At its most extreme, Jenkinson's approach would allow the archival legacy to be perverted by administrative whim or state ideology."[36] In this sense, Reavis's forgeries typify the mediated nature of all records. Though Reavis was a counterfeit records creator, he nevertheless demonstrates the extensive power that all records creators wield as they not only record but also create evidence.

This evidence has different values depending on its usage. Theodore Schellenberg, the "father of appraisal theory in the United States,"[37] separated what he referred to as the primary importance of records—that is, their value to their original creators—from the secondary value records had not to their creators but rather to future researchers.[38] Consequently, Schellenberg distinguished records, which encompassed the original body of materials, from archives, which were collections carefully cultivated with an eye toward the secondary value of the materials.[39] Whereas Jenkinson's theorization points to the power of records creators, Schellenberg identifies the power archivists wield by appraising materials and deciding what to include and exclude from archival collections. Reavis not only harnessed the authority of records creators, he also usurped the appraisal process by designing his forgeries specifically with an eye toward their secondary value. Because they documented a fictitious grant, Reavis's forgeries had no primary value whatsoever. They did, however, have immense secondary value, providing Reavis with the evidence he needed to carry out his con and steal the land that formed the fictitious Peralta Land Grant.

Though Reavis's forgeries could be seen as the exceptions that prove the rules that Jenkinson and Schellenberg outlined, they in fact take the unforeseen consequences of both modernist theories to their logical extremes. By taking over the role of records creators and archivists, Reavis shows the extent of their power to shape historical evidence and, consequently, historical narratives. In the years following the publication of Jenkinson's and Schellenberg's work, scholars in the archival sciences have engaged a postmodern perspective to reinterpret and redefine the field's core principles and account for and analyze the archives' obscured power. For example, scholars have expanded the seemingly straightforward concept of the provenance, or origin, of records to include what Tom Nesmith defines as "the social and technical processes of the records' inscription, transmission, contextualization, and interpretation which account for its existence, characteristics, and continuing history."[40] Within this framework, archival records are shaped by the archivists who process and interpret them, the patrons who use them, and the social environment in which their work happens. Though Reavis's alter-archiving process took the extreme form of the outright falsification of the provenance of certain texts, it nevertheless underscores that there is no such thing as unmediated origins when it comes to archival records, all of which are fundamentally shaped by their inclusion within archives.

Though Reavis forged the origins of the Peralta Land Grant papers over a century ago, his actions foreshadowed the need for this more expansive approach to archives. As Cook explains, the recent reformulations of the archives emerging from the archival sciences "move the theoretical (and practical) focus of archives away from the record and toward the creative act or authoring intent or functional context behind the record," shifting focus from "the physical record—that thing which is under our actual physical custody in archives"—to "the context, purpose, intent, interrelationships, functionality, and accountability of the record, its creator, and its creation processes, wherever these occur."[41] Though the content of Reavis's records was entirely false, there was a clear "authoring intent"[42] that underlay them—that is, they were intended to alter the chain of title to thousands of acres of land so that Reavis could claim to be the rightful owner. The records had no meaning or importance apart from the context in which they were created, underscoring the need to account not just for the limited value of individual records but also for the wider influence of archives as they circulate within particular historical and geographic contexts.

The impact of Reavis's forgeries and the counterfeit narrative they created *when they were believed to be true* provides a glimpse of the magnitude of the influence on society of archives and the historical narratives they produce. Reavis exploited the invisible gap that separates all archives from the pasts they preserve, in his case widening the gap until the archival record preserved a past that never even happened. In this light, Reavis's scheme productively unsettles assumptions about archival authority that conceal the fact that archives, whether overtly forged or not, are always already an invention. Though their authority stems from their perceived status as the definitive protector and preserver of historical evidence, archives are not separate from the histories they keep, meaning that how history is perceived impacts how it is preserved and vice versa. Examining the varied strategies Reavis employed to alter the archival record demonstrates how archives themselves, and consequently the authority they wield, are always malleable and mediated.

Unsettling the West

In addition to preying on the misconception that archives are objective and reliable sources of information, the success of Reavis's scheme equally depended on a second misconception, that of the United States' Manifest Destiny to expand westward into a virgin land. Homesteaders, corporations, and private investors all relied on this narrative to legitimize their presence and ease their settlement within the newly acquired southwestern territories. However, as Reavis's successful swindling of these stakeholders proves, U.S. westward expansion was neither inevitable nor unobstructed. Reavis's counterfeit narrative exposed the wide chasm that separated the doctrine of Manifest Destiny from the reality of U.S. westward expansion. That an invented story about an eighteenth-century Spanish land grant could so profoundly impact the late nineteenth-century U.S. Southwest demonstrates the instability inherent within Manifest Destiny, which obscured the suppressed yet sustained influence the pre-1848 history of the Southwest continued to have within the territory.

While the archives formed the immediate context for Reavis's counterfeit narrative, the doctrine of Manifest Destiny shaped the contours of its content. In Reavis's day, affirmations of national superiority combined with the idea that what became the West was a virgin land to form the dominant narrative of U.S. settlement. This narrative was inherently temporal and spatial; as Wai Chee Dimock explains, "The familiar strategy for antebellum expansionists was to invoke some version of 'Providence,' whose plans for the future happened to coincide exactly with America's territorial ambitions. American expansion in space and providential design in time turned out to be the same."[43] Nevertheless, there were cracks within the time and space of Manifest Destiny. Western lands were not without people or a past, an unsettling reality that made the doctrine of Manifest Destiny vulnerable to critiques—and counterfeits.

Reavis's nearly successful plot to steal land in the late nineteenth-century U.S. Southwest by inventing a counterfeit narrative about an eighteenth-century Spanish land grant brings to light the temporal and spatial fissures within the doctrine of Manifest Destiny. Temporally, westward expansion proved to be more planned than providential. The war between the United States and Mexico, through which the United States gained most of its western territories, was in fact a calculated and deliberate land grab. Spatially, the sudden incorporation of such a large amount of territory at the close of the war was unwieldy and uneven. Far from a virgin land, the territories were marked by a palimpsestic history that continued to shape the region's diverse people and places. Daniel Cooper Alarcón proposes the palimpsest, "a site where a text has been erased (often incompletely) in order to accommodate a new one" and is therefore composed "of competing yet interwoven narratives," as a paradigm for analyzing "the nexus of power, empire, and discourse" in the U.S. Southwest.[44] Likewise, María Josefina Saldaña-Portillo argues that "An investigation into the spatial production of the racial geographies of the region allows us to see how colonial and contemporary geographies are related palimpsestically, as a plurality that exists in the heterotemporality of the present."[45] The myths that underpinned Manifest Destiny erased the Southwest's palimpsestic history, making Reavis's victims susceptible to a counterfeit narrative of that history. Tracking the brief success of Reavis's counterfeit narrative simultaneously reveals how pervasive the myths underpinning Manifest Destiny were even as it also exposes the long-standing incommensurability of those myths with the time and space of the Southwest.

John L. O'Sullivan, the man credited with coining the term Manifest Destiny, elaborated the temporal myths that underpinned the justification for U.S. westward expansion in his 1839 essay "The Great Nation of Futurity." As the title suggests, O'Sullivan portrays the future as belonging to the United States, which had broken from corrupt and backward Europe to uphold the principles of liberty and equality for all. He claims, "We are the nation of progress, of individual freedom, of universal enfranchisement."[46] His celebration of these principles unsurprisingly does not take into account the many enslaved people living within the nation's borders, nor does it acknowledge the countless tribal nations that were removed or destroyed to make way for this U.S. national progress. That O'Sullivan can paint the United States as a republic founded on the principle of liberty for all even as its founding depended on the disenfranchisement of many highlights the tension at the center of what Thomas Allen calls the paradox of

U.S. expansion. Though the U.S. republic purported to oppose Europe's tyranny and imperial powers, U.S. westward expansion nevertheless very much resembled imperial growth. Allen argues that O'Sullivan's resolution to this apparent contradiction is temporal, "making time the medium for an effusive nationalism, in which the future itself would become American territory."[47] In his essay, O'Sullivan affirms that "the expansive future is our arena,"[48] claiming not territory but time as the domain of the United States. According to Allen, this "temporal nationalism" allowed O'Sullivan to shift the focus "away from space and toward time, a utopian horizon in the future where the nation's contradictions would resolve themselves into a coherent republic."[49] This convenient displacement of the inconsistencies of expansion onto the future absolved O'Sullivan from having to account for their incoherence and allowed him to conclude his essay by asking, "Who, then, can doubt that our country is destined to be *the great nation* of futurity?"[50]

Shortly after the publication of O'Sullivan's 1839 essay, the United States did in fact expand, first into Texas and then into what would become the western territories, in seeming fulfillment of O'Sullivan's predictions. Six years later, in his 1845 essay "Annexation," O'Sullivan describes the U.S. acquisition of Texas as "the fulfillment of our manifest destiny to overspread the continent allotted by Providence for the free development of our yearly multiplying millions."[51] Citing exponential population growth, O'Sullivan asserts that U.S. westward expansion is not only necessary but inevitable. The fact that Mexico ruled the region to the west posed no problem for O'Sullivan, who describes the neighbor nation as "imbecile and distracted," incapable of maintaining control over said territories or blocking the inescapable expansion of the United States.[52] In "Annexation," O'Sullivan explicitly maps the temporal nationalism of "The Great Nation of Futurity" onto the western United States, tying the future of the nation to the space of continental expansion.

This continental expansion happened in barely over a decade, as the United States suddenly acquired not only Texas but also what became part or all of California, New Mexico, Nevada, Utah, Wyoming, Colorado, Kansas, Oklahoma, and Arizona.[53] This vast territory encompassed a complex cultural landscape marked by centuries of uneven Spanish conquest in the far northern frontier, where Native Americans had mounted revolts and resistance to fight back against first the Spaniards and later the Mexicans to defend native sovereignty. Small communities of Spanish-speaking people, however, did exist throughout the region, maintaining strained relationships with both their Native American neighbors and the faraway colonial and later national center of power to the south. When the United States expanded into these lands, it acquired not only the territory's physical but also its cultural landscape, complicating the forward-looking dreams of expansionists like O'Sullivan by undermining the coherence of an exclusively Anglo-American continental republic.

The 1848 Treaty of Guadalupe Hidalgo, the treaty that ended the war between the United States and Mexico and authorized U.S. westward expansion, in fact foreclosed the possibility of establishing the exclusionary republic O'Sullivan imagined by granting citizenship to the conquered Mexicans and recognizing their Spanish and Mexican land grants. Articles VIII and IX of the treaty guaranteed that Mexicans residing in the territories acquired by the United States could choose to become U.S. citizens and enjoy all the rights associated with citizenship, including the right to retain their private property.[54] Nevertheless, as Richard Griswold del Castillo observes, "In the end the U.S. application of the treaty to the realities of life in the Southwest violated its spirit."[55] The system the United States established for verifying land claims subjected Mexican landholders to complex legal battles that either resulted in the outright denial of their claims or were so costly that petitioners were forced to sell their land in order to pay high legal fees.[56] Though the United States used the court system to disenfranchise many Mexicans who held title to land grants in the Southwest, the government's recognition, even in name only, of the continued applicability of a previous political and economic system was at direct ideological odds with the temporal and spatial myths of Manifest Destiny, which denied the existence, much less relevance, of pre-Anglo history to post-U.S. expansion in the Southwest.

However, the ideological incongruence of the myths of Manifest Destiny and the provisions of the Treaty of Guadalupe Hidalgo did not prevent the promulgation of those myths. Nearly fifty years after the treaty was signed, Fredrick Jackson Turner immortalized the idea that the West was uniquely and exclusively American in his 1893 essay, "The Significance of the Frontier in American History." In the essay, Turner elaborates what became known as the frontier thesis, or the idea that U.S. expansion along the western frontier shaped the core characteristics of the nation. Essential to Turner's thesis was the idea that the United States expanded into what was "free land" that was only tamed by "the advance of American settlement westward."[57] In Turner's estimation, any settlement that predated or was external to U.S. expansion was either nonexistent or inconsequential. After all, it was U.S. settlers who led the way "in crossing a continent, in winning a wilderness, and in developing at each area of this progress out of the primitive economic and political conditions of the frontier into the complexity of city life."[58] Like O'Sullivan, Turner collapses the time of U.S. progress with the space of the western frontier. Writing half a century later than O'Sullivan, however, Turner portrays this progress as not only part of the nation's future but also a critical component of its still developing history.

Both Reavis's plot and Turner's thesis appeared at nearly the same time, and Reavis's counterfeit narrative depended on the prevalence of the myths that underpinned Turner's frontier thesis for its success. The pervasiveness of the ideas that Turner espoused about a virgin land meant that U.S. settlers had no metric by which to evaluate anything to the contrary, including Reavis's wildly unbelievable story about a land grant named after a man no one had ever heard of. Referring to the Maxwell Land Grant case, a similar case regarding an actual land grant in New Mexico, María E. Montoya affirms, "The Turnerian conception of the American West as unsettled, unappropriated, unsocialized nature conquered by intrepid pioneers prevents ordinary observers . . . from even imagining how the West could be a place where different people, much less different property regimes, collided with one another."[59] Because Reavis's victims were unable to imagine such a past, they were incapable of identifying a counterfeit version of it. Their gullibility resulted from their ideological adherence to the exclusive time and space of Manifest Destiny, neither of which matched the palimpsestic reality of the Southwest.

The counterfeit narrative Reavis created was so disturbing to his late nineteenth-century contemporaries precisely because of the way it disrupted the neat distinction between Anglo and Spanish temporal and spatial occupation of the Southwest. According to the doctrine of Manifest Destiny, Anglo-American settlement superseded the communities and conquests that came before it. While the Spanish may have conquered the space that became the Southwest, the United States settled it, a semantic difference that invokes the Black Legend, an anti-Spanish trope that framed Spanish conquest as violent and backward and Anglo settlement as providential and beneficial.[60] This differentiation was foundational to the moral framework of Manifest Destiny, which, as Brickhouse argues, justified "the premise of English (and, later, U.S.) predominance in the hemisphere."[61] That predominance, however, was precarious. That Reavis's manipulation of *Spanish* archives nearly allowed him to alter the borders of the *United States* points not only to the existence but also to the enduring impact of the Spanish conquest of what became the Southwest. Fifty years after the United States expanded from one shining sea to another, the havoc Reavis's invented land grant wreaked on the settlers living within the Southwest exposed the inconsistencies inherent within the not-so-seamless time and space of Manifest Destiny, underscoring how non-U.S. history continued to shape the Southwest well beyond the close of the U.S.-Mexican War.

The ubiquity of the temporal and spatial myths of Manifest Destiny foreclosed the overt recognition of non-Anglo peoples and pasts within the story of the Southwest, but Reavis's counterfeit narrative offers a competing reading of westward expansion that critiques this misleadingly myopic representation. Though his counterfeit narrative was based on falsehoods, its content nevertheless exposes what Dana Luciano calls a "fault line" inherent within the narrative of U.S. westward expansion—that is, a place "where competing readings, foreclosed historically, persist in and as critique."[62] U.S. victory in the war against Mexico historically foreclosed Mexico's dominance north of the border. That victory, however, did not foreclose the possibility of other readings of the war and its consequences. Reavis's counterfeit narrative unsettled what the war meant for the future of the United States, interrupting the narrative of easy expansion and uncovering the complexities inherent within national growth. Through a counterfeit narrative, Reavis remapped the Spanish past onto the space of the Southwest, activating a different recognition of its formation.

Though the dominant narrative of U.S. westward expansion depicted the region as providentially belonging within the nation's borders, Reavis's victims soon learned that quite the opposite was true. If, as Ian Haywood argues, "forgeries are subversive artefacts,"[63] then the Peralta Land Grant forgeries subverted the decisiveness of the U.S. settlement of the Southwest by unsettling its claims of inevitable expansion and complete domination. The physical forgeries Reavis presented to the court were not what accomplished this subversion. Rather, it was the counterfeit narrative they wove together that unsettled the temporal and spatial foundations of the Southwest.

Unsettling Futures

Even today, over a century after Reavis attempted to claim the Peralta Land Grant, his counterfeit narrative continues to unsettle dominant narratives about the time and space of the Southwest. Recent legislation in Arizona, where the majority of Reavis's Peralta Land Grant was situated, confirms that the temporal and spatial myths that underpinned westward expansion in the nineteenth century are still very much alive in the twenty-first. Laws like Senate Bill 1070,[64] which required authorities to demand documentation from any person who could reasonably be suspected of living in the United States illegally, and House Bill 2281,[65] which banned the teaching of ethnic studies in the state's public schools, are a transparent denial of the palimpsestic history that Reavis's counterfeit narrative indirectly reveals. In an era of alternative facts about the Southwest, Reavis's counterfeit narrative reminds us of the dangerous consequences of the incompleteness, if not total inaccuracy, of dominant narratives about the region's people and past.

In the end, the very unsettling implications of Reavis's counterfeit narrative are what make an otherwise amusing case profoundly instructive, highlighting how archival records and the historical narratives they produce shape not only our understanding of the past but also the trajectory of our future. Unsettlement is, after all, a future-oriented concept. As Luciano affirms, "Unsettlement *moves* rather than mourns the state of things, activating both utopian and pragmatic attempts to imagine other ways of being."[66] And what better place to make this move than in the future-oriented gaze of the archives? Though often thought of as repositories of the past, archives are always grounded in the present with an eye toward the future. Preservation of the past is never for the past; archives are organized with a present and future audience in mind, representing an attempt

to anticipate what documents, what experiences, what stories the following generations will want and need to access. This future vision is of course limited by
the assumptions and biases of the present, as well as the countless unknowns of
what might lie ahead. Nevertheless, as Reavis's counterfeit narrative so powerfully illustrates, archival collections and the historical narratives they produce
are profoundly implicated not only in recording what we have been but also
imagining what we might yet become.

CHAPTER 2

Searching for Sofia

RACE, GENDER, AND AUTHENTICITY AT THE 1895 COURT OF PRIVATE LAND CLAIMS

In the summer of 1895, all eyes were on the U.S. Court of Private Land Claims in Santa Fe as people near and far anxiously awaited the conclusion of the contentious Peralta Land Grant case. Despite Surveyor General Royal A. Johnson's 1890 *Adverse Report*, James Addison Reavis and his wife, Sofia Loreto Peralta-Reavis, filed a lawsuit against the federal government demanding the immediate confirmation of their title to the over twelve million acres of land in the territories of Arizona and New Mexico covered by the Peralta Land Grant. Everyone from small landowners to large corporations followed the trial with unease and anticipation, waiting nervously to find out whether their titles were secure.

While the archives formed the foundation of Reavis's claim, as the image in figure 5 so powerfully demonstrates, his forgeries were meaningless without the identity he forged for Peralta-Reavis. Reavis had altered the archival record to not only invent the Peralta Land Grant but also create a chain of inheritance that led directly from Don Miguel Nemecio Silva de Peralta de la Córdoba y García de Carrillo de las Falces, otherwise known as the first Baron of Arizona, to Peralta-Reavis, whose full name (according to her husband) was Doña Sofia Loreto Micaela de Peralta-Reavis née Maso y Silva de Peralta de la Córdova. At the trial, the case presented by U.S. attorney Matthew G. Reynolds and his special assistant Severo Mallet-Prevost to discredit Reavis's claim was as dependent on discrediting Peralta-Reavis's forged identity as it was on discrediting the forged archival documents. Though Reavis, who represented himself at the trial, insisted his wife was the long-lost heiress to the Peralta Land Grant, Reynolds contended that her real name was in fact Sofia Treadway and that she was the daughter "of one John A. Treadway by an Indian squaw commonly known and called Kate."[1] For both Reynolds and Reavis, the case hinged on proving who Peralta-Reavis really was, either a nobody or Spanish nobility.

Figure 5. Photograph of Sofia Loreto Peralta-Reavis next to a rock with markings that supposedly indicated the boundaries of the Peralta Land Grant. Image courtesy of Special Collections, the University of Arizona Libraries.

The climax of the trial came on June 17, when Peralta-Reavis herself took the stand. Reynolds grilled her about her childhood, her relationship with Reavis, and her awareness of the large inheritance she now claimed. After an intense back-and-forth in which Peralta-Reavis became increasingly agitated, Reynolds finally asked her directly,

Q: In other words, all you know about [the Peralta Land Grant] is what [James Reavis] told you?

A: I have looked at [the documents], as I say, but I have never looked them all over, to study them.

Q: You have never read it, to know of your own knowledge?

A: No, sir; because, if you want to know, I have never gone to school but three months in my life; everybody has been jumping on me and keeping me from everything—(Witness here burst into tears).[2]

At this point, Reavis interjected, "It seems to me the government ought to be more considerate. The government insists upon repeating questions that we think she has answered fully enough."[3] The court agreed, but Peralta-Reavis did not shrink back: "I want to get through to-day; I am not coming back here again."[4]

Resolute, Peralta-Reavis braced herself for Reynolds's final question: "There is one more question, under my duty as United States Attorney, I deem it neces- sary to ask. I desire to ask the witness whether or not she does not know that she is personating, as claimant here, a person who does not exist, and never did exist, to wit, the great-granddaughter of the original grantee, Don Miguel Nem- ecio Silva de Peralta, and so-forth."[5] The court immediately intervened: "We think she is entitled to be protected from answering that question, unless she voluntarily wants to do it. She is under no obligation to answer it."[6] Reavis affirmed that while his wife had nothing to hide, she did "not wish to stay in the court room any longer than is necessary to answer the government" and should not be required to answer.[7] Reynolds maintained that he had "not mistreated the lady" and only "wanted her statement" on the record.[8] The court concluded that Peralta-Reavis could "answer the question, or decline to do so, as she sees fit."[9]

Decades of careful plotting and the planting of evidence all led to this one moment. For Reavis, a scheme that he had spent the better part of twenty years planning was on the line. The vast and valuable territory of the Peralta Land Grant would either finally be his or stay firmly in the hands of the federal gov- ernment. For Peralta-Reavis, even more was at stake. Her very existence hung in the balance. With that, she uttered her last recorded words: "No, sir; I did not know that I was personating anybody but myself."[10]

This dramatic scene records more than one woman's bold claim to a vast inher- itance. In her study of another contentious Spanish land grant case, María E. Mon- toya argues, "The problem of land grants in the American Southwest is largely a problem of translation."[11] Reavis saw an opportunity to exploit this problem of translation by inventing and claiming a land grant that never existed, preying on the ignorance that allowed for mistranslations and, in his extreme case, counter- feits. However, because of the central role the identity of Peralta-Reavis played in her husband's con, the trial to confirm Reavis's counterfeit land claim transformed into a heated debate over Peralta-Reavis's claim that she was the Spanish heiress to the vast and valuable grant. Precisely because her claim was eventually shown to be baseless, the arguments presented by both sides to prove or disprove Peralta-Reavis's identity point directly to the fluidity and fragility of racial cate- gories, gender, and authenticity in the nineteenth-century Southwest.

The nearly successful transformation of Peralta-Reavis from a poor, mixed- race, illegitimate child into a wealthy Spanish baroness is a testament to the unstable positionality of late nineteenth-century Mexicans and Mexican Amer- icans in general, and women in particular, and the far-reaching consequences that instability provoked. Though its victory against Mexico introduced a new racial hierarchy within the Southwest, the United States' decisive political tri- umph did not translate into a similarly definitive cultural conquest. The binary racial hierarchy the United States introduced did not fully replace the gradated Spanish system, and the testimonies of the various witnesses called by both Reavis and Reynolds affirm that within this context, proving (or disproving) a person's "authentic" racial identity was easier said than done. Though the government did eventually prove that Peralta-Reavis was not in any sense who she claimed to be, the conversations surrounding her identity reveal lingering anxieties about how the U.S.-Mexican War altered not only the physical but also the cultural borders of the United States, and what the lasting consequences of those shifted borders would be. Read in this way, the Peralta Land Grant trial transcript archives not only a historical land fraud but also the fault lines of the late nineteenth-century U.S. racial imaginary.

If the near believability of Reavis's alter archive reveals how the U.S.-Mexican War unsettled the temporal and spatial borders of the Southwest, then the nearly successful racial, national, and cultural passing of Peralta-Reavis as a Spanish baroness exposes how that unsettlement impacted the people living there. The ambiguity the war created made the counterfeit narrative of Peralta-Reavis as a Southwest Cinderella both possible and precarious. As coverage of the Peralta Land Grant trial gripped the nation, Peralta-Reavis's disputed identity quickly became a shorthand for debates about belonging in the Southwest, highlighting the simultaneous centrality and instability of race and ethnicity to questions of citizenship and its accordant rights. Consequently, a close reading of the legal adjudication of Peralta-Reavis's forged Spanish identity allows for a recovery of the always already forged nature not only of Mexican American identity but also of racial identity writ large.

INVENTING A BARONESS: SPANISH FANTASIES AND RACIAL UNCERTAINTIES

When Reavis took the stand in Santa Fe, Reynolds grilled him about one of the more unbelievable parts of his story: his chance meeting on a train in California with his future wife, Peralta-Reavis, the lone heiress for whom he had been searching. Though Reynolds's questions highlight the implausibility of such a serendipitous encounter, the terms both he and Reavis used to describe the meeting further underscore the fluidity of racial identity in general, and Mexican American identity in particular, in the late nineteenth-century U.S. Southwest. Reynolds began,

Q: Now, what name was she going by at the time you so met her on the train?

A: The name she gave me as her adopted name was Treadwell.[12]

Q: You suspected by reason of her appearance that she was of Spanish origin?

A: Certainly. That was the only inducement for speaking to her.

Q: You were then looking for a long lost heiress to the property?

A: That idea had not occurred to me when I spoke to her. It was simply that she was a Spanish beauty and I a young man—quite natural, in my opinion.[13]

It is not surprising that Reavis would describe the first interaction he had with his wife in terms of "natural" attraction. His comments, however, also strategically position Peralta-Reavis's identity, her "Spanish origin," as immediately and unequivocally obvious. In his testimony, it is clear that Reavis intends to bolster his wife's claim to the Peralta Land Grant by affirming the irrefutability of her Spanish identity. Legally, to be a credible heiress for the Spanish land grant, Peralta-Reavis of course needed to be able to claim Spanish ancestry. However, proving it was easier said than done. Reavis knew that the forged documents he presented to the court were meaningless without the identity he had forged for his wife, who brought those documents to life in a specific social reality that depended on the legibility of her identity in order to validate his claim. Reavis's careful construction of Peralta-Reavis as an "heiress" and a "Spanish beauty" is therefore more than just a detail; it is evidence of Peralta-Reavis's undeniable identity and, consequently, the validity of her inherited claim.

Of course, the irony of Reavis's plot was that it depended simultaneously on the belief that identity was indisputable and the reality that it was mutable. In this way, the debates that consumed the trial regarding Peralta-Reavis's racial identity and that were foreshadowed in the exchange between Reavis and Reynolds underscore the falsity of the fixity of Mexican American identity in particular and racial categories in general. In his study of *The Woman in Battle*, an 1876 narrative that describes a cross-dressing Cuban woman named Loreta Janeta Velazquez who had fought as a Confederate soldier in the U.S. Civil War, Jesse Alemán affirms that the debate surrounding the accuracy of Velazquez's story "speaks to the impossibility of authenticity altogether. Gender, race, and nation are sartorial performances that dislodge stable identity markers, wreaking havoc . . . on ideologies, national institutions, and literary histories that demand readable signs of subjectivity."[14] The Peralta Land Grant trial transcript similarly forecloses appeals to authenticity by recording the vigorous debates surrounding Peralta-Reavis's identity. That such debates could happen in the first place is proof that late nineteenth-century racial and national categories were fluid, subjective, and, ultimately, impossible to define.[15]

The specifics of how this racial uncertainty operated and what its consequences were are clear in the contradictory testimony of two key witnesses, one called by Reavis and the other by Reynolds, who provided contrasting accounts of Peralta-Reavis's ancestry. Reavis's key witness, R. C. Hopkins, was a translator in the Surveyor General's Office who had traveled with Reavis to Guadalajara to verify the authenticity of the Peralta Land Grant papers.[16] There Reavis and Hopkins became such good friends that Peralta-Reavis later lived with Hopkins as a boarder in his home.[17] When Reavis called Hopkins to the stand, he questioned him about his impression of Peralta-Reavis:

Q: During the time that Sofia was at your house, wasn't it distinctly understood that she was Spanish, and nothing else?

A: That is my recollection. I do not now remember anything to the contrary.

Q: If there had been an intimation that she was Indian, would you certainly remember it?

A: I have no recollection of any suggestion that she was an Indian.[18]

In contrast to Reavis's earlier affirmation of his wife's Spanish identity as self-evident, here he prompted Hopkins to confirm her identity in relation to another racial category, that of Indian. Hopkins in fact confirmed that Peralta-Reavis was Spanish by *denying* that she was Indian.[19] In the late nineteenth century, such a claim had complex racial resonances and important consequences for U.S. citizenship. Half a century before Hopkins took the stand, the Treaty of Guadalupe Hidalgo had promised the rights and privileges of citizenship, including the right to own property,[20] to Mexicans living in what had been northern Mexico and was now the southwestern United States, so long as they were not Indians.[21] This demand to distinguish a national identity (Mexican) from an imagined ethnic identity (not Indian) provoked confusion regarding which U.S. racial categories Mexican people fell into and instigated a national conversation about the "Mexican Question,"[22] or how to categorize these new subjects within U.S. racial hierarchies. Whereas Indians were wholly discounted as barbaric others,[23] Mexicans, whose mestizo heritage meant that they were part Native American and part European, occupied a more liminal position in this hierarchy, embodying an ambiguous, "off-white" racial identity.[24]

While this ambiguity allowed for the systemic discrimination against and disenfranchisement of many Mexicans, it also shaped one key resistance strategy: asserting a Spanish identity. Many Mexicans strategically shored up their claims to citizenship by emphasizing their European ancestry and downplaying their Native American heritage. This racial reframing, what Carey McWilliams calls the "fantasy heritage" and Raymund Paredes the "hacienda syndrome," was a survival mechanism.[25] As Martha Menchaca explains, "Given the nature of the U.S. racial system and its laws, the conquered Mexican population learned that it was politically expedient to assert their Spanish ancestry."[26] For these Mexicans, appealing to their Spanish identity allowed them to affirm their access to U.S. citizenship and all the rights and privileges that it afforded.[27] In this sense, Reavis's plan to base his wife's land claim on a highly manipulated appeal to Spanish ancestry is not unique. Though Peralta-Reavis's claim to a specific Spanish lineage was necessary to claim ownership of the Peralta Land Grant, it alludes to a wider strategic response employed by many Mexicans who suddenly found themselves on the margins of citizenship in the aftermath of U.S. expansion.

Though this so-called Spanish fantasy heritage has often been cited as evidence of Mexicans' and later Mexican Americans' desire to claim a white racial identity, its invocation is much more complex than an appeal to a binary division between black and white. As Anthony Mora argues, "Spanish identity was a quadrangulation, itself an empty signifier, created in the discursive interstice opened up through the triple negation of 'Indian,' 'Mexican,' and 'Anglo/white' identities."[28] When Hopkins's testimony is read alongside the reality of Peralta-Reavis's fraudulent claim to Spanish ancestry, his defense of her invented heritage calls attention to the hollowness of Spanishness as a racial category in this context. Hopkins's testimony in fact attests to the emptiness of *Spanish* as a signifier, as his affirmation consists of a series of negations: that he "do[es] not now remember anything to the contrary" and "ha[s] no recollection of any suggestion that she was an Indian."[29] Though Peralta-Reavis's blatantly false claim to Spanish ancestry is an extreme example of "an empty signifier," it points to the gaps and fissures that plagued the relationship among Spanish, Indian, Mexican, and Anglo/white racial categories in the late nineteenth-century Southwest, underscoring how racial categories are largely empty signifiers that must be litigated into fixity.[30]

The fragility of this quadrangulation is readily apparent in the opposing testimony of Jennie Mack, a key witness for the government who professed to have known Peralta-Reavis as a child and disputed her claim to Spanish ancestry in general and her connection to a Peralta family in particular. The repeated questions Mack answered in her deposition regarding Peralta-Reavis's parentage, the relationship between her mother and her father, and the character of her mother reveal the persistent anxieties surrounding mixed-race children, illegitimacy, and female sexuality in the late nineteenth-century Southwest. Mack insisted that Peralta-Reavis was the daughter of an Anglo man named John A. Treadway and "an Indian woman" named Kate.[31] Through repeated questions about the nature of their relationship, it became clear that Treadway and Kate were not married. Instead, Mack asserted that Kate had lived with Treadway through Peralta-Reavis's birth and then "ran off," after which time Mack had "not seen her."[32] This information discredits not only Kate but also Peralta-Reavis. If what Mack said was true, then Peralta-Reavis was a mixed-race child who had been born out of wedlock and was abandoned by her mother, a heritage that clearly negated the pure "Spanish" identity that formed the basis of her property claim.

Because Kate was crucial to the government's case to discredit Peralta-Reavis's claim, the control of female sexuality became a central focus of Mack's testimony. As María Elena Martínez affirms, from Spanish colonial times, this control extended beyond taboos against sexual relationships between people of different races to the offspring of those relationships, who were seen as a threat to the "hierarchical and racialized social order."[33] To neutralize this threat and maintain a strict social order, these children were denied "access to economic resources and political rights and offices."[34] U.S. expansion into the Southwest added another layer of complexity to ethnically mixed relationships and the offspring they produced. According to Miroslava Chávez-García, during the time that Peralta-Reavis would have been a child in California, "The records indicate that . . . 954 Spanish-speaking women and 231 native women (20 to 30 percent of the women in those ethnic groups) formed intimate relationships with men of various ethnic backgrounds and social classes to whom they were not married."[35] The many impetuses for these relationships included an imbalance in the ratio of women to men in California and the decimation of the Native American population by disease and forced displacement.[36] In this context, it is not surprising that "among ethnically mixed couples—particularly those consisting of indigenous women and Euro-American or Spanish-speaking men—the rate of illegitimacy was even higher than among couples made up of a man and a woman from the same or similar ethnic backgrounds."[37] Though the impact of illegitimacy varied greatly, it undoubtedly complicated the lives of all people involved, disproportionately affecting economically and socially marginalized women of color.[38]

Mack's deposition therefore points to the deep roots of the marginalization of Native American and mixed-race women in the Southwest. Though the specific currency changed over time, the sexual economy of the Americas always positioned women who were not white as highly vulnerable. The remainder of Mack's deposition describes precisely the vulnerability that a mixed-race or Native American woman would experience in a relationship with an Anglo man after U.S. expansion, giving some clues to explain Kate's departure. Mack was familiar with Peralta-Reavis's parentage because she too was a Native American woman who was living in the same community as Kate with a man named Alfred Sherwood "as his wife" and who saw Peralta-Reavis "when she was born."[39] Further questioning revealed that Mack "was a little girl" when she lived with Sherwood and that other women were living with him as well. She declared, "He got my sister first, Ann," and, "He got another one by the name of Ellen."[40] Her age when she was with Sherwood and her description of how he "got" the other women reveal that their relationship was more predatory than partnership. That the questioner did not appear to react to Sherwood's status as not only a polygamist but also a child molester clearly indicates how little value was ascribed to the life of Native American or mixed-race women like Mack. It is hardly surprising, then, that despite having children with Mack, Sherwood eventually left her to marry "a white woman."[41]

As the testimonies of Hopkins and Mack demonstrate, the credibility of Peralta-Reavis's claim to the Peralta Land Grant hinged on her ability to claim an authentic Spanish identity. The terms each used to settle her identity, however, expose such claims to authenticity as socially constructed at best and as dubious forgeries at worst. The contradictions in their testimonies reveal that the racialized and gendered delimitations of Peralta-Reavis's identity were anything but clear. Mora affirms that racial categories at the time were marked by ambivalence, as "the Euro-American representatives of the U.S. nation-state never secured absolute control over the contours of racial and national identification, despite their having erected and policed those borders themselves."[42] The debates surrounding the racial and national identification of Peralta-Reavis, embodied by the incongruous statements made by Hopkins and Mack at the trial, reveal the very real lack of control and coherence when it came to U.S. policing of racial identity at the turn of the century. This uncertainty often facilitated the legal and extralegal disenfranchisement of people of color in general and women in particular, but as Peralta-Reavis's own testimony at the trial indicates, it also opened up new possibilities for survival and resistance.

Romancing a Baroness: Intermarriage and Property

The testimonies of Hopkins and Mack highlight the centrality of Peralta-Reavis's ancestry and childhood to the trial. Nevertheless, it was her marriage to Reavis that set in motion the official filing of her claim, and it was Reavis who was the clear driving force behind the legal pursuit of her title to the Peralta Land Grant. As Reynolds continued his interrogation of Reavis on the stand, he pressed him on the motives and purpose of his marriage to Peralta-Reavis. Reynolds probed,

Q: You really married your wife because of the fact that you were getting, or at least that you had information enough to verify the fact, at least, as to her identity as the great-granddaughter of Miguel Peralta, and wasn't that the reason of the marriage contract, and is not that the substance of the marriage contract, and does not the contract go to that and that alone?

A: I don't believe it would be possible for a man to segregate a combination of motives that consummate marriages, and I believe I would be just as incapable of doing that as any one else. I married her, as a fact.

Q: I am not speaking of the mere question of joining in marriage, but I am speaking of the contract or inducement for the contract, independent of any formal marriage. The inducement was the fact that you were preparing to set her up as the claimant for the grant?

A: The inducement for the formal contract was certainly to suit our case, without any question?

Q: To set her up as claimant?

A: I intended to set her up as claimant.[43]

In his questioning, Reynolds distinguished between "joining in marriage" and the "marriage contract," immediately drawing attention to the division between a romantic and a legal relationship. Though Reavis quipped that the division was a false one, for no man could "segregate a combination of motives that consummate marriages," he later admitted that "the inducement for the formal [marriage] contract" was in fact "to set [Peralta-Reavis] up as claimant." Reynolds's line of questioning clearly accused Reavis of having ulterior motives for marrying Peralta-Reavis—namely, to access the property that he had taken great pains to prove belonged to her. Reynolds knew that Reavis's "research" into the Peralta Land Grant was of no use to him without the formal marriage contract that granted him access to Peralta-Reavis's wealth.

Just as the contradictory testimonies of Hopkins and Mack illuminate the larger circulation of the Spanish fantasy heritage in the late nineteenth-century Southwest, the exchange here between Reynolds and Reavis underscores the broader legal and cultural dynamics at play in intermarriages between Anglo men and Mexican and Mexican American women following the U.S.-Mexican War. As the United States expanded into territory that had for centuries been governed by Spanish and later Mexican laws, it introduced new legal codes that often clashed with the former systems. Laws governing marriage were no exception. As María Raquél Casas notes, U.S. law drew on "British common law and the traditions of Germanic northern Europe," whereas Spanish and Mexican law was rooted in "ancient Roman law."[44] Though marriage laws in all these patriarchal societies favored men, ancient Roman law, and its subsequent Spanish and Mexican interpretations, allowed women more independence during and after marriage. Casas explains, "Under British and U.S. law, marriage transformed a man into a husband; however, a woman became not only a wife but also a *femme covert*, a legal dependent 'covered over' by her husband. . . . Married couples had a singular identity around the law, but the husband's identity structured and intertwined around the wife's, never the other way around."[45] For women, that meant limited rights "when they sought to separate from or divorce their husbands, tried to protect their property, or sought custody or authority over their children."[46] Spanish and Mexican law, on the other hand, "allowed women to retain a separate legal identity when they married. . . . As legally recognized persons, wives could buy, purchase, inherit, or maintain separate property and could enter into contracts and sue in court."[47] These varied legal regimes collided in the post-1848 U.S. Southwest and came to a head in intermarriages between Anglo men and Mexican and Mexican American women.

As Casas and others have shown, these intermarriages did not have a monolithic cultural significance, varying greatly by region, time period, and, of course, individual couple.[48] Casas's recovery of so-called daughters of the land in California reveals a long and complex genealogy of intermarriage, first among Spanish and Native American women and then among Mexican and Mexican American women and Anglo U.S. settlers.[49] After U.S. expansion, these intermarriages led to the slow loss of wealth of Mexican and Mexican American women and their families.[50] In the case of New Mexico, Deena J. González notes a stark difference, writing that it would be a misconception to say that Mexican and Mexican American women married Anglo men for social mobility. In fact, she affirms that due to the relatively small number of Anglo men and the infrequency of intermarriage, it was the Anglo men who became Hispanicized.[51] Katherine Benton-Cohen and Eric V. Meeks both describe a fluidity of racial categories in Arizona that fostered intermarriages in the mid-nineteenth century but that waned by the late nineteenth and early twentieth centuries as the racial distinction between Mexican and Anglo became sharper.[52] Sal Acosta clarifies that this decline was in the percentage of overall marriages, though the raw number of intermarriages continued to increase. This shift, then, is also an indicator of demographic changes in Arizona, as more Anglo families, not just Anglo unmarried men, began to move into the territory.[53]

The marriage of Sofia Peralta-Reavis, a counterfeit Californiana, to James Reavis, an ex-Confederate soldier from Missouri, and their subsequent attempt to claim land in Arizona at a trial in New Mexico draws attention to the geographic and cultural fault lines of the relationship between intermarriage and property in the late nineteenth-century Southwest. As a counterfeit version of a supposedly advantageous intermarriage between a "Spanish baroness" and an Anglo man, the relationship between Peralta-Reavis and Reavis as presented by Reavis at the trial is a romanticized vision of nineteenth-century interethnic unions and the property transfers they made possible. Papering over geographic differences and cultural specificity, the fictional romance Reavis forged about his marriage to Peralta-Reavis points to the inauthenticity not only of his own relationship but also of the broader romanticization of similar Spanish-Anglo unions in the Southwest and the larger conquest to which they alluded.

By the time Peralta-Reavis and Reavis presented their claim to the Peralta Land Grant to the court in Santa Fe in 1895, the multilayered history of conquest and colonization in the Southwest had already entered the realm of romance. In her analysis of the development of what she calls "romantic California," Casas highlights the centrality of romantic desire to the normalization of conquest.[54] She writes, "Californianas supposedly desired to marry 'white' men, 'white' men desired access to land, and the United States desired to portray the invasion of California as largely untraumatic for the invaded peoples."[55] Intermarriage between Spanish women and Anglo men was central to this image, as they "became false symbols of peaceful invasion and control by the United States."[56]

These interethnic relationships were popularized in literature, from fiction to nonfiction, that introduced the rest of the nation to the unique and romantic Spanish history of the Southwest. As Reavis was setting the stage to lay claim to the Peralta Land Grant, these literary accounts were gaining in popularity. From novels such as Helen Hunt Jackson's *Ramona* (1884) to magazines like *Sunset*, easterners seemingly could not get enough of tragic tales of beautiful señoritas and glossy images of Spanish revivalist architecture, all of which served to bolster tourism to the Southwest.[57] After the Peralta Land Grant trial ended, it too became part of this canon of cultural production as it was recounted in magazine articles, novels, and films.[58]

Yet the counterfeit nature of the individual romance between Reavis and Peralta-Reavis points to the dark reality that the broader romanticization of the Southwest obscured. Though intermarriage had by the late nineteenth century declined, Reavis's characterization of his relationship with Peralta-Reavis tapped into an idealized vision of mid-nineteenth-century bonds and the cultural and legal consequences they provoked in the immediate aftermath of the U.S.-Mexican War. The rosy representation of this history that had become prevalent in popular culture elided the realities of conquest, including its reliance on the ability of Anglo men like Reavis to control the bodies, sexuality, and property of women like Peralta-Reavis.

Embodying a Baroness: Passing and Possibility

In addition to her ancestry and her marriage, who Peralta-Reavis was perceived to be—that is, who outside observers believed she was—was the final test of the credibility of her claim to the Peralta Land Grant. Consequently, the counterfeit narrative that produced Peralta-Reavis was, at its core, a narrative about passing. Elaine Ginsberg affirms that "passing is about identities: their creation or imposition, their adoption or rejection, their accompanying rewards or penalties."[59] The court's adoption or rejection of the counterfeit narrative Reavis created about Peralta-Reavis promised to bring, respectively, a reward, the confirmation of Reavis's claim to the Peralta Land Grant, or a penalty, the discovery of his deception. Nevertheless, more was at stake in Peralta-Reavis's passing than the title to a piece of land. Ginsberg continues, "Passing is also about the boundaries established between identity categories and . . . the individual and cultural anxieties induced by boundary crossing."[60] The construction of and responses to the counterfeit narrative that created Peralta-Reavis demonstrate the unsettling permeability of these boundaries. A wide cultural chasm separated Sofia Treadway from Sofia Peralta-Reavis, yet one woman was nearly able to bridge that divide by appearing and behaving convincingly as someone she was not.

Passing has long been associated with appearance, and Peralta-Reavis's appearance played a predictably key role at the trial. Returning to Reavis's and Hopkins's testimonies reveals how important appearance was to the substantiation of Peralta-Reavis's racial identity. Reynolds framed his question to Reavis about his wife's identity in terms of appearance, asking, "You suspected *by reason of her appearance* that she was of Spanish origin?" to which Reavis responded,

"Certainly. That was the *only inducement* for speaking to her," crediting Peralta-Reavis's appearance as the stimulus for approaching her and, by extension, as the foundation of his entire claim.[61] Similarly, Hopkins's affirmation that he had no "recollection of any suggestion that [Peralta-Reavis] was an Indian, and *her appearance did not indicate she was an Indian*," demonstrates how his perception of her identity ("suggestion") was inevitably tied to the way she looked ("appearance").[62] For both men, there was no question as to who Peralta-Reavis really was; the truth was as plain as the look of her face.

The long history of mixture and passing that marked the Southwest, however, complicated their claims. Though blood purity, or *limpieza de sangre*, was prized by the Spanish settlers, such purity was all too elusive in the isolated northern reaches of New Spain. Mixing was inevitable, and the Spanish responded by classifying the offspring produced through interracial relationships in an elaborate system, the *sistema de castas*, which they then categorized and named visually through *casta* paintings.[63] As Carolyn Dean and Dana Leibsohn argue, these paintings, by "lending mixing and its complexities visible form[,] . . . throw into relief the presumption that mixing will manifest itself physically and thus be visually apparent."[64] That same presumption undergirded the arguments made centuries later by Reavis and Hopkins at the Peralta Land Grant trial, as both men attempted to read Peralta-Reavis's appearance for tangible evidence of her racial identity, as if she were a late nineteenth-century embodiment of a *casta* painting.

While the *casta* system was intended to distinguish different racial categories from each other, the borderlands tested the limits of its logic. In his study of racial identity in eighteenth-century Spanish New Mexico, Ramón Gutiérrez affirms that "there was no direct correspondence, except perhaps at the extreme ends of the classification scale, between race and actual physical color. . . . Comments that a person 'appeared to be,' 'was reputed to be,' or 'was known to be' of a certain race indicated the degree to which racial mixing and passing existed on this remote fringe of northern New Spain and complicated the classification system."[65] The borderlands not only complicated but also destabilized centuries of *casta* and subsequent racial classification systems, exposing their own volatility and, more importantly, the incoherence of the racial identities they attempted to define.

Despite this incoherence, from Spanish colonial times to the period following U.S. expansion, how a person looked directly impacted the rights, privileges, and opportunities he or she would enjoy. The Spanish ruled the New World with what Chilean sociologist Alejandro Lipschütz has called a pigmentocracy, or a system that privileged those with lighter skin.[66] Though U.S. expansion altered the specifics of how this racial hierarchy functioned, it continued to privilege people who appeared lighter. For the people of the Southwest, this visually based calculation shaped their legal and cultural citizenship within the United States.

Menchaca confirms that the "skin color of Mexican-origin people strongly influenced whether they were to be treated by the legal system as white or as non-white."[67] This was a crucial calculation, as "Mexicans who were White were given full citizenship, while mestizos, Christianized Indians, and *afromestizos* came under different racial laws."[68] As the debates surrounding Peralta-Reavis's appearance attest, though these calculations carried important consequences, their foundation was shaky at best.[69] In such an environment, passing was prevalent, as were the anxieties that surrounded its transgressive potential.

That transgressive potential went beyond defying racial boundaries to also include the contestation of gender norms. In the testimony of another of Reavis's key witnesses, José Ramón Valencia,[70] Valencia appealed to both gender and race in order to affirm Peralta-Reavis's identity. Valencia, who claimed to be a friend of the Peralta family, described his immediate recognition of Peralta-Reavis as the heiress to the Peralta Land Grant. Upon seeing her at the trial for the first time in twenty-three years, he insisted that he "recollected her right away" as the once-young daughter of Maso, the son-in-law of Miguel Peralta.[71] In his statement, the importance of his recognition of Peralta-Reavis as the Spanish heiress to the Peralta Land Grant resonates beyond the limits of her land claim. As Casas explains, by the late nineteenth century, to be perceived as a Spanish woman was to be "racially of pure Spanish decent, protected by a patriarchal family whose honor was beyond reproach, and endowed with personal virtue and sexual chastity beyond question."[72] In recognizing Peralta-Reavis as a Spanish woman, Valencia also recognized her as the embodiment of the gendered norms that sustained the Spanish fantasy heritage. His description of her appearance therefore placed her at the top of the racialized and gendered hierarchy of the Southwest.

Reynolds's cross-examination of Valencia gives some idea of what kind of treatment those who did not occupy the upper echelons of that mutually constitutive hierarchy could expect. Reynolds began,

Q: You have not seen her from 1872 to this time?
A: Yes sir. She was not so stout as she is now.
Q: She was not so tall either?
A: No sir; she has grown.
Q: She was about ten years old the last time you saw her?
A: Yes sir.
Q: And she is about 32 or 33 now, and the mother of children?
A: Yes sir, she is about that.
Q: Has she not changed some?
A: She has changed in height and flesh.
Q: Very materially, has she not?
A: But her face has not changed.[73]

In this exchange, Reynolds implied that the passage of over two decades would make it difficult, if not impossible, for Valencia to recognize Peralta-Reavis. He referred specifically to gender in order to plant the seeds of doubt, emphasizing that her status as "the mother of children" and her related physical changes would render her unrecognizable. Though Valencia maintained that "her face has not changed," Reynolds did not back down, continuing his line of questioning by asking,

Q: She has not changed in the face?
A: No sir.
Q: She is very much larger in the face?
A: A little larger.
Q: Her face is very much more gross, fat, fleshy than before?
A: Yes sir.
Q: Has her face wrinkled any?
A: No sir.
Q: Any grey hairs?
A: No sir.
Q: You are satisfied if you met her on the street and took a good look at her you would have remembered her?
A: I think I could.[74]

This exchange between the two men is deeply disturbing in its detached, dehumanizing description of Peralta-Reavis's height, weight, and age. The dissection of her physical appearance, from Reynolds's questions about her "gross, fat, fleshy" face to whether she has "wrinkled" or grown "grey hairs," is degrading but not surprising. The verbally violent rhetoric betrays an underlying logic that dehumanizes women and people of color. For centuries, this logic enabled not only verbal but also physical violence. As Chávez-García affirms, "Native Americans as well as 'half-breed Mexicans,' who were despised and viewed as a degraded race by Euro-Americans, bore the brunt of the vigilantism and racial violence" that occurred in the Southwest.[75] Although Peralta-Reavis was the linchpin of the Peralta Land Grant case, her centrality did not shield her from the ruthlessness of a racial regime that was at its core based on the violent rejection of people, and especially women, of color.

The debates surrounding Peralta-Reavis's appearance reveal how the desire to classify people according to race in the Southwest has long existed alongside the reality that such classifications are inherently unstable and therefore transgressible. As Amy Robinson contends, "The 'problem' of identity, a problem to which passing owes the very possibility of its practice, is predicated on the false promise of the visible as an epistemological guarantee."[76] That Peralta-Reavis was able to pass successfully in many circles is certainly a testament to the falsity of this promise. Even more significantly, her passing testifies to the fundamental instability of the racial classifications on which the visual regime she transgressed was based, an instability that long preceded, and has extended far beyond, mid-nineteenth-century U.S. expansion into the Southwest.

Of course, racial identity is a social construct tied to more than just appearance, meaning that passing can take other forms as well. As Ginsberg affirms, "Racial categories refer not only to persons with discernible and visible physical characteristics such as skin color but also to persons who share language, nationality, and religion."[77] At the trial, in addition to appearance, each side used language to make its case for or against Peralta-Reavis's Spanish heritage. This is not surprising when one considers that both appearance and language are easily observable, though not necessarily reliable, external indicators of racial identity. Just as the debates surrounding her appearance expose how U.S. westward expansion revised Spanish colonial ideas regarding racial visibility, the arguments regarding Peralta-Reavis's Spanish fluency reveal how U.S. expansion transformed the language ideologies that shaped the Southwest.

Though the United States began as a multilingual nation, by the late nineteenth century English was gaining dominance as not only a form of communication but also a symbol of (Anglo) U.S. national identity.[78] Speaking of U.S. westward expansion, Elise DuBord affirms that "Anglo newcomers reproduced the dominant nativism as part of their expansionary nation-building project," creating a "linguistic ideology . . . that conflated language, race, and citizenship as defining factors for full membership in the nation."[79] In this context, language became racialized, serving as another metric for determining whether a person should be included within or excluded from the full rights of citizenship.

The racialization of language in the Southwest extended beyond a simple white-nonwhite binary relationship between English and the second most dominant language, Spanish. Wealthy Mexicans appealed to their bilingualism, biliteracy, and Spanish fluency as a way of distancing themselves not only from the U.S. Anglo community that sought to displace them but also from Native Americans and poorer, more recently immigrated and less educated Mexicans.[80] As José del Valle and Ofelia García explain, this elite "defense of Spanish . . . was often grounded in purist ideologies that reproduced class inequality and . . . a (transatlantic) historical narrative that linked their culture and language to Europe via a supposedly uninterrupted and untarnished descent from Spain."[81] Here again the long reach of the racialized *limpieza de sangre* doctrine is clear. Language, like appearance, played a key role in these elites' strategic invocation of a pure-blooded Spanish identity in order to shore up their claim to whiteness within the U.S. racial hierarchy.

The mutually constitutive relationship between linguistic and racial ideologies is clear in Reynolds's interrogation of Reavis. In reference to the languages Peralta-Reavis spoke, Reynolds asked Reavis,

Q: Could she speak Spanish when you first met her?

A: A few words.

Q: Does she speak it now?

A: She does not speak much Spanish, although what she does speak, I am told, is very clear Spanish, without any accent whatever.[82]

Here Reavis attempted to reinforce Peralta-Reavis's credibility by affirming that even though "she does not speak much Spanish," when she does speak in her ancestral tongue, it "is very clear . . . without any accent whatever." This is a strange argument, as Spanish ancestry would not translate into Spanish fluency. Unlike appearance, language is not passed on genetically, and the fact that she was raised in the United States by an adopted Anglo father should be explanation enough for her inability to speak the language. Nevertheless, Reavis's insistence that Spanish *comes naturally* to her—that is to say, that her Spanish is instinctively "clear" and "without any accent whatever"—is an unmistakable appeal to a language ideology that associates racial identity with linguistic ability.

The racialized dimensions of the language ideologies of the Southwest are even more obvious when this excerpt is read in the context of Reynolds's and Reavis's larger exchange. Their discussion about Peralta-Reavis's Spanish fluency at first appears oddly unrelated to the litany of other questions Reynolds asked Reavis regarding the history of the Peralta Land Grant. Nevertheless, its significance becomes clear when read against the question that immediately preceded it, in which Reynolds asked Reavis, "Didn't she claim herself, and don't you know it to be the fact [sic] that she claimed herself that her father was John A. Treadway?"[83] By questioning Peralta-Reavis's ability to speak Spanish immediately after accusing her of lying about her familial history, Reynolds made clear the centrality of language to the determination of familial and, consequently, racial identity.

When Peralta-Reavis took the stand, she was even more resolute in defending her Spanish fluency. Unlike how Reavis responded in his more evasive comments, Peralta-Reavis insisted she had spoken Spanish since she was a child, prompting Reynolds to ask whether she ever spoke Spanish with Mrs. Snowball, a Mexican woman with whom she lived as a child. Peralta-Reavis replied, "I tried not to, because she nearly broke my head whenever I tried to speak to her. She would not have it. She was determined to brand me an Indian, and an Indian she would have me."[84] Here Peralta-Reavis clearly invoked the "linguistic capital" of Spanish, which served to "elevate" the "racial status" of elite Mexicans and distance them from Native Americans.[85] She refuted any accusations that she did not speak Spanish as conspiratorial attempts to deny her true ancestry and the rightful inheritance that accompanied it.

Peralta-Reavis's physical and linguistic passing was predicated on her ability to exploit the ambiguities U.S. expansion introduced to the racial hierarchy of the U.S. Southwest. Though her counterfeit narrative of Spanish ancestry was entirely false, it developed in response to real uncertainties regarding how racial identity was defined and detected in the region. Her nearly successful claim highlighted the permeability of this racial hierarchy and the possibilities for passing that such instability introduced.

Searching for Sofia

How complicit was Sofia Peralta-Reavis in the invention of her forged identity? Did she know of and actively participate in the creation and performance of her husband's scheme? Or did she truly believe his story about her family genealogy? Such questions are impossible to answer, as the archive is largely silent on Peralta-Reavis's own thoughts. The transcripts of her testimony on the stand during the 1895 trial are the only part of the archive to record her exact words, and those remarks are highly mediated both by the questioning of U.S. attorney Reynolds and by the interruptions and objections of her husband, James Reavis. Beyond these few indirect glimpses, any deep exploration of who Peralta-Reavis was or what she thought about the case and her relationship to it is plagued by abundant and frustrating silences.

Still, those silences speak volumes about the hemispheric crossroads that determined racial identity in the U.S. Southwest. Heeding Ann Laura Stoler's call to read "along the archival grain," what the archive does say about Peralta-Reavis can be read as what Stoler calls a "condensed [site] of epistemological and political anxiety."[86] In the post-1848 U.S. Southwest, the epistemological and political anxieties surrounding the hemispheric relocation of borders, both physical and cultural, were great. At the trial, Peralta-Reavis came to embody those anxieties as a living representation of the threats those new borders created, including the threat of the exposure and perhaps even alteration of the exclusionary racial foundation on which U.S. citizenship was built, as well as the imaginary nature of racial categories themselves.

Furthermore, Peralta-Reavis's trial testimony, though mediated, is an important part of the Peralta Land Grant archives. As González cautions, "To suggest that the evidence is scanty or impossible to find, as many historians do to justify excluding women or gender, is to ignore the sources or the women in them."[87] Looking specifically at land grants, Karen R. Roybal likewise looks to the interstices of the archival record to locate Mexican and Mexican American women's voices and "contribute to an expanding alternative archive of the Borderlands that challenge nineteenth- and twentieth-century male-centric narratives of land grants and the male bias in more generalized treatments of land issues."[88] Following the example set by González and Roybal, in an effort to comb the interstices of the Peralta Land Grant archives and acknowledge the woman in the source, I conclude by returning to where I began, with Sofia Peralta-Reavis, in her own words.

Before disappearing from the archival record, Peralta-Reavis responded to Reynolds's accusation that she was an impostor with an unwavering affirmation of her claim: "No, sir; I did not know that I was personating anybody but myself."[89] Perhaps she knew that the narrative Reavis told her of her extraordinary inheritance was false but played along anyway. Referring to the testimony of Spanish Mexican women in court, González affirms, "Women . . . adjusted their behavior to achieve the results they desired. Whether they were consciously or unconsciously manipulating powerful structures or the men who controlled them is unclear, but in the majority of cases in which women appear as plaintiffs or defendants, both women and men repeatedly resurrected the notions of modesty, honor, and reputation. In this way, women codified their behavior to suggest the resolutions they desired."[90] Perhaps Peralta-Reavis codified her behavior to usher along the resolution that both she and her husband desired: the confirmation of the Peralta Land Grant. Or perhaps after years of hearing her husband repeat the extraordinary story of her identity and inheritance, she had begun to believe it. Regardless of what she believed or why she believed it, reading along the archival grain of her statement reveals an extraordinary image: that of a mixed-race woman from a poor family in California confidently and unapologetically claiming to be a Spanish baroness and the rightful owner of a large amount of valuable property.

Discounting the boldness behind Peralta-Reavis's statement due to the unanswerable questions surrounding the context in which it was uttered risks missing its remarkable implications. Peralta-Reavis's words reveal the real threat that her husband's invented Peralta Land Grant posed: not that his story about her identity was false but that it could not be disproved. When Peralta-Reavis claimed that she was not "personating anybody but [her]self," she left unresolved the question of who she really was, foreclosing the possibility of absolutely and conclusively determining her racial identity. As a result, the lingering ambiguity of her statement resonated beyond the confines of the late nineteenth-century Santa Fe courtroom, casting doubt on not only the validity of the Peralta Land Grant but also the salience of the mutually constitutive conceptions of race, gender, and authenticity on which it depended.

CHAPTER 3

Southwest Speculation

NEWSPAPER COVERAGE OF THE
PERALTA LAND GRANT

An 1887 article that originally ran in San Francisco and was later republished in places as disparate as Illinois, Utah, Georgia, and New York announced the recent organization of the Casa Land Company, a corporation that James Addison Reavis formed to confirm and develop the Peralta Land Grant,[1] the Spanish land grant Reavis fabricated to steal valuable land in central Arizona Territory. After describing the original grant, the article, which was alternately titled "A Strange Story: A Company Organized to Improve the Peralta Land Grant in Arizona,"[2] "The Great Peralta Grant: Sensational Developments in Regard to the Old Spanish Grant,"[3] and, most tellingly, "Claiming an Estate: A Girl Who Says She Is Heiress to 5,000,000 Acres of Land,"[4] went on to describe the person through which Reavis claimed title to the land:

No claimant appeared to the estate until three years ago, when Reavis appeared with a dark complexioned native California girl about 18 years of age whom he had married and whom he claimed to be the granddaughter of Don Peralta and heir to the now very valuable Peralta grant. To strengthen his claims he made a trip to Spain and about six months ago returned, bringing with him an elaborate parchment from the authorities at Madrid, conveying to his wife, who was then recognized as the daughter of Don Peralta, a perfect title to the Peralta grant and she was further honored by having the title of the Baroness of the Colorados conferred upon her. The *Examiner* of this city [San Francisco] prints an interview with a resident of Woodland, Yolo County, Cal., claiming that the girl is the daughter of a Missourian named Treadwell by an Indian woman. She worked for a number of Woodland families until married to Reavis. On the other hand Director [John] Benson [of the Casa Land Company] asserts that she is Spanish, and makes the statement that the girl's mother died at San Diego at the girl's birth, and that the latter accompanied Peralta to

Woodland where he died, and the girl fell into the hands of Treadwell, who was a sheep herder.[5]

The widely reprinted article provides a window into the reaction to Reavis's counterfeit narrative outside the walls of the archives and the courtroom. In addition to the trial at the Court of Private Land Claims, the Peralta Land Grant was put on trial in the court of public opinion through extensive newspaper coverage. As this short excerpt demonstrates, the public reaction to Reavis's plot was far from uniform. Some, like the resident of Woodland, California, dismissed Reavis's farfetched story, especially when it came to his assertion that the humble Sofia Treadwell was actually the long-lost Sofia Peralta. Others, like John Benson, who was one of Reavis's San Francisco–based backers and a director of the Casa Land Company, wholeheartedly defended the validity of Reavis's claim and his elaborate explanation for it. While reactions varied, one thing was certain: the Peralta Land Grant was important news, and people across the country were talking about it.

As the wide republication of this article demonstrates, coverage of the Peralta Land Grant extended far beyond the territories of Arizona and New Mexico, where the grant itself was situated and where the trial at the Court of Private Land Claims took place. Before, during, and after the 1895 trial, people evaluated the legitimacy of Reavis's counterfeit narrative by following the developments of the case in their local newspapers. Though today the Peralta Land Grant case is all but forgotten, it dominated newspaper headlines for the better part of two decades, from the mid-1880s to the early 1900s. In the pages of major newspapers in financial centers like New York and San Francisco and regional papers in seemingly every city in between, readers across the country followed the ups and downs of Reavis's scheme to invent and claim his legendary Peralta Land Grant.

The Peralta Land Grant filled the pages of these papers just as a new trend in journalism was emerging: yellow journalism. The style, which emerged from battles to increase circulation in New York City, was a perfect match for the outrageous details of the case. Yellow journalists, who were known more for style than substance, recounted the sensational story for their readers without much regard for its validity. In the vast majority of the articles, Sofia Loreto Peralta-Reavis became a central focus of the reporting. Though the forgeries that formed the basis for the Peralta Land Grant proved to be fertile ground for the yellow journalists of the 1890s, ancient documents, even forged ones, were not nearly as interesting as a mysterious orphan who was either a secret baroness or an imposter who had fooled Spanish royalty. From small towns to big cities, from East Coast to West, newspapers endlessly debated Peralta-Reavis's identity. Whether the coverage was sympathetic or hostile, it was dominated by hearsay, rumors, and misinformation. The coverage developed its own counterfeit narrative that was not accountable to facts, instead underlining the desirability of upholding national fictions about race, gender, and class and foreshadowing how the Peralta Land Grant would evolve from legal debate to legend.

BETWEEN FACT AND FICTION: YELLOW JOURNALISM AND THE PERALTA LAND GRANT

The Peralta Land Grant, from its romantic Spanish origins to its Cinderella-like orphaned heiress, was a yellow journalist's dream. As rumors spread that the grant had been forged, the saga, and the newspaper coverage of it, became even more salacious. The combination of the already sensational Peralta Land Grant story and yellow journalism's tendency to embellish the facts created a perfect storm of irresponsible reporting about the large grant and its purported owners that reached a fever pitch when the Peralta Land Grant came to trial in the mid-1890s.

The U.S. newspaper industry, from its financial structure to the form and content of its reporting, changed dramatically over the course of the nineteenth century. Throughout the 1800s, newspapers fought to expand circulation in order to increase subscription and advertisement sales and, therefore, profits. As Gerald J. Baldasty has shown, newspapers in the early part of the nineteenth century functioned largely as wings of various political parties, which supported the papers financially. As this arrangement became less predominant, newspapers sought other paths toward financial solvency. The most obvious solution was to increase profits by growing circulation and, consequently, advertisement revenue. In order to increase circulation, however, newspapers needed to appeal to a wider public—that is, they needed to produce something that many people would want to read.[6]

By the end of the century, the battle to expand readership had prompted the creation of a new style that eventually came to be known as yellow journalism.[7] Matthew Arnold first identified this shift in 1887, calling it "new journalism" and praising its innovative style while cautioning that its brand of reporting "throws out assertions at a venture because it wishes them true; does not correct either them or itself, if they are false; and to get at the state of things as they truly are seems to feel no concern whatever."[8] Yellow journalism was the logical outcome of the push to expand readership, as reporting shifted toward entertaining readers in order to garner the largest audience possible.[9] The success of this strategy is clear; between 1830 and 1900, newspaper circulation jumped from seventy-eight thousand to a staggering twenty-two million.[10]

As the influence of yellow journalism spread across the nation, news of Reavis's villainy, Peralta-Reavis's impersonation, and the Peralta Land Grant's ultimate demise was exaggerated and exploited in newspapers across the country. Whether a particular newspaper was associated with the yellow journalistic style or not, the Peralta Land Grant saga presented a particularly tempting opportunity to play with fact and fiction. For those who lived far from the southwestern territories in which the grant was situated, anything seemed believable regarding these faraway foreign lands. In an article from May 15, 1892, for example, Portland's *Oregonian* reported that Peralta-Reavis claimed the land through her position as the "Last of the Aztecs" and that her husband, Reavis, who was very much alive, was already dead.[11] This sort of misinformation, though not uncommon before the Peralta Land Grant went to trial in 1895, increased exponentially after the case was closed and became the stuff of legend. On October 5, 1900, the *Kansas Semi-weekly Capital* included a dramatic report that Reavis's scheme was exposed when Peralta-Reavis tearfully broke down at the trial while on the stand, confessing everything. Of course, Peralta-Reavis had not confessed anything, resolutely maintaining her identity as Sofia Peralta and her claim to the Peralta Land Grant throughout the entire trial, but it made for a good story.[12]

While the Peralta Land Grant filled the pages of papers across the country, one western paper that was associated with the yellow journalistic style became especially preoccupied with the saga: the *San Francisco Examiner*. The 1849 California Gold Rush prompted newspapers to move westward as more people and a more industrialized economy developed.[13] In the West, the capital of this new economy and the newspapers that accompanied it was San Francisco.[14] By the 1880s, San Francisco had risen to become the ninth-largest city in the United States and the most significant center of trade west of Chicago.[15]

Because of its financial and political prominence, San Francisco became a point of convergence for supporters and critics of the Peralta Land Grant. Reavis turned to San Francisco's wealthy elite to back his claim, but not everyone in San Francisco was enamored with Reavis and his Peralta Land Grant, including William Randolph Hearst's *San Francisco Examiner*. Hearst's father bought the paper in 1880 and, after much lobbying on the part of the younger Hearst, allowed his son to assume control of the paper in 1887.[16] Hearst capitalized on the changing dynamics of the city, whose sudden economic and population boom had created an increase in corruption and the gap that separated the rich from the poor.[17] In response to this shift, Hearst employed xenophobic and populist rhetoric to appeal to a wide readership and increase the *Examiner*'s circulation.[18]

The *Examiner*'s anti-elite and antiforeigner bent shaped its reporting on the Peralta Land Grant. Reavis was an ideal target to help bolster the *Examiner*'s reputation as a populist paper that was on the side of the common man and not big business or corrupt government officials. Reavis's association with the Southern Pacific Railroad, which Hearst believed to be "the worst of all public villains," and other powerful corporations and political leaders did not earn him any favor from the newspaper.[19] The paper's coverage of Baroness Peralta-Reavis likewise consolidated its xenophobic rhetoric regarding foreigners who threatened to displace "real" Americans. For his part, Reavis dismissed the *Examiner*'s reporting, declaring, "They have taken up the evidence in the case at a certain point and presented it from there on. I have traced back far beyond where the Examiner started in and I have established facts and worked up evidence that will speak for itself when the proper time comes."[20]

Thanks to the newspaper exchange system, the *Examiner*'s negative coverage of the Peralta Land Grant traveled far beyond San Francisco. Before the telegraph, a wide network of exchange between newspapers served as an informal national news service.[21] Because of this system, the news, including the latest reports about the status of the Peralta Land Grant, reached almost every corner of the nation. These reprinted stories were sometimes credited, other times not. Many appeared in local Arizona newspapers, where negative coverage of the highly unpopular Peralta Land Grant was always sure to please readers.[22] This coverage was not always accurate; as Barbara Cloud clarifies, the system of formal and informal exchange of information "facilitated the movement not only of news but also of misinformation and outright hoaxes."[23] Because the Peralta Land Grant was itself a hoax, it became even more difficult to separate the facts of the case from misinformation, fomenting a reporting culture in which rumors, hearsay, and falsehoods flourished.

MIXED-RACE UNCERTAINTIES:
SOFIA PERALTA-REAVIS IN THE PAPERS

Much of the misinformation that circulated in reference to the Peralta Land Grant had to do with Peralta-Reavis, whose allegedly mixed racial identity was the source of great confusion and contention. Before, during, and after her racial identity became a focus of the 1895 Peralta Land Grant trial at the U.S. Court of Private Land Claims in Santa Fe, it was a central concern of newspapers across the country. Characterizations of her racial identity varied greatly, from those that affirmed her claim to Spanish ancestry to those that belittled her as a "half-breed Indian." The latter connected Peralta-Reavis and the newspaper coverage of the Peralta Land Grant to the long history of the disenfranchisement of people of mixed ancestry in the Americas. Though the Spanish and the English developed very different racial categories through which they organized their colonies in the New World, they both ascribed positive characteristics to people of pure European descent, who were then bestowed with political, economic, and cultural power, and developed negative stereotypes about people with a mix of ancestries, who were then marginalized in colonial society.[24] In the late nineteenth-century U.S. Southwest, the legacy of Spanish and English colonial racial hierarchies, as well as the gender and class norms they promoted, combined with Progressive Era fears of racial and class mixing and the rise of scientific racism in order to solidify the marginalization of people of mixed ancestry.[25]

The increasingly hostile newspaper coverage of Peralta-Reavis's racial identity reveals the contours of this multilayered marginalization, as well as the internal fractures that allowed Peralta-Reavis, if only for a time, to convincingly pass as someone she was not.

Newspaper coverage relied on norms associated not only with race but also with gender and class in order to make the case for or against Peralta-Reavis's claim to Spanish ancestry. On August 6, 1887, the *Tombstone Epitaph* ran "The Peralta Claim. Array of Public Men Who Are Interested in the Scheme. Opinions That It Is Bolstered Up by Manufactured Testimony" on its first page. The article, which originally ran in the *Examiner*, quotes at length from an interview with Mrs. Isaac C. Smith, who claimed to be "a friend of Sophia Treadwell when she was engaged in Mrs. Hopkin's [sic] household."[26] In the interview, Smith declares, "When I knew Sophie she was as poor as anybody, but I have heard she has got tony lately. That man Reavis took her to Europe and pushed her up. He first taught her to read and write decently, after which she took lessons in the arts. I hear she paints now. Well isn't it funny the way people spread themselves when they get hold of money?"[27] Smith's hostility toward Peralta-Reavis is clear in her disparaging remarks. Though Smith does not at first explicitly mention Peralta-Reavis's racial identity, her invocation of class and gender norms—namely, Peralta-Reavis's newfound access to international travel, literacy, and the arts—also functions as a coded rebuttal of Peralta-Reavis's racial identity. As Lauren Basson explains, in the late nineteenth-century United States, "education, fluency in English, proper etiquette (i.e., the ability to comport oneself as a lady or gentleman), social class, and ownership of private property all figured into . . . assumptions about racial status."[28] The intersection of these class, gender, and racial codes becomes clear as Smith continues, laughing at the suggestion that Peralta-Reavis was the granddaughter of a Don Peralta and adding, "I have always thought she was the daughter of an Indian squaw and never in the world considered her to be an aristocrat."[29] Here Smith more explicitly connects gender and class with race, dismissing Peralta-Reavis's claim "to be an aristocrat" by affirming that she was actually the "daughter of an Indian squaw." By invoking the offensive term "squaw," Smith puts Peralta-Reavis in her place, so to speak, at the bottom of the U.S. racial hierarchy.

In the article, Smith's statements are contradicted by Reavis, who is also quoted at length. When asked by the reporter about the reception of Peralta-Reavis in Spain, Reavis affirms, "The striking personal resemblance my wife bore to the living and pictured Peraltas was so positive that there was absolutely no room for doubt; nor indeed did they think it worth while to entertain any. She was received with open arms and treated as one of the family at once."[30] This affirmation then appears to be seconded by the article's author, who describes Peralta-Reavis as a "lady" with "quite a high type of Castillian [sic] air and a most pleasant genial presence. She is apparently about 30 years of age, medium height, with clear dreamy complexion, already inclining to fleshiness."[31] Though the author does not go as far as Reavis in drawing a direct connection between Peralta-Reavis and the Spanish Peraltas, the reference to "quite a high type of Castillian [sic] air" suggests that the author does believe that Peralta-Reavis at least has a claim to European ancestry. The disagreement within the article regarding how to interpret Peralta-Reavis's appearance and behavior speaks to the instability of racial categories and the class and gender norms that were ascribed to them in the late nineteenth-century United States. Nevertheless, the fact that papers like the *Examiner* and the *Epitaph* would deem the debate over Peralta-Reavis's racial identity newsworthy also indicates that, despite this instability, racial categories and the assumptions they carried were a fundamental concern for late nineteenth-century U.S. society.

Smith was not the only person to use Peralta-Reavis's uncertain racial identity against her. Many newspaper articles, particularly after it became clear that the Peralta Land Grant was a fraud, appealed to negative stereotypes about so-called half-breeds in order to discredit the claim further. Though when the term *half-breed* first appeared in print in 1760 it was not necessarily derogatory, by the nineteenth century it had gained in popularity as a wholly negative epithet.[32] Culturally, mixed ancestry carried with it a host of negative associations, including an untrustworthy, manipulative, and crafty nature.[33] Legally, people of mixed descent also faced limited rights, as they "could be barred from voting, practicing law, or becoming naturalized citizens, and in many states the selection of their marriage partners was restricted."[34] Facing such formal and informal discrimination, many people with mixed ancestries were incentivized to pass.[35]

In this context, Peralta-Reavis's passing as a Spanish baroness in the case of the Peralta Land Grant highlights the larger dynamics that shaped why and how people with mixed ancestry passed in the late nineteenth-century United States. As the August 6, 1887, *Epitaph* article indicates, assumptions related to race, class, and gender shaped how a person's appearance and behavior would be evaluated. As the contradictions within the article demonstrate, however, there was no guaranteed uniformity as to how such assumptions would be applied or interpreted in the case of any given person. Peralta-Reavis's temporarily successful passing is a testament to not only the irregular application of racial categories but also the variable assumptions that defined the categories themselves.

The flexibility of these racial categories and the assumptions they carried allowed characterizations of Peralta-Reavis in the papers to change over time. These changes were most marked as the conclusion of the Peralta Land Grant trial neared and Reavis's fraud became clear. For Peralta-Reavis, this shift meant that descriptions of her racial identity moved from ambiguous to overtly mocking. This change is clear in a June 3, 1895, *New Mexican* article entitled "Peralta-Reavis Grant Case. Wonderful Structure Founded on Fraud, Perjury and Forgery About to Fall. Baron Peralta a Myth—The Alleged Grant a Fraud—Pretended

Baroness a Half-Breed Indian." As the title of the article suggests, emboldened
with the information that Reavis had forged the Peralta Land Grant, the contradictions and uncertainties that marked the *Epitaph*'s August 6, 1887, article
disappeared, as the *New Mexican* article does not hold back in its overt, racialized ridicule of the supposed heiress to the invalidated claim. The article describes
"Mrs. Peralta-Reavis" as

> a large, heavy-featured, plain looking woman of about 30, showily dressed and
> glittering with jewels, calmly posed as the baroness of Arizona, and the great
> grand daughter and only living heir of Baron Miguel de Peralta who easily
> traced her lineage back 700 years among the real grandees of Spain. When
> the ladies of Phoenix called upon her she would sometimes be found sitting
> luxuriously in her "drawing room" with an elegant bit of fancy work lying in
> her lap, and at other times she would appear, as if taken by surprise, in a neg-
> ligee costume with a half finished painting in her paint-besmeared fingers. Yet
> no one ever saw her ply a needle or touch canvas with a paint brush.[36]

The description echoes many of the same sentiments provided by Smith in the
August 6, 1887, *Epitaph* article. The resentment that marked Smith's description,
however, here turns to ridicule, as the now discredited baroness can be safely
mocked as an imposter. Her performance of wealth turns into a caricature as
her "glittering . . . jewels" cannot hide her "plain" features and her artistic ability is shown to be an artifice. The *New Mexican* article appeals to the inadequacy
of her performance of gender and class norms in order to discredit her supposed
Spanish racial identity and expose her for who she really is: "the daughter of one
John Treadway by a Digger Indian squaw known as Kate" who is "in nowise
related to any Spanish family."[37]

The racialized ridicule aimed at Peralta-Reavis was not limited to an Anglo,
English-speaking audience. The June 3, 1895, *New Mexican* article was translated
into Spanish for the paper's Spanish-language version, *El nuevo mexicano*, and
then reprinted in *El fronterizo*, a Spanish-language paper serving Tucson, Arizona.[38] The Spanish-language versions of the article are no less vitriolic and no
less disparaging of Peralta-Reavis, whom they call "un fraude y un engaño," (a
fraud and a fake) though how they denigrate her claim is specific to the Spanish
American context.[39] For example, *El nuevo mexicano* translates the subtitle of
the English-language version, "Pretended Baroness a Half-Breed Indian" as "La
Supuesta Baronesa no Pasa de Ser una Coyota."[40] *Coyote* was a label used in the
Spanish colonial racial categorization system, or *sistema de castas*, in order to
name the offspring of an *indio* and a mestizo.[41] As Mary Dashnaw argues, "Those
labeled coyote were visually positioned as one of the lowest members of the *casta*
and of questionable quality as humans, given their comparison to wild
canines."[42] The classification of Peralta-Reavis as a *coyota* is clearly meant to be
derogatory, though the specific context of the insult, unlike that of the insult in

the English-language version of the article, is grounded not in U.S. racial codes but rather in Spanish colonial categories. The linguistic and cultural translation of this racialized hostility toward Peralta-Reavis clearly indicates that the elite Mexicans and Mexican Americans who ran Spanish-language newspapers in the Southwest were as invested in maintaining a racial hierarchy as their Anglo counterparts, though the genealogy and specifics of that hierarchy differed.

Despite the certainty with which these English- and Spanish-language papers mocked Peralta-Reavis's claim to Spanish ancestry, her actual racial identity was never legally determined. Though the government attorneys who prosecuted the Peralta Land Grant case later went after the false witnesses Reavis paid to lie under oath, they never brought charges against Peralta-Reavis, likely because her identity was never discredited in the same way. Though she could not claim the specific parentage Reavis had forged for her, who she was remained a mystery. The government attorney who represented the United States at the trial, Matthew G. Reynolds, strongly believed the testimony of the witnesses he brought to the stand who affirmed Peralta-Reavis's mixed ancestry, and he condemned her impersonation of a Spanish baroness as harshly as he did Reavis's forgeries. At the conclusion of the trial, the *New Mexican* quoted Reynolds as saying that "the people of this country [will never] hear anything more of the 'Peralta grant,' except as a myth; nor will Reavis and his alleged wife have occasion or opportunity to protect the noble status and purity of blood of a half-breed Indian."[43] In this remarkable quote, Reynolds equates the threat posed by Reavis's claim to the land with the threat posed by Peralta-Reavis's claim to "purity of blood," framing both as a grave danger to "the people of this country."

The chief justice of the Court of Private Land Claims, however, did not corroborate Reynolds's assessment. In his verbal dismissal of the case, Chief Justice Joseph R. Reed "said that the evidence adduced conclusively proved that the so-called grant was purely fictitious, being clearly founded on fraud, forgery and perjury," but "that it was unnecessary to go into the question as to the ancestry of Mrs. Peralta-Reavis."[44] The chief justice even went so far as to say "that the court was persuaded from her appearance and other reasons that she was of Spanish origin, but whether or not she was a descendant of Miguel Peralta was a question that could not be passed upon nor did it concern the court as to its present judgment."[45] The official conclusion of the case sidestepped the question of Peralta-Reavis's racial identity, leaving its determination unsettled.

The diverging opinions of Reynolds and Reed and the legal sidestepping of the subject of Peralta-Reavis's racial identity underscore the uncertainty surrounding late nineteenth-century racial categorizations and their relationship to the physical space of the nation. The widely conflicting descriptions of Peralta-Reavis in newspapers across the country point to the ambiguity that defined racial identity, which created enough flexibility for Peralta-Reavis to both pass as a Spanish baroness and be mocked as a "half-breed" Indian. This ambiguity was then mapped onto the physical space of the nation. It was not by accident that Reynolds equated the threat that Reavis posed to U.S. territorial borders with the danger that Peralta-Reavis represented for U.S. racial categories. Following the end of slavery and in the wake of territorial expansion that incorporated large swaths of formerly Mexican territories and people, as Basson affirms, "the links that once connected prevailing definitions of the American nation and state to visibly distinguishable human and territorial bodies became increasingly tenuous."[46] As a purportedly mixed-race woman, Peralta-Reavis represented the weakening link between U.S. national identity and actual racial and national borders.

In this way, the debates that took place in newspapers around the country surrounding Peralta-Reavis's racial identity mirrored the debates that took place in the halls of Congress surrounding Arizona's bid for statehood. In 1891 and then again in 1893, Arizona's territorial leaders presented statehood bills that the U.S. Congress summarily dismissed. As historian Mark E. Pry explains, "Pointing to the territory's small population and aridity, among other negative characteristics, opponents of the bill attacked Arizona's claim to statehood as pretentious and premature, arguing that the territory needed to attract more immigrants and capital before applying for admission."[47] Implicit within the call to attract more immigrants was an expectation that Arizona's Anglo population should outnumber its non-Anglo, primarily Native American and Mexican, people. One of the principal reasons that Arizona statehood remained delayed for another twenty years was national anxieties about "whether people of Mexican descent should fit within the nation in the context of statehood, and the extent of their incorporation as Americans in terms of full citizenship as well as social recognition and equal treatment."[48] National policy makers worried what impact granting statehood to a largely non-Anglo territory would have on national identity. That is, they worried what would happen if a racialized U.S. national identity was suddenly required to expand in order to incorporate Mexican people who were mestizo, or of mixed ancestry.

Despite these concerns, Arizona was eventually granted statehood in 1912, not long after the conclusion of the Peralta Land Grant case. The incorporation of so many mestizo people into the union, however, did not lead to a redefinition of national identity. Quite the opposite, as Basson explains: "As the citizenry of the United States became less white, efforts to preserve and protect whiteness accelerated."[49] The increasingly vigilant policing of racial divisions is clear in the evolution of newspaper coverage of Peralta-Reavis's identity. As the Peralta Land Grant went from national news to western lore, the dismissal of Peralta-Reavis as a deviant mixed-race woman in a moralizing tale about the perils of fraudulent behavior became solidified.

The Making of a Legend: Remembering
the Peralta Land Grant

Three short years after the trial in Santa Fe had ended and Reavis was sentenced to the penitentiary, the Peralta Land Grant saga had already moved from legal debate to legend. An article that appeared on January 27, 1898, in the *Weekly Phoenix Herald* began with the following melodramatic description: "The most audacious and stupendous fraud ever incubated—and perhaps the most romantic—was the 'Peralta Grant,' which came very near robbing the United States of more than twelve million acres of land in Arizona and New Mexico."[50] The *Herald's* retrospective description of the Peralta land Grant is both aggrandized and romanticized, prefiguring the main themes that would appear again and again in remembrances of the Peralta Land Grant: assertions of authenticity regarding the characterization of events, superlative descriptions of the exceptional nature of the crime, and a romanticized nostalgia for the old days of the Wild West.

The *Herald* article is in fact an advertisement for a forthcoming "inside statement of this unparalleled (and almost successful) plot," which the author affirms would be "the first authentic story"[51] of the whole complicated affair: a two-part tell-all titled "The Prince of Impostors" by Will M. Tipton, expert graphologist who had worked for the government in the Peralta Land Grant case,[52] that appeared in the February and March 1898 issues of Charles Fletcher Lummis's *Land of Sunshine*. In the article, Tipton carefully goes over the incredible details of the case. His firsthand experience with the subject matter, combined with the incredible detail with which he recounts the events that led to the trial and Reavis's eventual downfall, lend the article an air of credibility, which is further bolstered by its straightforward, no-nonsense tone.

The inclusion of Tipton's article in Lummis's *Land of Sunshine* provides a window into how the Peralta Land Grant fit into the larger narrative that Lummis and other late nineteenth-century boosters were developing about the West. Lummis, who was an author, editor, and promoter of all things Southwest,[53] used his tenure as the editor of the *Land of Sunshine* to disseminate a carefully curated image of the region, as he explains in this excerpt from the January 1896 issue:

A "local magazine" this is and always will be—but never a narrow one. . . . Geographically, its area is California, New Mexico, Arizona, and whatever further patches constitute the Southwest. In that area there is probably a wider range and variety of subject-matter than in all the rest of the Union together; besides which, this is exclusively the romantic corner of the United States as well as the wonderland of the continent. The tallest and noblest peaks in the United States, the deepest and noblest chasms in the world, our finest (and our only) ruins, the strangest and grandest scenery, the most remarkable geographic contrasts—all are in this extraordinary area. So, too, is the latest and highest development of modern civilization, the climax of human achievement to date, the most radical and important experiment ever made by the race which just now stands at the head of the world.[54]

In this extended quote, Lummis outlines the contours of the image he and others were crafting for the Southwest, which combined remarkability, romance, and race to argue for the extraordinary uniqueness, yet fundamental Americanness, of the area. The geography ("strangest and grandest scenery") and history ("finest . . . ruins") were unlike those of any other region, making the Southwest "exclusively the romantic corner of the United States as well as the wonderland of the continent." Lummis is careful to cast the region as distinctive, yet not foreign. The Southwest was, after all, "the climax of human achievement to date . . . by the race which just now stands at the head of the world"—that is, by U.S. Anglos. As Martin Padget affirms, "Travel westward for Lummis meant a deliberate move away from the East he perceived as economically and morally corrupt, subject to race mongrelization, and scourged by a cruel climate in which the full bodily and mental potential of the individual could not be realized."[55] Of course the irony of Lummis's Southwest boosterism "was that while it was a self-conscious departure away from the perceived threat of immigration to the Anglo-Saxon racial and cultural purity in the East, it was a move into one of the most racially and ethnically diverse regions of the U.S."[56] This tension would haunt the *Land of Sunshine* and the rest of Lummis's writings, as well as remembrances and fictionalizations of the Peralta Land Grant, which selectively acknowledged the role of non-Anglo people in the past, present, and future of the Southwest.[57]

Tipton's recounting of the Peralta Land Grant saga was an ideal fit for the image of the Southwest that Lummis was creating. Not only the outlandish details but also the context for Reavis's crime contributed to an overall air of exceptionality. That is, the history of Spanish land grants, which was unfamiliar to many *Land of Sunshine* readers in the East and Midwest, was as remarkable as Reavis's manipulation of it. This Spanish past also contributed to the romance of the story, which transcended the actual romance between Reavis and Peralta-Reavis. Like Helen Hunt Jackson's 1884 novel *Ramona* and other popular narratives circulating at the time in magazines like the *Land of Sunshine*, Tipton's descriptions of knights and baronies created a romantic nostalgia for the Spanish history of the Southwest in a way that was sure to captivate the imagination of readers who had never visited the region. The exotic locale and subject matter of Tipton's story, however, were tempered by its heroes, who were all U.S. Anglo men. The lawyers, judges, and experts who eventually exposed Reavis and convicted him of attempting to defraud the government anchored the story in a safe hierarchy in which U.S. laws—and U.S. Anglo men—were the ultimate authority. Tipton's "Prince of Impostors" was the perfect embodiment of Lummis's vision of the Southwest's uniqueness, romance, and racial order.

Like other *Land of Sunshine* articles, "The Prince of Impostors" was also richly illustrated, making equal use of words and images to create its desired effect. Lummis prioritized visuals in the magazine, increasing the number of illustrations by 50 percent within the first five months of his editorship.[58] As Jennifer Watts asserts, this visual focus helped Lummis "make real" his vision of the Southwest for his readers.[59] Tipton's article is no exception, including twenty-three images that range from full-page copies of Reavis's forgeries to portraits of important people involved in the case. Like the written narrative, the images fit within the larger image of the Southwest that Lummis was developing. Eight of the images are of documents Reavis forged, old manuscripts with elaborate handwritten Spanish script. An additional five images are portraits Reavis submitted of the imaginary Peralta family, depicting people who appear to be Spanish aristocrats (figure 6). Together, these images of the forgeries and the family underscore both the exceptionality of the story and its articulation with a romanticized Spanish past. Five of the images are of prominent Anglo men involved in the case, from the panel of judges who presided over the Peralta Land Grant trial to a portrait of Tipton himself. These images contrast with the forged documents and portraits, alleviating the threat they posed by exposing their deception and anchoring the article in the U.S. context. The remaining images include a map of the area the Peralta Land Grant threatened to upend should it have been confirmed and four images of Reavis, Peralta-Reavis, and their children.

The images and accompanying captions of the Peralta-Reavis family foreshadow how each person would be remembered as time went on. Reavis appears in a striped prison uniform alongside a caption that reads, "In the penitentiary at Santa Fé [*sic*]. [Made especially for this magazine. The first photograph of the infamous claimant ever published.]" (figure 7).[60] It is significant that the first photograph ever published of Reavis is of him as a prisoner, ensuring that he will always be remembered as a criminal. The photograph of the children of Reavis and Peralta-Reavis pictures the twin boys posed, one with his head resting on his folded arms and the other with his head leaning against one arm, both with long, cherub-like hair that is curled at the ends (figure 8). They wear matching white, long-sleeved, starched shirts with elaborate ruffles that give off a Spanish aristocratic air. The caption reads "REAVIS'S TWIN SONS. These beautiful little boys were a feature of the trial of Reavis, and made great sympathy for his claim."[61] The combination of their age (they appear to be around three or four years old) with their angelic hair, poses, clothing, and expressions paints the boys as innocent bystanders and victims. They are also unnamed, prefiguring later remembrances that either do not mention or do not name the boys.

Figure 6. A painting supposedly depicting the first Baron of Arizona. Image courtesy of Special Collections, the University of Arizona Libraries.

Figure 7. Mug shot of James Addison Reavis. Image courtesy of Special Collections, the University of Arizona Libraries.

Though Tipton focuses his article principally on Reavis and his plotting, he does include two images of Peralta-Reavis, with captions that are quite telling. One image shows Peralta-Reavis standing next to a rock with markings on it, which Reavis claimed were related to the boundaries of the Peralta Land Grant (see figure 5 in chapter 2). Tipton captions this image "MRS. REAVIS AND THE 'BARONY.' (The arch conspirator even 'found' an old map of the Peralta grant carved on a rock near the center of this mysterious domain; and had it and the

Figure 8. Portrait of James Addison Reavis and Sofia Loreto Peralta-Reavis's twin
sons. Image courtesy of Special Collections, the University of Arizona Libraries.

'Third Baroness' photographed in conjunction.)."[62] By putting "barony" and
"Third Baroness" in quotes, Tipton likens Reavis's invention of the Peralta Land
Grant to his invention of Sofia Peralta-Reavis. Expanding on the nature of this
invention, in a caption to a different image, this time a profile portrait of
Peralta-Reavis, Tipton writes, "'THE THIRD BARONESS OF ARIZONA.' 'Da. Sofia
Loreto Micaela de Peraltareavis, neé Masó y Silva de Peralta de la Córdoba.'
Alias, Reavis's half-breed wife" (figure 9).[63] Here Tipton's tone is much more
cutting, as the contrast between the long aristocratic title and "half-breed"
serves to not only discredit but also mock Peralta-Reavis's claim to the Peralta
Land Grant.

The disparagement of Peralta-Reavis that Tipton hints at only intensified with
time. Nearly fifty years after Tipton's "Prince of Impostors" appeared in the *Land
of Sunshine*, Clarence Budington Kelland's "Red Baron of Arizona" graced the
pages of the October 1947 issue of the *Saturday Evening Post*. Kelland was a prolific author who moved to Arizona in 1937,[64] later writing the novel on which
the 1940 film *Arizona* was based. Just as Lummis's *Land of Sunshine* was instru-
mental in forming and disseminating a particular image of the Southwest at the
turn of the century, Kelland's *Arizona* was a nostalgic reminder of that image
in the prewar era. As Geraldo L. Cadava asserts, *Arizona* "not only foreshadowed

Figure 9. Portrait of Sofia Loreto Peralta-Reavis. Image courtesy of Special Collections, the University of Arizona Libraries.

the Southwest's rise as an iconic film location and tourist destination but also offered a snapshot of racial and cross-border dynamics in Arizona on the eve of World War II," presenting "a tale based on frontier myths about the advance of white civilization, legends that cast the area's people of Mexican and Native American descent as outsiders and downplayed [Arizona's] connections with Mexico."[65] For Cadava, the narrative that Kelland and others were promoting was a twentieth-century reinvigoration of nineteenth-century myths surrounding Anglo ingenuity, progress, and civilization.[66] His depiction of the history of the Peralta Land Grant serves exactly this purpose, becoming particularly apparent in the way he portrays Peralta-Reavis.

Kelland published "The Red Baron of Arizona" seven years after *Arizona*. In the intervening time, the United States had entered and exited a world war and solidified its place as a global superpower. Against this backdrop, the nationalist undertones that had marked nineteenth-century coverage of the Peralta Land Grant are amplified in Kelland's retelling. The captions of the images on the first page of the story demonstrate how the tone of what had by then become the distant history of the Peralta Land Grant shifted in the intervening half a century. The caption for the image of Reavis reads, "James Addison Reavis as he looked when the money was showering down and he was deep in clover. A few years later he was in a cell in Santa Fe."[67] Though the tone is a little more glib, the content is not so different from Tipton's description many decades earlier. Kelland differs from Tipton more starkly in his caption for the image of Peralta-Reavis, which reads "Carmelita, the illiterate kitchen drudge who fully believed Reavis's story that she was descended from Spanish kings, heiress to titles and vast wealth."[68] The mocking tone of Tipton's caption pales in comparison to Kelland's description, which not only misidentifies Sofia as Carmelita, a diminutive and more stereotypically Mexican name, but also belittles her as an uneducated and poor woman who, the caption insinuates, must have been a fool to believe Reavis's story about her heritage. The ridiculing tone of the caption is amplified by its contrast with the drawing of Peralta-Reavis, which portrays her wearing a black lace mantilla. While the drawing alone could be an innocuous portrayal of a Spanish lady, the caption recasts the image as a derisive caricature.

Kelland also has much more to say about Peralta-Reavis than Tipton did, using her to amplify both the romance and the absurdity of the Peralta Land Grant story. When he first introduces Peralta-Reavis into his tale, he writes,

> So here, for the first time, romance enters the plot. And with romance [Reavis] was as patient as he was with building his bridge of world-wide forgeries. James Addison Reavis set out in quest of a woman. He was not looking for beauty or love, but for a dupe. It could not be any woman, no matter how young and desirable she might be. She must possess certain specifications. She must be of a certain age—approximately fourteen years old. She must be a waif. She must be Spanish or Mexican, and she must know practically nothing of her origin or who her parents were. He wanted a girl who had no background and no history, a girl out of whom he could create a living character, as by forgeries he had created a whole family of dead characters.[69]

Kelland's characterization of the relationship between Reavis and Peralta-Reavis as a romance is disturbing, particularly as he elaborates the nature of their affiliation. Kelland highlights that Reavis was looking for a vulnerable girl who was young ("fourteen years old"), poor ("a waif"), isolated ("no background and no history"), and naive ("a dupe"). This description emphasizes that Reavis's intentional pursuit of such a woman was predatory, horrifying, and clearly abusive.

Despite Reavis's intentional deception and exploitation of this woman, Kelland goes on to affirm that "in [Reavis's] favor it must be said that always, until the debacle, he treated [Peralta-Reavis] with respect and gentleness and kindness, perhaps even with sincere love."[70] The disparity between James Reavis the abuser and James Reavis the lover is a tension that many twentieth-century retellings would smooth over, most notably in the film *The Baron of Arizona*. Despite explicitly acknowledging that Reavis used Peralta-Reavis, Kelland's article and later fictionalizations simultaneously depict his relationship with her as altruistic and their relationship with each other as romantic. This romance is hard to find in what few traces there are of the real-life relationship between Reavis and Peralta-Reavis. Reavis, who was perhaps as much as thirty years older than Peralta-Reavis, wielded incredible control over not only the identity he created for her but also the life she led. Unsurprisingly, their relationship ended in tragedy, as after the conclusion of the case and the dissolution of their claim Peralta-Reavis eventually filed for divorce on grounds of nonsupport.[71]

In addition to the romance between Reavis and Peralta-Reavis, Kelland's article also alludes to how the romanticization of Peralta-Reavis's unknown origins would evolve. Clearly, as the trial at the Court of Private Land Claims proved, Peralta-Reavis was not who her husband, Reavis, claimed she was. However, it remained unclear what her lineage actually was. After thoroughly mocking her claim to a Spanish/Mexican identity, Kelland suggests a different yet "equally glittering lineage; that she was descended from an American line, lofty if savage, that ran back into the mists of aboriginal antiquity . . . that Carmelita was granddaughter to the noble Cochise, who, foreseeing the defeat of his people, had given her for safekeeping into the hands of a trusted white friend."[72] Kelland perhaps picked up this legend from William Atherton DuPuy's 1940 novel *The Baron of the Colorados*, which incorporates this ancestry into its narrative. Though Kelland clarifies that the connection was a "legend," the fact that it appears in several places is a testament to the spread of misinformation related to the Peralta Land Grant in general and Peralta-Reavis in particular, especially as the actual history of both grew distant.

The Allure of Fake News

On March 9, 2018, the journal *Science* published an article entitled "The Spread of True and False News Online," which described the findings of an ambitious study of news stories, both true and false, that had been shared on Twitter between 2006 and 2017. The authors found that "falsehood diffused significantly farther, faster, deeper, and more broadly than the truth in all categories of information."[73] They determined that this difference was likely attributable to the fact that false news is more novel than true news, triggering "fear, disgust, and surprise."[74] Despite the recent focus on the role of so-called bots in spreading false information online, the authors also found that "robots accelerated the spread of true and false news at the same rate, implying that false news spreads more than the truth because humans, not robots, are more likely to spread it."[75] False information is enticing, as it turns out, in a way that the truth simply is not.

Though so-called fake news has received more attention in the wake of the 2016 U.S. presidential election, as the extensive and often inaccurate coverage of the Peralta Land Grant attests, the existence and attraction of false information are not new phenomena.[76] Nineteenth- and twentieth-century audiences from across the political spectrum were fascinated by the false story that James Reavis invented about his wife the baroness and her claim to a Spanish land grant. When Reavis's story turned out not to be true, people embellished the actual history of what happened with their own accounts of how Reavis and his wife, Sofia Peralta-Reavis, had nearly won and then lost a fortune.

The implications of the rapid spread of news related to the Peralta Land Grant, however, extend far beyond the history of the Peralta Land Grant itself. As the popularity of western-focused publications like Lummis's *Land of Sunshine* and Kelland's *Arizona* attest, falsified narratives about the past, present, and future of the western United States that place Anglo "pioneers" at their center captivate readers and viewers in a way that the actual history of the conquest and settlement of the area simply does not. To this day, as popular representations of the western United States prove, the triumphant "fake news" associated with the doctrine of Manifest Destiny is more pervasive and captivating than the often complex, violent, and tragic realities that it elides. Considering the coverage of the Peralta Land Grant in its full context is a preliminary step toward recovering these other, more complex realities, which continue to lurk beneath the surface of the false narratives that have threatened to erase them.

(RE)MEMBERING THE PERALTA LAND GRANT

CHAPTER 4

Counterfeit Nostalgia

WILLIAM ATHERTON DUPUY'S *BARON OF THE COLORADOS* (1940)

William Atherton DuPuy's 1940 novel *The Baron of the Colorados* opens with a tense meeting at the end of the Southern Pacific rail line in Phoenix, Arizona. There, a group of homesteaders gather to await the arrival of James Addison Reavis and Sofia Loreto Peralta-Reavis, the couple claiming to be the rightful owners of the homesteaders' growing settlement in Phoenix and the territory that lies beyond it. Among those waiting is John Travers, an older man who is aged further by his many years spent farming in the harsh Arizona desert. With him is his daughter, the beautiful Helen Travers, who accompanies her father to witness the first appearance of the so-called baron and his wife in Arizona Territory. Waiting along with the settlers is an unfamiliar face in these parts: that of Will Tipton, special agent in the U.S. General Land Office and the man assigned with the daunting task of evaluating Reavis and Peralta-Reavis's claim.

Even before they step off the train, Reavis and Peralta-Reavis make an entrance unlike anything the humble homesteaders have ever seen. Railcars hauling provisions and a few passengers are new enough in Phoenix, but Reavis and Peralta-Reavis's coach is a world apart from the freight cars that normally pull up to the platform. Audible murmurs arise from the crowd as attendants begin to unload a seemingly endless array of luggage from the luxurious private car. Finally, Reavis himself emerges, his tall figure made even more imposing by a silk hat that sits atop his head.

As Reavis makes his way across the platform, the sound of a gunshot cuts through the settlers' hushed whispers. Old John Travers has pointed his ivory six-shooter at Reavis and fired. Nevertheless, no sooner has Travers pulled the trigger than Tipton, who is standing next to him, springs to action and diverts the weapon so that the bullet goes up toward the sky instead of across and into Reavis's chest. Reavis, who appears unfazed by the attempt on his life, merely tips his hat to Travers and then turns to thank Tipton for saving his life. Tipton, however, brushes past Reavis's gratitude, as his attention is gripped by the beautiful woman standing next to the would-be assassin. The chaotic scene ends with a warm handshake between Helen Travers and Tipton, who appear destined to meet again.

In this opening scene, DuPuy takes some artistic license with the history of the Peralta Land Grant, imagining real-life con man James Reavis and federal agent Will Tipton meeting the fictional John and Helen Travers at a train station in Phoenix. By adding John Travers to this fictionalized encounter, DuPuy evokes images of the Wild West that existed before the closing of the frontier, one in which men battled against the land and each other to carve out a living. Reavis, the wealthy (fake) Spanish baron who appears economically and culturally out of place in this remote and rugged landscape, is cast as a foreign threat who jeopardizes the land claims of homesteaders like Travers. When Travers pulls out his revolver to shoot Reavis, he is a reminder of the violent way frontier justice dealt with foreign threats to Anglo settlements. But Travers is not successful, implying that the early tactics of U.S. westward expansion were, even in Reavis's late nineteenth-century moment, passing away. Instead, it is Tipton, federal agent, who controls the scene by coming to Reavis's rescue and winning the girl. If Travers represents the methods that facilitated the first wave of Anglo expansion, then Tipton represents a later stage of that growth: the formal, federalized incorporation of newly acquired territories into the political, economic, and cultural fabric of the United States.

While the preceding chapters examined the historical import and impact of the Peralta Land Grant by closely reading contemporaneous government reports, the trial transcript, and newspaper coverage, this and the following chapter read later fictionalizations of Reavis's scheme as markers of how racialized narratives about U.S. expansion evolved in the years following the official closure of the frontier and the commencement of U.S. formal and informal expansion overseas. When the U.S. Census declared the closure of the frontier in 1890, it brought to an end the first stage of U.S. imperial growth, which transformed thirteen small colonies huddled along the Atlantic Ocean into a combination of states and territories that stretched from one sea to another.[1] This expansion had been facilitated by peaceful acquisitions as well as wars against other nations, including many wars with Native Americans across the continent and a war with Mexico.[2] When the continental frontier closed in 1890, another war, this time with Spain, opened up new possibilities for expansion overseas, including the island territories of Puerto Rico, the Philippines, and Cuba.[3]

Analyzing how DuPuy fictionalized Reavis's story in his 1940 novel, which was written after this overseas expansion but set in the time before it, allows us to trace Arizona's role as a multiethnic proving ground for the racialized narratives that underpinned U.S. continental and overseas growth. In the years that separated Reavis's scheming and DuPuy's publication of *The Baron of the*

Colorados, Arizona transitioned from a territory to a state and the United States expanded beyond its contiguous land borders to islands in the Pacific and the Caribbean. Like Arizona, many of these islands were formerly ruled by Spain, and all had majority non-Anglo populations. Debates at the turn of the century about the fitness of these multiethnic overseas territories to join the United States as states strongly resembled the debates that had plagued Arizona's own arduous path to statehood, which lasted from the close of the U.S.-Mexican War in 1848 to the official granting of statehood in 1912. During its sixty-four-year territorial period, Arizona's Anglo political leaders purposefully crafted a whitewashed image of Arizona that downplayed its Native American and Mexican population in order to appeal to national policy makers, who worried that Arizona was not culturally similar enough—that is, not Anglo enough—to join the union as its own state.[4]

Once the territory was granted statehood, the whitewashed image that supplanted Arizona's multiethnic reality became the state's official history. The racial hierarchy that this historical revision made possible was then amplified by heavy federal investment, from infrastructure to transportation to military installations, that bolstered Anglo dominance in the state. Arizona therefore became a model for how racialized revisionary historical narratives laid the ideological groundwork for the political and economic incorporation of majority non-Anglo territories into the United States. Though the many island overseas territories that the United States gained at the turn of the century did not follow exactly the same path of national incorporation as Arizona, or each other, thinking about these seemingly unrelated desert and island spaces together reveals a pattern of U.S. expansion: narratively erasing non-Anglo populations in order to make way for formal or informal U.S. rule that ensured Anglo dominance.

DuPuy's *Baron of the Colorados* is part of this narrative erasure, characterizing the progress and modernization of the Arizona Territory as an Anglo phenomenon. In prewar Arizona, increased economic opportunity driven by federal investment led to explosive population growth and the quick rise of Sunbelt metropolises in the state.[5] Anglos involved in these modernization projects saw themselves as the direct inheritors of their nineteenth-century pioneering predecessors.[6] In his own twentieth-century moment of change, DuPuy returned to the late nineteenth-century period to ground his story in a familiar narrative of Anglo superiority, celebrating not only the triumphs of Arizona's (Anglo) past but also the promises of its (Anglo) future. Though the frontier may have been closed, the future was still open for the (Anglo) people of Arizona.

Of course, this story of Anglo-driven progress and modernization was a counterfeit narrative. Native and Mexican Americans were central to the development of Arizona's political, economic, and cultural landscape. In order to downplay the role of non-Anglo people, in *The Baron of the Colorados*, DuPuy deploys what I call a counterfeit nostalgia about the settlement of Arizona in particular and U.S. expansion in general. As Houston Baker Jr. argues, nostalgia is always a warped remembrance, "a purposive construction of a past filled with golden virtues, golden men, and sterling events" that "substitutes allegory for history."[7] Counterfeit nostalgia is an important subset of this broad category, purposefully constructing an inaccurate vision of the past in order to legitimize the structure of the present. In DuPuy's case, this counterfeit nostalgia takes the form of remembering U.S. expansion as inevitable and unobstructed in the past in order to legitimize continued Anglo hegemony in the present and future.[8] As DuPuy's novel attests, counterfeit nostalgia is central to the enduring logic of Manifest Destiny and its political, economic, and cultural consequences on the continent and around the globe.

The Writings of William Atherton DuPuy: Celebrating U.S. Continental and Overseas Expansion

The Baron of the Colorados was the last thing DuPuy published before his death in 1941.[9] DuPuy was born in Anderson County, Texas, in 1876,[10] but his family soon relocated to the Salt River Valley in central Arizona Territory, near what is today the city of Phoenix, to homestead a plot of land.[11] Their move coincided with Reavis's suit to claim the Peralta Land Grant, placing DuPuy and his family among Reavis's potential victims.[12] Whether due to Reavis or some other obstacle, the family left Arizona Territory before the Peralta Land Grant case was settled, and DuPuy did not learn of its conclusion until many years later.[13] In the meantime, DuPuy joined the army, eventually earning the rank of captain,[14] and worked as a journalist in Washington, D.C.[15] After spending years as a freelance writer, he secured employment in the Department of the Interior, rising to the level of executive assistant to the secretary.[16] It was in the Department of the Interior that he again came across the Peralta Land Grant in the records of the General Land Office.[17] Based on the information he discovered, DuPuy wrote *The Baron of the Colorados*, a fictionalized account of the story of Reavis and his forged Spanish land grant.

Though *The Baron of the Colorados* at first appears oddly unrelated to DuPuy's other writings, it nevertheless takes up a theme that is common across all of his works: the racialized superiority of the United States over all other nations. During his life, DuPuy was a prolific writer. In addition to the articles he produced as a journalist, he also authored a popular series of books that celebrate the achievements of "Uncle Sam": *Uncle Sam, Wonder Worker* (1913) and *Uncle Sam's Modern Miracles* (1914), both of which commend the work of various departments within the federal government; *Uncle Sam, Detective* (1916), a novel that sings the praises of a fictional FBI detective; and *Uncle Sam, Fighter* (1919), a tribute to U.S. military achievements in World War I. Though DuPuy's Uncle Sam series is generically, temporally, and geographically distinct from *The Baron of the Colorados*, the works are united in their exceedingly overt celebration of U.S. government institutions through a rhetoric of Anglo superiority. Focused mostly on U.S. achievements in the twentieth century, the Uncle Sam series celebrates the superiority of the U.S. government in everything from military prowess to public health. The racialized dimensions of this superiority become clear when DuPuy compares the United States to other nations, in particular Spain, which he demonizes as a cruel empire that stunted the progress of its island territories. In contrast, DuPuy characterizes the United States as a benevolent and humanitarian nation that serves as an example of how to rule over citizens and territorial subjects properly. DuPuy makes a similar comparison in *The Baron of the Colorados*, in which he sets Will Tipton, the Anglo federal agent charged with investigating the authenticity of the Peralta Land Grant, against James Reavis, the would-be Spanish baron who threatens to displace helpless homesteaders like John and Helen Travers. DuPuy's admiration for Tipton, who protects the Anglo homesteaders against foreign threats, is as racially charged as his veneration for his unmistakably Anglo Uncle Sam.

This racialized rhetoric is what enables DuPuy to connect U.S. continental and overseas expansion.[18] DuPuy makes this connection explicit in a 1932 report about Hawaii that he authored in his capacity as executive assistant to the secretary of the Department of the Interior.[19] DuPuy writes, "Since it is a psychological fact that interest in any object decreases as the distance to it increases, the Hawaiian Islands are at a material disadvantage as compared to those other units that go to constitute the United States. Once the handicap of distance is overcome, however, this community, which occupies the position of a Territory and is as much a part of the United States as was Arizona before it was admitted to statehood, is likely to become an ambitious claimant for attention."[20] By explicitly naming Arizona as a model for incorporation, DuPuy characterizes the state as a meeting point for continental expansion, overseas administration, and federal state formation. Just as Arizona, which was once physically and culturally distant from the rest of the United States, was eventually incorporated within the boundaries of the nation, so too will Hawaii be. Far from a wild western outpost, Arizona becomes the crossroads for the development of U.S. national identity and institutions. This short excerpt foreshadows the themes that DuPuy would return to eight years later in *The Baron of the Colorados*, in which Arizona and its road to statehood take center stage.

THE BARON OF THE COLORADOS:
COUNTERFEIT NOSTALGIA AND COGNITIVE DISSONANCE

Set before statehood, *The Baron of the Colorados* claims to recover not only the specifics of Reavis's case but also an authentic portrait of the early days of Anglo settlement and homesteading in Arizona. In the foreword to *The Baron of the*

Colorados, DuPuy emphasizes the authenticity of his fictionalized history of the Peralta Land Grant: "This book should not be regarded as history although most of the characters in it are real, most of the events set down actually took place, and, especially, the color of the time and place in which the author was steeped during his impressionistic youth, may be taken as almost photographically correct. Into this background he has woven a few threads of romance to hold the story together."[21] These opening lines are key for DuPuy to establish both the authenticity of the story the novel tells (despite the few fictional threads of romance) and his own authority to tell it.[22] The foreword cues readers to treat this novel, though fiction, as an "almost photographically correct" and therefore reliable representation of "the color of the time and place" of the late nineteenth-century Southwest. This accuracy is important, as DuPuy's stated objective in writing the novel is "saving . . . from oblivion . . . what probably was one of the most remarkable interludes that grew out of that fantastic clash of bold spirits incidental to the unfolding of the West."[23] As the West was modernizing and the days before the closure of the frontier grew more distant, DuPuy saw his novel as a kind of archive, reconstructing this episode from the early pioneer days in order to save it from erasure and preserve it for generations to come.

Nevertheless, *The Baron of the Colorados* is less about authenticity and more about authenticating a particular version of western history, one that was based on a racially and culturally exclusive hierarchy that celebrated Anglo political, economic, and cultural superiority. DuPuy's fictionalizations show how the counterfeit nostalgic lens through which this period of westward expansion was remembered strategically justified and bolstered Anglo dominance in the region fifty years later. This counterfeit nostalgia is evident in the way DuPuy describes the novel's main characters. Whether they are based on real-life people or fictional creations, DuPuy takes significant artistic license with their characterization. James Reavis becomes the personification of the anti-Spanish Black Legend, despite the fact that he is an Anglo man from Missouri. Will Tipton becomes the epitome of benevolent, beneficial U.S. imperial expansion, despite some highly unsettling behavior. Sofia Peralta-Reavis becomes the romanticized vanishing Indian, despite passing as a modern subject. And the completely fictional John and Helen Travers become the real, authentic Arizonans, despite being newcomers to the area. Though DuPuy's counterfeit nostalgia attempts to smooth over these contradictions, in the end his fictionalization cuts both ways, showing the ideological inconsistencies inherent within the racialized hierarchy of westward expansion that had by 1940 become accepted as a natural part of national history.

JAMES REAVIS AND THE BLACK LEGEND

In the novel, Reavis's attempted usurpation of territory based on Spanish law serves as a foil to U.S. expansion and is fundamental to DuPuy's narrative of

American exceptionalism and Anglo superiority. Though the real-life Reavis was an Anglo man from Missouri, DuPuy characterizes Reavis as not only depending on Spanish law to carry out his scheme but in fact "assum[ing] an air which he considered Castilian."[24] Instead of "going native," Reavis "goes Spanish," allowing DuPuy to distance him from the Anglo settlers to whom he is otherwise identical and cast him as representative of Spanish imperial growth and governance.

DuPuy's vilification of Reavis and, consequently, of the Spanish Empire is central to his celebration of U.S. empire. In *The Baron of the Colorados*, Reavis functions as what María DeGuzmán calls a "figure of Spain," a historical foil that she argues was central to the elaboration of Anglo-American identity and history.[25] In the novel, DuPuy portrays Reavis as a figure of Spain in order to constitute and elaborate the dominant fictions of Anglo-American identity. As the novel's villain, Reavis bases his claim on an antiquated and antidemocratic land grant from a king from the previous century. From the opening scene, it is clear that Reavis's way of life is incommensurate with life in the Arizona Territory, as he arrives in an opulent train car and is accompanied by myriad servants. By contrast, Anglo settlers like John Travers, whom Reavis threatens to displace, base their land claims on the modern, democratic, and egalitarian practice of homesteading. The juxtaposition of Reavis's land claim to that of homesteaders like Travers underscores the idea that, unlike European empires, the United States expanded naturally (Manifest Destiny), democratically ("American" exceptionalism), and benevolently (antiempire).[26]

DuPuy specifically appeals to stereotypes associated with the Black Legend in order to vilify Reavis's, and consequently Spain's, land claims and justify U.S. control of formerly Spanish colonies. The Black Legend first developed in the sixteenth century, when the Spanish Empire was one of the most powerful empires in the world, if not the most. As a response, rival European empires began demonizing Spanish imperial practices as particularly cruel or violent. These rival European empires often cited Bartolomé de las Casas's 1542 *Brevísima relación de la destrucción de las Indias*, in which Las Casas criticizes Spanish treatment of indigenous peoples, as proof of the Spanish Empire's brutality and, implicitly, the superior nature of their own, less brutal European empires. DuPuy's portrayal of the "menace of James Addison Reavis,"[27] as he calls it, is clearly informed by the anti-Spanish attitudes that constituted the Black Legend. DuPuy portrays Reavis's arrival in Arizona ominously, writing, "The shadow over their homes, faint in the beginning, had darkened, and now the mysterious figure that had threatened from a distance was to appear in person."[28] Reavis is the personification of the Black Legend, literally darkening the territory with his threat to displace the Anglo settlers living there.

Writing in the twentieth century, DuPuy appealed to the Black Legend's characterization of Spanish imperial growth as morally corrupt and therefore illegitimate in order to bolster the legitimacy not of another European empire but rather of U.S. empire. The ideas that undergirded the Black Legend evolved as they moved across time and space. According to DeGuzmán, with time, figures of Spain shifted from symbolizing the alter egos of other European empires to symbolizing the alter egos of the United States. The growth of this vilification of Spain indirectly corresponded to its actual power, which dwindled by the eighteenth century, around the same time that the U.S. empire began to grow.[29] As a result, DuPuy's casting of Reavis as the Spanish villain that would undo Anglo settlement is entangled with U.S. territorial expansion into formerly Spanish territories on the continent and overseas. During the 1848 U.S.-Mexican War, the United States appealed to stereotypes associated with the Black Legend in order to discredit Mexico, which it argued had inherited Spain's inability to govern fairly and effectively.[30] Fifty years later, the United States again invoked the Black Legend in order to cast itself as the liberator of islands in the Pacific and the Caribbean from their cruel and inept Spanish overlords.[31]

The glorification of U.S. imperial control in formerly Spanish colonies was not a new theme for DuPuy. Nearly thirty years earlier, he praised the practices of U.S. empire at length in his book *Uncle Sam's Modern Miracles: His Gigantic Tasks That Benefit Humanity* (1914). In it, DuPuy discusses the wide-ranging achievements of the U.S. federal government, including the national Public Health Service, the Weather Bureau, the Bureau of Indian Affairs, the Reclamation Service, the Army Corps of Engineers, the Department of Agriculture, the Land Office, the Office of Public Roads, the creation of wireless stations and infrastructure, the Postal Service, the U.S. Census, the Treasury Department and U.S. Mint, the Army Medical Corps, the Secret Service, the War College, the Bureau of Immigration, and the occupation of the Philippines and Puerto Rico. At first, the inclusion of the U.S. occupation of these overseas territories seems at odds with the other chapters of the text. Nevertheless, DuPuy unites them all under the umbrella of the United States as a model for democratic values and efficient institutions. At home, this takes the form of various offices within the federal government. Abroad, it takes the form of democratic ambassadorship— that is, the growth of the empire.

In discussing U.S. occupation of the Philippines and Puerto Rico, DuPuy invokes the Black Legend in order to distinguish U.S. imperial control, which is both benevolent and beneficial, from Spanish imperial control of the territories. In the second chapter, entitled "Awakening the Filipino," he writes,

Uncle Sam is governing these people of the Philippines as no conquered people has ever been governed before since the world began. He has, in his administration of their affairs, one central idea—the improvement of the condition of the native. All other nations in all times have exploited conquered peoples for the profit of the conquerors. The conquerors have planned to keep their subjects well under control, to keep them poor, weak, ignorant, that this might be the easier. The United States has sought to develop its subject race into strength, wisdom, prosperity, that it might ultimately be given independence. Thus are the Philippines being made an object lesson in colonial government to all the nations of the world. Thus is the United States demonstrating the great, humanitarian sentiment that underlies its government and which constantly lifts it above mere commercialism.[32]

According to DuPuy, the United States is distinct from Spain and all other empires in that it is fundamentally "humanitarian." Though DuPuy does not cite Spain by name in this passage, as the immediately preceding "conqueror" of the Philippines, its presence is palpable. Whereas Spain had exploited and profited off the Filipinos in its own self-interest, the United States was educating and empowering the Filipinos for self-governance thanks to its selfless benevolence. DuPuy's patronizing language positions the United States as uniquely capable of helping the Filipinos, who are otherwise unable to help themselves.

Elsewhere in *Uncle Sam's Modern Miracles*, DuPuy more explicitly compares the impact of U.S. and Spanish imperial governance in the Philippines and Puerto Rico, employing a twentieth-century invocation of the Black Legend to vilify Spain as exploitative and harmful to the native people of the islands. While "the rule of the Spaniard" in the Philippines "had been high-handed and cruel," U.S. rule improved the people and their island by providing education, sanitation, transportation, and industrial development.[33] In Puerto Rico, whereas Spanish rule depended on "the exploitation of the masses for the benefit of the governing class," U.S. rule was "converting 1,120,000 tyranny-ridden descendants of the Spanish buccaneers into prosperous and productive Americans."[34] Whether or not the Puerto Ricans wanted to be Americans in the first place does not register in DuPuy's description, which unequivocally affirms the benefits of U.S. rule for Filipinos and Puerto Ricans alike.

In addition to U.S. expansion overseas, DuPuy's invocation of the Black Legend also resonates with the continental growth of the United States and anti-Mexican stereotypes. Just as supporters of U.S. imperial pursuits overseas vilified Spain in order to construct a positive image of U.S. empire, supporters of U.S. continental expansion maligned Mexico in order to justify the takeover of the Southwest. Though Mexicans had overthrown Spanish imperial control, within the United States, stereotypes associated with the Black Legend evolved to apply to Mexicans postindependence. These stereotypes, which circulated in the mid-nineteenth century to justify the U.S.-Mexican War, became even more prevalent in the early twentieth century as the Mexican Revolution brought an influx of people across the border.

DuPuy's characterization of Reavis manifests these twentieth-century fears about the Mexican Invasion, or the fear that Mexicans were poised to displace

Anglo settlement, not through outright war but through more subtle means such as population growth and the accrual of economic and political power. Clearly, Reavis's plot threatened to not only physically displace the Anglo settlers but also jeopardize their political and economic power. In response, DuPuy discredits Reavis's claim by appealing to anti-Mexican stereotypes, which portrayed Mexicans as lazy, nonindustrious, and unassimilable. Even if Reavis's Spanish grant were not forged, under this logic it would still be illegitimate because, unlike the homesteaders who had planted and plowed and worked for the land, Reavis did not do anything to earn its title. Relatedly, by casting not only the land claim but Reavis himself as foreign, DuPuy alludes to fears that Mexicans would refuse to assimilate and remain perpetual foreigners who would undermine U.S. racial and cultural identity.[35]

Nevertheless, DuPuy's characterization of Reavis, an Anglo man, as the embodiment of the Black Legend is inherently unstable. Though DuPuy demonizes Reavis to bolster Anglo-U.S. superiority, DuPuy cannot deny that neither Reavis's Spanish land grant nor his Spanish identity is real. The counterfeit nostalgia with which DuPuy remembers Reavis is a double-edged sword. On the one hand, characterizing Reavis as a villainous figure of Spain who threatens to displace hardworking Anglo settlers with an ancient royal land grant allows DuPuy to uphold dominant fictions about U.S. territorial expansion as egalitarian. On the other hand, the fact that Reavis bases his claim not on a real Spanish land grant but rather a forged one and that Reavis adopts the false Spanish identity of a baron that never existed undermines DuPuy's characterization. No amount of rhetorical maneuvering can change the fact that Reavis is not in fact Spanish but is in actuality an Anglo man from Missouri whose land grab is more similar to that of the other homesteaders than DuPuy would care to acknowledge.

The instability of DuPuy's representation of Reavis as Spanish therefore has the unintended consequence of undermining the Anglo-American superiority DuPuy so desperately tries to establish throughout the novel. Channeling the doctrine of Manifest Destiny and the idea of the West as a virgin land in order to paint the Anglo settlers as innocent, hardworking victims, DuPuy describes Reavis as "a somber figure in the background of the consciousness of these settlers ever since they had begun to come straggling in from Tennessee, Texas, and Missouri, from all the lands of restless spirits, to apply here the miracle of irrigation to sagebrush-covered desert plains that they might forthwith yield those prodigious ready crops of barley and hay that hurried most expeditiously to market."[36] What DuPuy does not acknowledge is that, just like Reavis, these Anglo homesteaders displaced other people in order to work a land that was not theirs.

Though DuPuy vilifies Reavis for threatening to undo the settlers' hard work to irrigate the land and produce crops, neither the land nor the agricultural practice of irrigation originated with these "restless [Anglo] spirits." Irrigation was first applied to the land centuries earlier by the Hohokam, a pre-Columbian civilization that developed a complex network of canals in what is today central Arizona. By the nineteenth century, the Hohokam's descendants, the Akimel O'odham, were still living in the same area and continued to practice irrigation in order to cultivate the land. As David H. DeJong affirms, the Akimel O'odham's crops fed the first Anglo pioneers, who then learned about the irrigation system from these non-Anglo people. The Akimel O'odham's agricultural production did not begin to decline until those same Anglo pioneers diverted the Akimel O'odham's water source to irrigate their own crops.[37] In DuPuy's counterfeit nostalgic rewriting of the agricultural history of the territory, the Anglo settlers' displacement of the Akimel O'odham is erased and replaced with the threat of Reavis's displacement of the Anglo settlers. Nevertheless, the cracks in DuPuy's counterfeit nostalgia unintentionally point to these other displacements, suggesting that the impact of U.S. empire was not as different from its Spanish counterpart as DuPuy makes it seem.

WILL TIPTON AND THE FEDERALIZATION OF ARIZONA

The counterfeit nostalgia with which DuPuy depicts Tipton ties this U.S. Anglo fantasy about the history of expansion in general, and Arizona in particular, specifically to the federal government. From the first scene, in which they meet at the train station, to the last, in which DuPuy juxtaposes the families of the two men, Tipton represents the U.S. government's resistance to the foreign threat Reavis poses. The first scene also sets up another juxtaposition: that of Tipton and Travers. Though both men are associated with U.S. expansion, Travers is a picture of its frontier past, while Tipton embodies its federal future. DuPuy's depiction of Tipton therefore crystallizes the modernization of U.S. empire, as exemplified by the transition of the Arizona Territory from lawless, multiethnic frontier to settled, Anglo state.

The real-life Will M. Tipton was the U.S. government's expert graphologist who worked as a special agent of the Court of Private Land Claims on the Peralta Land Grant case.[38] Along with Matthew G. Reynolds, U.S. attorney for the Court of Private Land Claims, and Severo Mallet-Prevost, associate counsel, Tipton deposed witnesses around the country in preparation for the Peralta Land Grant trial. At the trial, Tipton was a key government witness, corroborating Surveyor General Royal A. Johnson's condemning report by affirming that the evidence Reavis had provided in support of the Peralta Land Grant was in fact forged.[39] Though Tipton was just one of a team of government experts, in DuPuy's novel he becomes a composite character who represents all those involved in making the government's case. DuPuy may have chosen to focus on Tipton because of the article Tipton later published about Reavis titled "The Prince of Impostors," which appeared a few years after the trial in Charles Fletcher Lummis's *Land of Sunshine*.[40] In his article, Tipton carefully recounts the details of the Peralta Land Grant case, from Reavis's biography to analyses of some of his forgeries to a synopsis of the trial and the eventual undoing of the Peralta Land Grant scheme. It is possible that, in addition to whatever records he found at the government office in Washington, DuPuy also based some of his novel on the information Tipton provides in his article.

In the novel, DuPuy uses Tipton to portray the very best of the U.S. government. DuPuy begins *The Baron of the Colorados* with a dedication: "To William M. Tipton, Special Agent of the General Land Office and a worthy forerunner of generations of G-men that were to follow."[41] This dedication gives the reader an idea of the novel's tone and the kind of heroism it will celebrate. As DuPuy's earlier writings, such as *Uncle Sam's Modern Miracles*, make clear, he was a longtime champion not simply of the United States as a national identity but specifically of the federal government and its accomplishments at home and abroad. In *The Baron of the Colorados*, DuPuy personifies these accomplishments in Tipton.

DuPuy introduces Tipton to the reader as an unassuming yet extraordinary "young representative of the government":[42]

> To the casual observer the Special Agent would have seemed merely a quiet, middle-sized, conventionally-dressed, brown-eyed young man such as might be met by the score in a stroll down any city street. The Federal Government selected for this service men who were physically inconspicuous. It was necessary that they should be able to lose themselves in a crowd, that they should be seen and not remembered. But, like Will Tipton, most of them were college graduates, were lawyers; often they were athletes. If they remained in the service they must show the tenacity, the intelligence, the imagination, the courage that the work demanded. . . . [Reavis] knew from the set of Tipton's shoulders that muscles of steel played beneath his tailored coat. He recognized the intelligence indicated by the rise of his brow and the determination in the glint of his brown eyes and the set of his jaw. He did not underestimate his man.[43]

In this extended passage, DuPuy portrays Tipton as an exemplary federal agent thanks to his winning combination of physical strength, intelligence, and unassuming appearance. Tipton here is the picture of modern U.S. masculinity. Unlike Travers, who uses the formulaic pistol to try to neutralize Reavis's threat with brute force, Tipton is an intelligent, educated man who knows how to defeat an enemy without resorting to vigilante justice. That is not to say, however, that Tipton is not physically strong. Like a government Superman, Tipton's "muscles of steel" hide "beneath his tailored coat" and inconspicuous appearance as he goes about his day job. And like Clark Kent, DuPuy warns that Tipton's hidden powers should not be underestimated.

In a moment in which fears about foreign threats were high, DuPuy's characterization of Tipton reassured readers of the federal government's ability to protect the nation's borders, both physical and cultural. Foreign infiltration worried the prewar United States, and it was especially concerning for those who lived along what was perceived as a vulnerable entry point, the U.S.-Mexico border.[44] Notably, Tipton represents a very different kind of U.S. border security from Travers. In setting up the conflict as being between Reavis and Tipton as opposed to Reavis and Travers, DuPuy shows the transition from frontier to federal justice in Arizona. When Tipton visits Reavis later that night, he shows Reavis the very gun that almost ended his life earlier that day, which Travers has awarded Tipton in gratitude for having stopped him from committing such an impulsive act. Admiring the weapon, Reavis remarks, "But had you noticed this? There are two notches filed on its barrel," to which Tipton replies, "Yes. It evidently has a record of greater success in the past than that of today."[45] While Tipton is speaking of the events of the day, the symbolic value of his commentary suggests the end of frontier justice and an increasing proximity to settled society and an Anglo-U.S. identity. Arizona was at the time a picture of this shift, as federal investment in border security and military bases brought new economic opportunities that attracted predominantly Anglo people from other states.[46] The vigilante justice Travers almost executes in the beginning of the novel is relegated to the past, as DuPuy uses Tipton to show that the Anglo, federalized future had already arrived.

But this juxtaposition breaks down when Tipton is confronted with a group of Tohono O'odham men. In a chilling and outrageously offensive scene, DuPuy depicts a confrontation between the men and a group of Anglo women, including Helen Travers. The "blonde young wom[e]n . . . were students from the University of Arizona" who had decided to ride their horses from the campus to the nearby Mission San Xavier del Bac, a mission built by the famed priest Father Kino to proselytize the local Tohono O'odham community.[47] The girls arrive just as the Tohono O'odham are performing a ceremony that is, according to DuPuy, "freely interspersed with bounteous libations of tiswin, the native beverage of the tribe."[48] As the ceremony concludes, the two groups collide in a nearby stockade corral. The scene, which evokes the familiar tropes of a captivity narrative in its description of aggressive and violent Native American men and defenseless Anglo women, is interrupted by Tipton, who is conveniently also at the mission, researching the Peralta Land Grant in its archives.[49] Hearing the commotion, Tipton goes to the corral to see what is going on, and at the "exact moment the circling Indian dancers surge[] madly toward the cowering girls," Tipton comes to their rescue using the very gun given to him by John Travers, "mow[ing] them down with broken heads until the ground [is] covered with the fallen, and few remain[] standing. Those who [do take] to their legs and [flee]."[50] Here Tipton embodies a more familiar frontier masculinity, using his pistol to save a group of vulnerable Anglo women from a mob of angry non-Anglo men. While he had earlier prevented the same weapon from killing Reavis, opting instead to let a more formalized federal justice run its course, here he uses that very weapon to execute frontier justice on this group of Tohono O'odham men. DuPuy justifies this execution by describing in great detail his repulsion at the alcohol-infused behavior of the men, and the scenario helps DuPuy build toward the concluding romance between Tipton and Helen Travers.

Nevertheless, this scene, which reads very differently from DuPuy's other depictions of Tipton, complicates DuPuy's portrayal of U.S. expansion. While DuPuy justifies the violence against the Tohono O'odham men with the threat they pose to the Anglo women, the brutality with which Tipton neutralizes this threat is at odds with DuPuy's other descriptions of him and, consequently, of the federal government that he represents. After using both Reavis and Tipton to create a narrative of the United States as an exceptional antiempire, this scene reminds readers that U.S. expansion was made possible not by benevolent bureaucrats but rather by genocide. Tipton's murder of the Tohono O'odham men is another crack in the counterfeit nostalgia with which DuPuy glorifies U.S. expansion and the federalization of the Arizona Territory, showing the violence that enabled the United States to bring Arizona and other continental and overseas territories within its jurisdiction.

Sofia Peralta-Reavis and the Myth of the Vanishing Indian

DuPuy's characterization of Sofia Peralta-Reavis provides an alternative justification for U.S. expansion into Native American land: the inevitable disappearance of Native American people from the modern world. His romanticized descriptions of Peralta-Reavis join a long history of rhetorical maneuvers that ideologically eliminate Native American people by narratively vanishing them from the modern U.S. cultural landscape. DuPuy's fictionalized version of the real-life Peralta-Reavis sides with Reynolds's characterization of her at the Peralta Land Grant trial—that is, that she was not a Spanish baroness but rather a half-Anglo, half-Native American mixed-race woman. However, DuPuy takes some artistic license with the details of this mixed ancestry. In DuPuy's retelling, Peralta-Reavis's father is an Anglo man who lived among the Apaches and earned the trust of their famous leader, Cochise, who allowed the man to marry his daughter, Carmelita.[51] DuPuy's choice to fictionalize Peralta-Reavis's ancestry as Apache geographically and temporally anchors her within the late nineteenth-century Arizona Territory, when the Apache Wars dominated the local and national media. The language that DuPuy uses to describe Peralta-Reavis taps into the gendered and racialized coverage of the Apache Wars, including the construction of U.S. modernity as exclusively Anglo and Native American people like the Apaches as inevitably vanishing.[52]

DuPuy first introduces Peralta-Reavis to the reader when Reavis, who has been searching for an heiress to his invented grant, meets her for the first time:

She must have been fourteen but was mature beyond what would have been expected of girls her age. She was tall and peculiarly erect, yet sturdy, her body rounded to a grace and strength that is given only to children of Nature. Her complexion was a rich olive, a bit darker than the girls of Spain whom he had come to know. Her eyes and hair were as black as the wing of a raven. Her features were of that even conformity which spelt beauty, and there was a dignity about her carriage which suggested, strangely, the American Indian. She was a handsome, dark, alluring child-woman who, in the eyes of a connoisseur, held possibilities that were beyond measure.[53]

Peralta-Reavis here is the epitome of noble savagery.[54] Her dark, racialized features combine with her beautiful, mature, dignified, graceful, and strong character to make her into an ideal and idealized child of Nature. Unsurprisingly, this colonial characterization is steeped not only in racialized rhetoric but also in sexualized language.[55] In this passage, the colonial ramifications of Peralta-Reavis's sexualization are twofold. First, DuPuy's characterization of her as an "alluring child-woman who, in the eyes of a connoisseur, held possibilities that were beyond measure" highlights the rhetorical role of Native American women in colonial discourse as the conduits of conquest. As Shari M. Huhndorf argues, Native American women from Pocahontas and Sacajawea in the United States to La Malinche in Mexico are often characterized as the gateway to colonization.[56] In a similar fashion, Peralta-Reavis becomes a conduit, albeit a counterfeit one, for Reavis's forged colonization of the territory of the Peralta Land Grant. Second, the passage also participates in the feminization of the New World as a "'virgin land' that ostensibly offered itself for capture."[57] In this passage, Peralta-Reavis represents not only the conduit to conquer the Southwest but also the territory itself, which possessed infinite potential if the right person controlled it. While Reavis's criminal behavior precludes him from being that person, DuPuy's description makes clear that Peralta-Reavis's actual and metaphoric value can only be realized by someone else.

By positioning Peralta-Reavis as a noble savage, DuPuy contradictorily portrays her as both strong and impotent. This oxymoronic picture comes to a head in the final trial scene:

Doña ... Peralta-Reavis, flawless in dress, her profile cameo-clear, the smooth cream of her complexion as transparent as a sun-kissed apricot, sat immobile. She who, until this day, had firmly believed in her descent from an ancient Spanish Grandee, had thought that royal blood coursed in her veins, received the blow of disillusionment without a quaver. The blood of Chief Cochise, which had lent her a quality never understood until now, provided a racial stoicism, composure, and dignity quite equal to meeting this emergency born of a complicated world to which her aboriginal forebears had never been a part.[58]

In this passage, Peralta-Reavis is a study in contrasts. She is on the one hand the doña who is "flawless" in dress and "cream" in complexion, a woman who fully believes herself to be Spanish royalty. On the other hand, she is the stoic, dignified granddaughter of Cochise whose people are not part of this complicated modern world. Her behavior is the embodiment of what Gerald Vizenor has termed manifest manners,[59] a U.S. fantasy that corroborates the myths that underpinned the logic of Manifest Destiny by affirming the inevitability of U.S. dominance and Indian removal. By writing that Peralta-Reavis does not belong to this complicated world, DuPuy naturalizes her disappearance and erases the culpability of others, either Reavis or the federal government, in it.

The passage also importantly connects Peralta-Reavis to Cochise, allowing DuPuy to anchor his romanticized narrative in a particular time and place. Though there is no evidence that Peralta-Reavis was Apache, DuPuy's fictionalization strategically connects her to Arizona and its role in one of the most dramatic chapters in the history of U.S. expansion: the Apache Wars. Though the United States fought many different Native Americans in the course of its westward expansion, the Apache Wars gained mythic proportions thanks to extensive coverage in the press and, later, their ubiquitous presence in popular culture. By the time the United States came into contact with the Apaches in the mid-nineteenth century, they already had a long-standing reputation as fearless, brutal, nearly unstoppable fighters who zealously defended their territory against intruders.[60] The Spanish had struggled to contain them for centuries, and the Mexicans were so ill equipped to deal with them that they wrote a clause into the Treaty of Guadalupe Hidalgo requiring the United States to prevent Apaches from crossing the newly formed border into Mexico.[61]

The Apaches were infamous for their raiding, which was as widely practiced as it was misunderstood. Raiding was a political and economic activity in which the Apaches sought to take property from their enemies in order to hurt them economically and weaken them politically. Raiding was distinct from war, in which life, not property, was the main target. While raiding was commonplace, warfare could only be provoked by the need for revenge.[62] In U.S. popular culture, however, Apache raiding and warfare were collapsed into one activity, creating a distorted picture of a people that were bloodthirsty, cruel, and savage.

In the U.S. Anglo imaginary, no Apache represented this savagery better than Geronimo.[63] Though Geronimo was not a chief, he gained notoriety as a warrior.[64] When the U.S. government attempted to remove the Apaches to reservations, Geronimo was one of the leaders of the resistance, breaking out several times and prompting a manhunt throughout the deserts of southern Arizona.[65] When Geronimo finally surrendered in 1886, his capture, which coincided with the U.S. Census's declaration of the closure of the frontier, signified the end of not only the Apache Wars but also the first stage of U.S. expansion.[66] Geronimo's capture became a national symbol of Anglo superiority and the fulfillment of U.S. Manifest Destiny.

Reavis filed his claim to the Peralta Land Grant in 1887, only one year after Geronimo's surrender. Each man represented a different version of the same threat to U.S. expansion; both were foreign, and both threatened to displace Anglo settlers from their land. While this characterization was rooted in racism and a severely anachronistic portrayal of territorial settlement, it gained widespread acceptance. As time wore on, the comfort of knowing the Apaches had been soundly defeated altered their representation. In the case of the Apaches, instead of being represented as fear-inspiring and savage criminals, they became romanticized warriors who belonged to a vanishing culture. Despite overwhelming historical evidence to the contrary, including a bloody war that lasted many decades and a persistent presence in the United States, the Apaches came to symbolize an already defeated enemy whose disappearance was inevitable. By tying Peralta-Reavis to Cochise, a powerful but defeated Apache leader, DuPuy heightens this romanticized portrayal of a vanquished and vanished enemy.[67]

Nevertheless, as is the case in DuPuy's depiction of Reavis and Tipton, here too there are cracks in the counterfeit nostalgia with which he imagines Peralta-Reavis. Though DuPuy portrays her as stoically accepting her fate as a landless, vanishing Indian, he nevertheless cannot account for how she is so convincingly able to navigate the complicated modern world. At the trial, Tipton himself reveals this tension:

> Mrs. Reavis . . . has been an innocent victim of this unprecedented hoax. As a young girl she was led to believe this fantastic story of her descent from Spanish grandees and her rights under this grant. The ranchman, Slaughter, and his wife, believed Reavis' representations to be true. The prospective heir was drilled to living up to her part. How well she has responded everybody knows. But all the time she believed herself to be the person Reavis represented her to be. Her actual identity is known to very few people and, of course, not to herself. And, strangest of all, though she has been accepted as possessing the royal blood of the Bourbons there is not in her veins a drop that in any way ties back to Spain.[68]

In this passage, the real impersonator is not Reavis but rather Peralta-Reavis. Although in the first half of his speech Tipton describes Peralta-Reavis as a victim, in the last line, he admits that the strangest element of the entire Peralta Land Grant scheme is her own deceptive performance. She is a masterful actress, "drilled to living up to her part" and responding remarkably well. So well, in fact, that she convinced Spanish royalty of her noble birth and gained entrance to the court as one of their own.[69] Just as Reavis's altered documents (temporarily) validate his land claim, Peralta-Reavis's acquired manners validate her identity claim. However, Peralta-Reavis's counterfeit is even more disconcerting. Reavis's forgeries could be dismissed by handwriting and document experts, but the convincingness of his wife's performance could not be explained away quite so easily.

DuPuy's portrayal of Peralta-Reavis as a vanishing victim is in tension with the subversiveness of her performative passing. Her racial shape-shifting resonates with Vizenor's answer to the dominant fiction of manifest manners, that of survivance. As Vizenor explains, "Survivance is an active sense of presence, the continuance of native stories, not a mere reaction, or a survivable name. Native survivance stories are renunciations of dominance, tragedy, victimry."[70] Though DuPuy portrays Peralta-Reavis as a victim, her nearly successful passing resists the story of total domination that Tipton tells at the trial. She is inexplicably convincing in her role as heiress, able to adapt and elude discovery by her captors. The implication is that, were it not for the errors in Reavis's forgeries, Peralta-Reavis would never have been exposed because her performance was so flawless. If she represents the romanticized vanishing Indian, then her ability to navigate so adeptly this modern legal environment is both a racial and temporal passing. As Philip Deloria argues, "Some Indian people—more than we've been led to believe—leapt quickly into modernity . . . because it became painfully clear that they were not distinct from the history that was even then being made."[71] DuPuy cannot explain Peralta-Reavis's passing without acknowledging that she is not separate from the history of the Arizona Territory and U.S. expansion but rather an active agent within it.

John and Helen Travers and the Idealization of the Homesteader

DuPuy's fictionalized versions of the real-life James Reavis, Will Tipton, and Sofia Peralta-Reavis celebrate the ideologies and institutions that made U.S. expansion possible. Alongside these real-life figures, DuPuy adds two fictional characters to the Peralta Land Grant story, John and Helen Travers, who represent the ordinary (Anglo) "Americans" who do the day-to-day economic and cultural work of carrying out that expansion. By making John and Helen Travers homesteaders, DuPuy alludes to the Jeffersonian concept of the yeoman farmer as the ideal democratic subject. While the political philosophy that associated agrarianism with democracy originated in Europe, it flourished in the United States, which benefited from the promise of seemingly infinite land available for farming.[72] U.S. political philosophers like Thomas Jefferson "saw the cultivator of the earth, the husbandman who tilled his own acres, as the rock upon which the American republic must stand."[73] This belief shaped Jefferson's political views, including his commitment to westward expansion and the allotment of public lands, and some of his most ambitious projects, including the 1803 Louisiana Purchase, which more than doubled the nation's available land.[74] Sixty years later, Jefferson's dreams became a reality when President Abraham Lincoln signed the Homestead Act in 1862. The act established a three-step process for acquiring the title to a 160-acre piece of public land: claim a section; make improvements to the land, such as constructing a residence and cultivating the soil; and, after five years, file for the deed of title.[75]

In the novel, John and Helen Travers appear to have used the Homestead Act to secure the title to a plot of land in Arizona Territory. Gazing out over their claim, John Travers says to Helen, "There it lies, Daughter. . . . At last we have established a home. How tall the cottonwoods have grown! We planted them as mere slips six years ago. Do you remember how we ran the drag over the sagebrush that had been sleeping through the ages beneath the sun and flattened it out for clearing? Our last dollar went to hire the teams. From there on it was bare hands against the desert."[76] This description does more than establish John and Helen Travers as landowners; it justifies their ownership by detailing the improvements they have made to the land through personal sacrifice. Their financial and physical sacrifice amplifies the threat Reavis poses, as John Travers laments to Helen, after "ten years of battle . . . now this man Reavis would take it all from us."[77] The Traverses' relationship to the land starkly contrasts with that of Reavis, who has made no apparent sacrifice to legitimize his claim. Reavis's Peralta Land Grant clearly violates the Jeffersonian ideal that "the only valid title to land was that of the man who applied his own physical labor to its cultivation."[78] Consequently, Reavis's claim threatens not only the homesteaders' land but also the ideological basis for their land claims.

Nevertheless, the counterfeit nostalgia with which DuPuy imagines the Traverses can only justify this settler colonialism by erasing the Native American and Mexican populations that U.S. expansion displaced. Patrick Wolfe affirms, "In addition to its objective economic centrality to the project, agriculture, with its life-sustaining connectedness to land, is a potent symbol of settler-colonial identity. Accordingly, settler-colonial discourse is resolutely impervious to glaring inconsistencies such as sedentary natives or the fact that the settlers themselves have come from somewhere else."[79] DuPuy writes Arizona as an Anglo agrarian utopia, despite the fact that this agriculture was facilitated by non-Anglo people like the Akimel O'odham. As Geraldo Cadava argues, the "narrative of white innovation, of course, depended on a fictionalized version of the border region's ethnic and racial past."[80] That fictionalization included anachronistic retellings of settlement. Though DuPuy does not specify where John and Helen Travers were before staking their claim to this plot of land, it is clear that they are not native to Arizona Territory. Nevertheless, through his own counterfeit nostalgic retelling, DuPuy legitimizes John and Helen Travers and the broader Anglo settlement they represent in this far-from-virgin land as undisputed and inevitable.

FAMILIES AND FANTASIES

DuPuy's counterfeit nostalgia about Anglo settlement reaches a fever pitch in the final scene of the novel, which juxtaposes the two romances at the heart of the narrative. On one side, there stands Peralta-Reavis with her twin sons, gazing on Reavis through the bars that surround the prison where he now lives. On the other side, there are Helen Travers and Tipton in "an exultant embrace while [their] yellow-headed children danc[e] in shrill exuberance about them."[81] While the former is a tragic scene of separation, the latter is a joyous scene of unity. The fate of each marriage is closely tied to the foundational fiction DuPuy has been elaborating throughout the novel about U.S. expansion, which ties nation building to Anglo superiority.[82] As Amy Kaplan argues, the domestic space of the home is inextricably linked to the foreign space of continental and overseas imperial expansion, and in DuPuy's novel, each family comes to stand in for opposing visions of the national family.[83] In *The Baron of the Colorados*, DuPuy's fictionalization of Reavis's scheme defines what it means to be an American, racially and culturally, as exclusive of other national and ethnic identities.

In DuPuy's counterfeit nostalgic retelling, the tragedy that befalls Reavis and Peralta-Reavis is the result of their inability to adapt and conform to the norms of the U.S. Anglo future. Though Reavis's scheme parallels that of the homesteaders who also seek to stake claims to land in the West, he bases his claim not on agrarian ideals of working the land in order to earn it but rather on an inherited land grant in which territory is given, not earned. Instead of justifying his conquest with the principles of democracy, he bases his claim on Old World aristocracy. Peralta-Reavis similarly belongs to a vanishing culture that, while possessing some admirable qualities, has no place in the modern U.S. future. Meanwhile, the marriage of Will Tipton and Helen Travers is the epitome of what Kaplan has termed manifest domesticity, uniting the nationalist and masculine arena of Manifest Destiny with the domestic and feminine space of the home and child-rearing.[84] DuPuy's counterfeit nostalgia naturalizes this racialized narrative, making it inevitable and all other histories unimaginable.

Despite the utopic vision with which DuPuy ends his novel, the counterfeit nostalgia he uses to construct this racialized national fantasy cannot fully erase the ambiguity embedded within U.S. empire. If, as Kaplan argues, "imperialism [is] a network of power relations that changes over space and time and is riddled with instability, ambiguity, and disorder, rather than as a monolithic system of domination,"[85] then DuPuy's counterfeit nostalgia cannot fully smooth over the contradictions inherent within the imperialism it celebrates, which is neither as inevitable nor as benevolent as he would like to make it seem.

CHAPTER 5

The Baron Is like a Battleground

SAMUEL FULLER'S *BARON OF ARIZONA* (1950)

Director Samuel Fuller's 1950 B movie *The Baron of Arizona* opens to the sounds of a grand orchestral score with blaring trumpets and soaring violins as a black-and-white image of an old parchment paper appears on the screen. It reads, "On February 14, 1912, at the home of the Governor of Arizona, there was cause to celebrate, for on this day President Taft signed the proclamation that made Arizona the forty-eighth state admitted into the Union." The parchment fades into a shot of a group of men dressed in black tie who stand in a circle. With glasses raised, the men make an exuberant toast "to the state of Arizona!" In the midst of their celebration, one of the men, a Mr. John Griff, offers a surprising toast "to a real lover of Arizona. To my friend, James Addison Reavis." As Griff tilts his head back to take a drink, the other men look around, visibly shaken by his words. As the camera closes in on Griff's profile, one of the other men asks, "The man who called himself the Baron of Arizona?" Griff explains that Reavis, the con artist who forged a Spanish land grant to try to steal territory in Arizona, was not so different from them. Reavis shared their love for Arizona and a desire to improve it, though his methods were less than conventional.[1]

The rest of the film is a flashback that begins on a dark and stormy night. In the first flashback scene, Reavis, who is played by the not-yet-famous Vincent Price, trudges through the rain to knock on the door of a run-down shack where a young orphan named Sofia lives. Inside, he informs the little girl and her guardian, Pepito Álvarez, that the girl is a baroness and the rightful heiress to a large land grant in Arizona and that he intends to help her take possession of her inheritance. *The Baron of Arizona* then follows Reavis around the world as he forges Spanish records, seduces beautiful women (including Sofia, whom he eventually marries), presents his case to the Court of Private Land Claims, narrowly escapes an angry lynch mob, and ultimately confesses his crimes to Griff, the government expert assigned to investigate Reavis's claim to the Peralta Land

Grant. In the final scene, which might be Fuller's only happy ending, Reavis emerges from the Santa Fe penitentiary to find none other than the now-grown Sofia Peralta-Reavis, played by Ellen Drew, waiting for him as his devoted wife.

With the budget of a B movie, the cinematography of film noir, the scenery of a Western, and the happy ending of a romance, *The Baron of Arizona* is a hybrid of early to mid-twentieth-century popular film genres that defies easy categorization. Unlike Fuller's other films, *The Baron of Arizona* has never enjoyed commercial or cult success. Fuller began his career in the early 1950s, at a time when large movie studios dominated the market, but was a freethinking and independent filmmaker. His first film, the low-budget Western *I Shot Jesse James* (1949), had surprising commercial success despite its homoerotic undertones and limited release. His third film, *The Steel Helmet* (1951), caused an even greater sensation as the first film to portray the still-unfolding Korean War. In between these two, Fuller made *The Baron of Arizona* (1950), a campy B-Western-noir-romance based on Charles Renshaw Jr.'s January 9, 1949, *American Weekly* article of the same name.[2] The film was not, in Fuller's own words, "a big success" and is one of his least studied today, lacking the journalistic style and gritty subject matter that would later become synonymous with his work.[3]

The film's content—that is, its dramatization of the Peralta Land Grant story—is as enigmatic as its genre. The most notable inscrutability centers on Reavis himself, as the film seems unable to decide whether he is the story's villain, hero, or something in between. Instead of presenting a definitive explanation of the significance of Reavis's forged Peralta Land Grant within the history of the conquest and settlement of the West, *The Baron of Arizona* offers a constellation of possible interpretations. Taken together, these sometimes incompatible readings chart the long-term instability not only of Reavis's counterfeit narrative but also of the contradictions inherent within the dominant narratives about U.S. westward expansion on which it relied.

PICTURING THE WEST

From its nineteenth-century setting to its hypermasculine leading man, *The Baron of Arizona* does have much in common with classic Westerns. With the advent of cinema, the Western leapt from page to screen and quickly became the quintessential film genre of the United States.[4] The starkly beautiful landscape of places like Monument Valley, the rugged masculinity of cowboy heroes like John Wayne, and the triumphant vanquishing of foreign enemies made the look and feel of Westerns an iconic part of U.S. national identity. Like *The Baron of Arizona*, Westerns often set their narratives in the nineteenth century, as Chon Noriega explains, during "the Border Conflict era, or the eighty years following the Mexican-American War in which Anglo Americans violated the Treaty of Guadalupe Hidalgo, solidifying legal and cultural control over the Southwest."[5]

Westerns celebrated this Anglo-American domination, as Noriega and other Chicano film critics like Gary Keller, William Anthony Nericcio, Rosa Linda Fregoso, A. Gabriel Meléndez, and Camilla Fojas have argued, by negatively depicting Mexicans, Mexican Americans, and Native Americans as foils to a superior Anglo-U.S. national identity.[6] As one of the most remarkable and racially charged episodes to occur during the Border Conflict era, it is no surprise that the Peralta Land Grant saga was eventually staged cinematically as a Western.

The Baron of Arizona was not, however, an A-Western. When sound first emerged in film in the 1920s, two different versions of the Western developed: the epic, high-budget A-Western and the often bizarre, low-budget B-Western. Throughout the 1930s, B-Westerns outnumbered their bigger, more glamorous counterparts. In his study *The Invention of the Western Film*, Scott Simmon notes that while there were "at most fifty films that can be labeled as A-Westerns," there were "more than one thousand B-Western features."[7] B-Westerns were subject to a different production budget and schedule from A-Westerns, making them more cost effective and faster to produce. B-Westerns typically showed second in a double feature, ran under one hour, cost as little as $15,000 to make, and took only days to shoot.[8] Prefiguring the popular Western television shows of the 1950s, B-Westerns also often featured recurring characters in a series of films. The tone of the films was generally light, and their fast and frugal production led to many uneditable errors that came to typify the genre. Though their production qualities make it easy to dismiss B-Westerns as comical and frivolous, they often produced their own social commentaries, dramatizing the past to make sense of present troubles.

A B-Western precursor to the *Baron of Arizona*, *The Night Riders* (1939),[9] used the Peralta Land Grant saga to glorify anti-immigrant vigilantism in the face of economic depression. *The Night Riders* was part of the Three Mesquiteers series, a B-Western franchise of films that featured "a shifting trio of stars and production companies," in this case including a young John Wayne.[10] Unlike *The Baron of Arizona*, *The Night Riders* was only very loosely based on the details of the Reavis case, using Reavis as inspiration to create an even more extraordinary plot. In the film, a former U.S. Mint engraver and his Mexican maid team up with a riverboat gambler to forge a Spanish land grant in California and claim the grant by impersonating a Spanish nobleman and his wife. The Three Mesquiteers enter on the scene when the U.S. government validates Don Luis de Serrano's grant and he begins to charge rent for all his land, including the Mesquiteers' eponymous 3M Ranch. When the settlers, including the Mesquiteers, cannot pay, the Don mercilessly evicts them from the land with his mercenary posse of enforcers. Though the Mesquiteers appeal to President James Garfield, he regretfully informs them that his hands are tied; the U.S. government must honor its treaty with Mexico and recognize the Spanish land grant. The brave Mesquiteers, not ones to stand idly by, then take matters into their own hands. Donning white masks and capes that eerily resemble Ku Klux Klan robes, the Mesquiteers become Los Capaqueros, riding around at night to rob the Don's henchmen and give the money to soon-to-be-evicted settlers so that they can pay their rent. In the course of their Robin Hood adventuring, the Mesquiteers discover that the grant is a forgery and expose the Don, his wife, and their friend the engraver as frauds. Having saved California from the evil fake Don, the Mesquiteers return to their ranch as heroes.

The Night Riders' glorification of Klan-style vigilantism reimagines the nineteenth-century Peralta Land Grant scheme through the lens of twentieth-century nativist resentment. Importantly, the film portrays the Mesquiteers donning their white capes and masks to rob the Don *before* they know that he is a fraud. From the very first shootout scene, in which the Don's men wear black cowboy hats and the Three Mesquiteers wear white ones, the film cues the audience to be on the Mesquiteers' side. The Mesquiteers and the audience do not need to know that the Don is a criminal to know that he must be stopped, since it is not the falseness of the papers but the foreignness of his Spanish claim that is so offensive to everyone, from the Mesquiteers and their fellow settlers all the way up to President Garfield. The 1939 release of *The Night Riders* notably coincided with the end of Mexican Repatriation, an effort led by the U.S. Immigration and Naturalization Service that successfully deported nearly half a million Mexicans, many of whom were citizens of the United States, as part of a series of nativist policies spurred by the Great Depression.[11] *The Night Riders* turns to the Peralta Land Grant case to bring to the screen the nativist resentment that plagued a nation on the heels of a decade of economic depression.

Premiering eleven years later, *The Baron of Arizona* did not reproduce the straightforward nativist nationalism that pervades *The Night Riders*. In the years that separated the two films, World War II pulled the country out of the Great Depression, but the United States soon sank into the Cold War, leading to the emergence of a new genre: the noir Western. According to Richard Slotkin, noir Westerns represented "a new and darker style" that either "centered on themes of revenge and featured psychologically damaged and alienated heroes" or "offered an ironic or inverted version of standard 'progressive' themes."[12] Triumphant tales of bravery and heroism like *The Night Riders* gave way to cynical films about tyrants, corrupt politicians, and conmen. While Westerns in general became more complex and critical in the postwar period, Imogen Sara Smith affirms, this "small group of postwar westerns exhibited distinctive aspects of film noir: chiaroscuro lighting, haunted heroes, dangerous women, confusing plots driven by secrets from the past, and a pervasive sense of anomie. . . . The noir western leads audiences not into the sunset but into the darkness beyond."[13] The combination is not surprising to Simmon, who sees a natural affinity between the two genres. After all, "noir revealed city life as the last frontier, where civilization and law is a veneered illusion and men must fight for whatever fragile order they care to invent."[14] The dark noir Western therefore had different preoccupations from its predecessors. In the postwar era, noir Westerns "played variations on the same basic concern: How had America's achievement and exercise of pre-eminent power affected our commitment to the democratic ideology for which we had nominally fought the war?"[15] These self-reflective films asked who benefited from the war and what they gained. Contrary to the celebratory tone of the prewar films, noir Westerns were gloomy, skeptical, and cynical. From its striking use of light and dark to its focus on a seemingly irredeemable main character, *The Baron of Arizona* employs many elements of the noir Western, though the film's happy ending complicates its relationship to this pessimistic subgenre.

SAMUEL FULLER: "A FILM IS LIKE A BATTLEGROUND"

In a cameo appearance in Jean-Luc Godard's 1965 film *Pierrot le Fou*, Fuller, when asked to define cinema, replies, "A film is like a battleground. It's love. Hate. Action. Violence. Death. In one word: emotions."[16] This oft-quoted line has become emblematic of Fuller's directorial style, which has been characterized as everything from primitive to offensive, but always raw. According to Lisa Dombrowski, "Fuller's storytelling goal is to arouse emotion, and his screenplays combine hard-boiled characters, ironic contradictions, excessive conflict, and a selective embrace of classical and generic conventions in order to shake the viewer up."[17] Inspired by his work as a crime reporter and soldier, as a filmmaker Fuller did not shy away from controversial storylines that were steeped in pulp and tabloid culture and full of ambiguity and contradiction.

As a director, Fuller drew from his personal experience as an immigrant, journalist, and soldier to create films that explored themes related to isolation, rejection, and social alienation. Fuller was a Russian Jew whose family immigrated to the United States when he was an infant, eventually settling in New York.[18] As a child, he sold newspapers in Manhattan and subsequently worked as a copyboy for the *New York Evening Journal*, a crime reporter for the *New York Evening Graphic*, and a freelance reporter in different parts of the United States.[19] These formative years spent working as a reporter would later shape the feel and focus of his films, which often explore the seedy underside of contemporary U.S. society. After the United States entered World War II, Fuller joined the army and saw a great deal of action in Europe and North Africa as a member of the First Infantry Division.[20] The horrors he witnessed during the war later emerged in his films, which frequently include intensely violent scenes.

Due to the unusual content and cinematic style of Fuller's films, their critical reception has been polarized. On the one hand, directors and critics alike have been drawn to Fuller's fearlessness when it comes to bending or breaking the rules of convention to tell a story narratively and visually. His "use of extreme close-ups and aggressive camera movements" has influenced well-known directors from François Truffaut and Godard to Martin Scorsese and Quentin Tarantino.[21] Despite these influential admirers, Marsha Gordon notes that "some critics and scholars have in fact dismissed Fuller's films as sensational, incoherent, or unsophisticated."[22] Like other B movies, the dialogue and acting in Fuller's films are often uneven and over the top. Critics also remain divided regarding the politics of the films Fuller produced, many of which emerged during the height of McCarthyism. While some have argued his films were aligned with Joseph McCarthy's fierce anticommunist stance, others have insisted that they rejected McCarthy's enforcement of censorship and uniformity.[23]

Though today retrospective reflections on Fuller's films are mixed, his eccentric cinematic style and gritty content were unilaterally disliked by the conservative large studios that ruled film production when he first began his filmmaking career.[24] Consequently, his first two films, *I Shot Jesse James* (1949) and *The Baron of Arizona* (1950), were produced as independent films by Robert Lippert.[25] *The Baron of Arizona* was shot on location in Florence, Arizona, just south of Phoenix.[26] It premiered to the general public in Phoenix on March 1, 1950, after a special screening for Arizona governor Dan E. Garvey a few weeks prior on February 14, 1950, to celebrate the thirty-eighth anniversary of Arizona's statehood.[27] Despite the film's ambitious script and staging, reviews of *The Baron of Arizona* were mixed and the film was a commercial disappointment for both Fuller and Lippert.[28]

Though *The Baron of Arizona* has never garnered significant critical attention, its complex, confusing, and even contradictory presentation of key aspects of the Peralta Land Grant saga importantly reflects how the story lived on as legend long after the actual court case concluded. As the following four key scenes demonstrate, the film's presentation of Sofia Loreto Peralta-Reavis's contested identity, the settlers' hostility toward Reavis and Peralta-Reavis and their Peralta Land Grant, and Reavis and Peralta-Reavis's unorthodox romance dramatizes the afterlives of late nineteenth-century ideologies about Manifest Destiny, race, and the western frontier. By exploring all of these themes without offering a clear message about any of them, *The Baron of Arizona* reveals the continued irresolvability of questions about race, gender, and land rights that remain at the center not only of the case but also of the settlement of the West in general and Arizona in particular.

Porous Identities, Racial Uncertainties: "Mr. Griff, Look at Me. Tell Me, Am I a Fake?"

Who Peralta-Reavis really was and how she was able to convince so many people she was a Spanish baroness were central parts of the Peralta Land Grant saga as it was happening and remained fundamental to its mythic afterlife. The film captures this uncertainty in a climactic scene in which Griff confronts Reavis at home about his bribing of witnesses to prove his wife's noble parentage. Though the scene is set up as a showdown between Reavis and Griff, it is Peralta-Reavis and the bribed witness, Mr. Martínez (played by Adolfo Ornelas), who are at the center of the action. The casting, costuming, and performances of Drew and Ornelas in the scene highlight lingering questions about the relationship among race, identity, and appearance in the Southwest. By caricaturing the stereotypical Hollywood Mexican, Ornelas subverts the stereotype's dehumanizing effects, using the assumptions that underpin its clichéd representation to empower instead of marginalize his character. Drew's portrayal of Peralta-Reavis has the opposite effect, whitewashing the real-life Peralta-Reavis's identity and mitigating the magnitude of the tragedy, and the threat, that her passing as a Spanish baroness caused. Despite this mitigation, the question with which Drew concludes the scene, "Mr. Griff, look at me. Tell me, am I fake?" underscores the ways that porous racial borders continue to haunt the history of the Peralta Land Grant and the settlement of the West.

The fade into the scene reveals the interior of a luxuriously appointed home. Reavis and Peralta-Reavis have their backs to the camera, which points toward two men whose footsteps echo off the walls as they enter the large room. The first, a tall Anglo man wearing a double-breasted suit, is Griff. He is followed by a shorter Mexican man wearing work clothes and holding a wide-brimmed hat.

As Griff and Reavis exchange how-do-you-dos, the camera pans to the side to reveal the profile of a woman standing beside Reavis. Reavis turns to the woman and says, "May I present Mr. John Griff of Washington D.C.," then turns to Griff to say, "My wife, the Baroness Sofia de Peralta Reavis." Peralta-Reavis and Griff lock eyes, and Griff is visibly taken aback by the beautiful woman, whose light skin appears even whiter against the opulent, black, off-the-shoulder, floor-length evening gown she wears. Griff gives a little bow to the lady, saying, "Forgive me. This is very important."

Griff then explains why he has come to call on Reavis and Peralta-Reavis in their home this evening. The Mexican man trailing behind Griff is Martínez, whom, as the audience is reminded in a jump cut to an earlier scene, Reavis previously paid to create false tombstones for Pedro and María de Peralta, Peralta-Reavis's supposed parents. Griff then proceeds to question Martínez in Reavis and Peralta-Reavis's parlor, saying "Is he [Reavis] the one who paid you to cut words on two unmarked tombstones in the Guadalajara cemetery?" In a heavily accented English, Martínez responds, "He pay [sic] me to cut flowers and keep the grave nice and beautiful." The visibly stunned Griff, who is shaken by this unexpected answer, responds, "Martínez, you know the seriousness of perjury?" to which Martínez replies, "What is 'perjury'?" highlighting his unfamiliarity with the term by placing the emphasis on the second syllable, so that the word becomes per-JUR-y instead of PER-jur-y. Griff, looking at Martínez, then Reavis, then Martínez again, asks Martínez, "Did you see this man today?" to which Martínez responds, "I see him. Eleven years ago. He were [sic] looking for Peralta family." Griff says, "You told me he bribed you," to which Martínez, with a shrug of the shoulders, asks, "What is 'bribe'?"

Turning to Reavis, Griff warns, "It won't do you much good," touching Martínez on the shoulder and turning to leave. As the backs of the two men approach the door, Peralta-Reavis runs after them, calling, "Mr. Griff," prompting Griff to turn around. She then asks him, "You think my husband is a fake?" In a close-up shot, Griff does not respond but instead averts his eyes from her gaze. Peralta-Reavis then responds, "Look at me." Griff raises his eyes to look at her, as the camera turns to a close-up of the woman in the formal evening dress. Defiantly, Peralta-Reavis demands, "Tell me, am I a fake?" but Griff does not respond. The scene fades to black over a shot of Peralta-Reavis, still waiting for the answer to her question, accompanied by the sounds of the retreating footsteps of Griff and Martínez.

———

In this scene, Martínez appears as a stereotypical Hollywood Mexican. He is short, has a large mustache, and wears heavily worn workmen's clothing. Most importantly, his complexion is dark, much darker than that of the other three characters who appear alongside him in the scene. Arnoldo De León notes that the derogatory term *greaser* originally developed in reference to the phenotype of many Mexicans, who were for the most part darker than U.S. Anglos.[29] Although Mexicans, unlike African Americans, were legally considered white, De León affirms, "color was a basic determinant of the way Anglos saw Mexicans. Anglos were not going to regard as equals people whom they thought to be colored, whom they therefore considered uncivilized, and whom they connected with filth and its foul implications."[30] These racist attitudes were prevalent in popular culture, first debuting in print culture like newspapers and dime novels and later appearing on screen.[31] William Anthony Nericcio notes that in the early twentieth-century, so-called greaser films, which featured disparaging depictions of Mexicans, were immensely popular and their cinematic themes remained influential for decades.[32] Martínez's appearance harks back to the "greaser" days, clearly positioning him as belonging to a different race and class from the other three characters. Martínez's behavior in the scene further underscores this divide. His heavily accented English marks him as foreign, while his grammatical errors mark him as ignorant and uneducated.

The way Ornelas embodies his role as Martínez, however, critiques the stereotypes he is called on to portray. It is clear that not only did Reavis bribe Martínez to forge the gravestones of Peralta-Reavis's purported parents, he also bribed him to lie to Griff and deny that he had any involvement with Reavis's scheme. When Griff realizes what is going on, he incredulously asks Martínez if he understands the seriousness of the crime he is committing. In response, Martínez relies on the assumption that Mexicans are ignorant in order to absolve himself, simply shrugging his shoulders and replying, "What is per-JUR-y?" and "What is 'bribe'?" Though it is obvious that Martínez understands more than he lets on, Griff simply lets the matter go, promising Reavis that he will get him some other way.

Ornelas's overperformance of anti-Mexican stereotypes mocks the inaccurate assumptions they promote, as well as the people who believe them. Scholars have analyzed how Latino actors can critique typecast roles through their performance of them. Charles Ramírez Berg proposes that Latino actors make these critiques through what he calls "performative excess"—that is, performances that lend depth, richness, and individuality to otherwise flat characters.[33] Drawing on Berg, as well as José Muñoz's theorization of disidentification, Marci McMahon posits that Latino actors' negotiation of cliché roles simultaneously sustains and challenges dominant discourses.[34] While Berg and McMahon both focus on actors who add complexity to formulaic characters through their performances, Ornelas's performance in *The Baron of Arizona* does the opposite. Instead of adding depth, Ornelas's over-the-top costuming, cartoonish accent, and exaggerated mannerisms emphasize the ridiculousness of the stereotypes he embodies and the foolishness of those, like Griff, who subscribe to them.

Drew's portrayal of the only other non-Anglo character in the scene contrasts sharply with that of Ornelas. Drew, who had starred in a number of films throughout the 1930s and 1940s, was a former Midwestern beauty pageant queen who had risen to stardom thanks to her girl-next-door charm.[35] Not only is Peralta-Reavis, as played by Drew, not dark, she is in fact the lightest person on screen. Her luxurious clothing, perfectly styled hair, extravagant jewelry, and accent-free speech further distance her from Martínez and the poor, working-class Mexicans he represents. Although at the end of the film it is revealed that Peralta-Reavis "has Indian blood," Drew's casting, costuming, and performance make this passing less transgressive. That is to say, there is nothing about Drew's appearance or behavior that would make the audience uncomfortable with the ease with which she navigates white spaces and passes for white herself.

Despite the palatability of Drew's portrayal of Peralta-Reavis's passing, her question, "Mr. Griff, look at me. Tell me, am I a fake?" haunts the film. Drew's question alludes to the bizarre and tragic role Peralta-Reavis's identity played in Reavis's scheme. While Reavis merely threatened to displace the Anglo settlers from their land, he destroyed Peralta-Reavis's life, inventing an identity for her that then unraveled in front of a national audience. Though the film version of their relationship ends happily, with Reavis ultimately repenting and falling in love with the woman he was formerly using, Peralta-Reavis's question troubles the ease with which the movie ends and gestures toward the unsettling implications of Peralta-Reavis's false identity, from the individual tragedy it prompted to the larger ambiguity it highlighted regarding the racialization of Mexicans and Mexican Americans in the Southwest.

Whitewashed Fantasies, Cold War Anxieties: "In God We Trusted, in Arizona We Busted"

A few scenes later, another showdown occurs, but this time, instead of Reavis and Griff, it is Reavis and one of the Anglo settlers, a man named Lansing, who exchange words. The racial tension of the previous scene continues, but this time it is played out in the context of Reavis's threatening to displace the Anglo setters from their land. The scene visually and narratively foments a Hollywood Western nostalgia, from a whitewashed retelling of Arizona's early days to an angry mob and a fistfight. As a noir Western, the film recasts this Western nostalgia through a Cold War lens, in which Reavis and Peralta-Reavis become foreign villains who threaten to infiltrate the domestic space with their anti-American land grant.

———

The scene begins with a close-up of the ringleader of the settlers, Lansing, who is in the middle of giving a speech. With a cloudless sky behind him, he points emphatically, shouting, "And not only that, but my father was the first white American to pitch a tent in Phoenix. Since I was eight years old I helped him plant and plow until we got enough to buy our own piece of land from the government. And then this fella comes along who says he's a . . . a baron . . . whatever that is . . . and every time I try talking plain horse sense to him, he told me to settle with one of his clerks. Well, I'm gonna settle with this baron himself." While Lansing speaks, the camera cuts away to the crowd of settlers, who listen attentively, anxious looks on their faces. The shot then jumps to a wide view of the scene from behind the crowd, revealing that Lansing is standing on a platform with a large hand-painted sign behind him that reads, "IN GOD WE TRUSTED, IN ARIZONA WE BUSTED." As the musical score swells, one man in the crowd yells, "There's your chance, Lansing! There they come!" The entire crowd turns to watch an open-air carriage pulled by four white horses approaching. The plush, fabric-lined carriage looks starkly out of place against the backdrop of an adobe house with a thatched roof. Even more out of place are the passengers, Reavis and Peralta-Reavis, whose opulent clothing is inconsistent with the rest of the scenery.

The camera turns to a close-up of Reavis and Peralta-Reavis. Reavis's black suit, silk tie, and black felt hat are only outmatched by Peralta-Reavis's black lace dress, oversize jewelry, dramatic black lace mantilla, and large white flower tucked behind her ear. With a look of disdain, Reavis booms, "Clear the road," prompting Lansing to grab his shotgun, descend from the platform, and move through the parting crowd to respond, "Clear the road. Next we'll have to pay you to breathe this air." After a tense exchange between the two men, Lansing fires his shotgun into the air, and Reavis jumps from the carriage to take a swing at the shooter. As the two struggle, Reavis gains the upper hand and wrestles Lansing's rifle away. He holds the rifle up, but just as he is about to bring it down on Lansing's head, Peralta-Reavis screams "James!" at which point a series of close-ups of the faces of Reavis and Peralta-Reavis reveal reluctant restraint and indignant horror, respectively. Ominous marching music plays as Reavis climbs back into the carriage, which drives through the crowd and disappears around a corner in a cloud of dust.

———

In the dramatic speech that opens the scene, Lansing appeals to the religious and racially infused arguments that underpinned the doctrine of Manifest Destiny and the policy of homesteading in order to cast Reavis and Peralta-Reavis as a threat not only to private property but also to the American way of life. The banner that forms the backdrop for Lansing's monologue, "IN GOD WE TRUSTED, IN ARIZONA WE BUSTED," reminds viewers of the religious justification for U.S. westward expansion. Lansing's affirmation that his "father was the first white American to pitch a tent in Phoenix" erases the peoples and histories that predated Anglo settlement and enables him to cast the other settlers as innocent victims of a foreign "baron . . . whatever that is." Reavis and Peralta-Reavis's incongruity with territorial Arizona is further underscored by their costuming. Their elegant clothes and luxurious carriage contrast sharply with the cowboy boots and hats of the settlers. The desert landscape is antithetical to, as Jane Tompkins puts it, "the fancy words and pretty actions of the drawing room, elegant clothes, foreign accents, dusky complexions, subservient manners, of women, Easterners, and nonwhite males."[36] The scene visually and narratively casts Reavis and Peralta-Reavis as foreign aristocrats who are a holdover from another time and for whom there is no place in Arizona.

Like the Three Mesquiteers in *The Night Riders*, Lansing uses Reavis and Peralta-Reavis's foreignness to reject the legitimacy of their claim even before he realizes it is a forgery. Because they are outsiders, they are already frauds, no matter what the legitimacy of their paper claim may be. In Lansing's estimation, they have not earned the land and therefore do not deserve to take possession of it. While Lansing appears to only be talking about his fellow settlers and their opponent Reavis, the two opposing claims that he identifies in his speech derive their legitimacy from the Homestead Act on the one hand and the Treaty of Guadalupe Hidalgo on the other. Lansing stakes his claim to the Arizona Territory by planting, plowing, and purchasing. The connection he makes between physical labor and property rights marks Lansing as a homesteader. Reavis, in contrast, stakes his claim to the Arizona Territory by presenting a land grant in accordance with the Treaty of Guadalupe Hidalgo. Ironically, the treaty was meant to safeguard the property rights of Mexicans who would otherwise find themselves in precisely the same situation as Lansing: dispossessed. Nevertheless, Lansing does not see the connection between his own circumstances and those of the Mexican landowners to whom Reavis's claim alludes. Instead, in rejecting the Peralta Land Grant, he also rejects the provisions of the Treaty of Guadalupe Hidalgo and the rights it supposedly guaranteed. By dismissing Reavis's Peralta Land Grant before he knows it is fraudulent, Lansing implicitly dismisses the legitimacy of the land rights of non-Anglo settlers in territorial Arizona.

The scene's characterization of nineteenth-century treaties and laws at first appears far removed from the film's 1950 post–World War II context, but Lansing's rejection of Reavis and Peralta-Reavis's land claim reflects the evolution of U.S. empire in the postwar era. Following World War II, the United States cemented its position as a global superpower, transitioning from the formal overseas governance of small islands to large-scale and informal yet influential political, economic, and cultural dominance within the hemisphere and around the world. Because of their close association with U.S. national identity, Westerns were ideally situated to reflect this transition and reached the height of their popularity in the postwar period.[37] As Stanley Corkin argues, "The repressed dimension of Westerns is their relationship to imperialism—and it is their indirect means of considering such activity that makes them *the* genre of the period after World War II."[38] During this time, Westerns functioned as a sort of shorthand for understanding and celebrating U.S. hegemony by allowing viewers to return to the imagined essence of what it meant to be an American. Lansing's speech clearly encapsulates this sentiment, affirming the legitimacy of U.S. Anglo settlement above all else and arguing that it must be protected at all costs.

Lansing's criticism of Reavis and Peralta-Reavis's foreignness also resonates with 1950s McCarthy-era xenophobia. The noir ambience of the film suggests that Cold War concerns about foreign infiltration of the United States on its own soil refracted Reavis's plot differently. As Jonathan Auerbach affirms, during the Cold War, "the question . . . became how to distinguish friend from foe, and, in the absence of clear markers of difference, how to uncover and deal with sedition at home."[39] Though Reavis based his claim to the land on Spanish laws, he himself was not Spanish. As an Anglo man using another empire's practices to displace fellow Anglo settlers, Reavis embodies the epitome of Cold War anxieties regarding sedition at home and people who were traitors to their own nation.

Frontier (In)justice: "What's Lynchin'
Got to Do with Provin' the Land Is Ours?"

The second-to-last scene of *The Baron of Arizona* is the film's visual and narrative climax. Shot in dramatic chiaroscuro lighting with quick jump cuts and a booming score, the mob scene in which the settlers attempt to lynch Reavis is a frenetic representation of frontier justice. The Cold War–infused Western nostalgia that marked the previous scene continues, but in this scene, the contrasting depictions of Reavis as a villain and the settlers as victims begin to blur. Reavis confesses to Griff and repents of his crime, but the settlers' angry lynch mob at first appears unstoppable. Though Reavis is eventually spared, the settlers' thirst for violence undermines their previously sympathetic portrayal, moving the audience to feel compassion for the reformed Reavis and paving the way toward the film's ultimately happy ending, in which Reavis is absolved of his past misdeeds.

The camera looks down on a crowd gathered in the town square under the cover of darkness. Lansing's familiar voice animates the crowd, shouting, "The land in Arizona don't belong to no baron! It belongs to you and me! We paid for it! We paid for it with money, and we paid for it with our hard work!" The crowd affirms Lansing's statement with shouts of acclamation. As he booms, "We gotta do somethin' now!" the scene cuts to Reavis and Peralta-Reavis's carriage and four white horses making their way along the dusty road. Reavis has just confessed to Griff that he forged the Peralta Land Grant and has promised to return the money he extorted from the settlers. Ominous music accompanies a cutaway shot to a man on horseback who watches the approaching carriage from a lookout spot on a nearby hill. The shot cuts back to the crowd in the square, where two men on horseback use ropes to pull down the sign hanging outside Reavis's headquarters. The lookout returns with shouts of "The Baron is comin'! The Baron is comin'!"

When Reavis and Peralta-Reavis's carriage arrives at the square, there is an eerie silence as the camera pans to the shadowy faces of the townspeople who are hidden behind storefronts surrounding the square. Suddenly, a gunshot pierces the silence and the settlers emerge from their hiding places. The scene immediately descends into chaos as images of men pulling Peralta-Reavis and Reavis out of the carriage are spliced with shots of townspeople running through the darkness holding flaming torches and signs that read, "Swindler get out," "Hang the Baron," and "Lynch the Baron." Reavis and Peralta-Reavis struggle as the horde throws a noose on an external support beam outside Reavis's headquarters. Peralta-Reavis's guardian, Pepito Álvarez, fires into the crowd so that he, Reavis, and Peralta-Reavis can run into Reavis's headquarters and barricade the door behind them with every piece of furniture they can find. Windows to the outside reveal settlers carrying flaming torches, and the sound of banging precedes an image of men with a log ramming the barricaded front door. The door gives way, and the men enter and hoist the noose yet again, this time inside Reavis's office. As the camera pans to the wall-size map of Arizona that adorns the area behind Reavis's gargantuan desk, the shadow of the men fitting the noose around his neck appears inside the outline of the map, as Lansing says, "This'll learn ya! You don't take land that don't belong to ya!"

A cutaway to the tearful Peralta-Reavis, who is being held back by more men, is interrupted by the fervent hissing of Reavis, who struggles to speak because the noose is now tightened around his neck: "Go on and hang me, you stupid idiots! Hang me, and the land'll never be proven yours. Go on and hang me! What's the matter? Haven't you got any brains? Isn't there one man among you with sense enough to realize that once I'm dead you'll never be able to prove anything? Ask the government man. He'll tell you. That's why he was with me—to question me, to save your property. You know the law. Tell 'em what'll happen if they hang me. Tell 'em what'll happen to their land!" Lansing responds, "What's lynchin' got to do with provin' the land is ours?" to which Reavis responds, "Hang me, and you hang your ranches and farms and shops and mines. Hang me, and you'll never give Griff a chance to get at me. He can't try a dead man. I've got to be alive if you want to prove that the land is yours. . . . Go on! Hang me!" As his words reverberate, the shot of Reavis, eyes bulging, hair wet with sweat, fades to a shadow of an empty noose swinging across the wall-size map of Arizona.

––––––

From a cinematographic standpoint, this dramatic scene is the most palpably steeped in noir of the entire film. The combination of light and shadow, abrupt transitions, and violent anarchy creates an overall mood of terror, danger, and darkness. In *The Baron of Arizona*, this darkness includes not just the darkness of Reavis's criminal plot but also the darkness of the settlers who are so readily willing to lynch him. As sympathy shifts from the settlers to Reavis, the film begins to move toward a neat resolution in which Reavis repents and emerges a reformed man. Nevertheless, the noir sensibilities of this second-to-last scene undermine the resolution that follows, as lynch mobs and conmen haunt the tidy end to a tumultuous story.

In over-the-top melodramatic fashion, Fuller combines cinematographic drama with the familiar Western trope of frontier justice, here embodied by the attempted lynching of Reavis, in order to create the dramatic climax of a winding and complex story. In one of the only critical analyses of *The Baron of Arizona*, Dombrowski focuses on this scene in particular as emblematic of techniques that would later become hallmarks of Fuller's films. Dombrowski affirms that, with the help of famed cinematographer James Wong Howe, "the attack of the mob and attempted lynching of Reavis is the visual high point of the film and the most complicated action sequence Fuller had yet directed."[40] The scene was meant to attract audiences who were hungry for action as well as historical melodrama, although the film's poor box office performance suggests that one action-packed scene was not enough to draw significant crowds.

The implications of this violent scene, however, are unsettling with regard to its relationship to both the nineteenth-century history of lynching and the twentieth-century history of Cold War witch-hunts. Many explanations of lynching in the West cite the absence of the formal rule of law as justification for extralegal methods. Nevertheless, as Manfred Berg argues, "The widespread notion that frontier vigilantes acted only where efficient law enforcement was nonexistent does not square with the historical record, which contains numerous lynchings of criminal suspects who were already in custody. Distrust of government played as large a role as lack of government."[41] This is precisely the case in *The Baron of Arizona*. Reavis has just confessed his crimes to Griff and is in government custody when the settlers seize him to execute justice on their own terms. The settlers are the embodiment of what Berg identifies as "the ugly specter of anarchy and mob violence" that loomed "behind the image of virtuous communities establishing law and order."[42] The settlers' lack of virtue is underscored by Lansing's question, "What's lynchin' got to do with provin' the land is ours?" Though the settlers supposedly lynch Reavis for justice, they themselves admit that the act of lynching has nothing to do with proving the land is theirs—that is to say, with the justice they supposedly seek.

This scene also highlights the racialized undertones of lynching beyond the regional frame of the South. Contrary to common conceptualizations of frontier justice made popular by dime novels, films, and television, which portray summary executions as a method to maintain order in the Wild West, as Ken Gonzales-Day has shown, many were actually motivated by racism and white supremacy.[43] That is to say, lynching in the West was not so different from lynching in the South. Though Reavis is Anglo, in the context of the film's earlier scenes that racialize him as foreign on account of his Spanish claim, this lynching scene also reads as an uncomfortable reminder of the racialized dimensions of lynching in the West as a method to dispose of unwanted populations in order to clear the path for Anglo settlement.

Moving from the scene's nineteenth- to its twentieth-century context, just as Lansing's racialized rejection of Reavis in the previous scene refracted Cold War fears regarding treasonous loyalties at home, this scene puts the dangerous and perhaps unforeseen consequences of those fears on full display. While McCarthy-era interrogations were supposedly intended to protect citizens, their actual impact was to create widespread terror and distrust, leading to a breakdown of civil society. Just like the angry lynch mob, they were more concerned with exposure and removal than with the restoration of justice and peace. This second-to-last scene captures the seamy underside of frontier justice and Cold War witch-hunts—that they were more about anarchy and mob violence than establishing law and order.

An Unbelievable Romance: "Arizona Seems So Small. You Suddenly Seem So Great."

Fuller took liberties with many details of the Peralta Land Grant case, but the most notable by far is his insertion of a classic Hollywood romance, complete with an inexplicably happy ending. At the end of the film, despite the deceit, public scandal, and questionable age difference, Reavis and Peralta-Reavis fall in love. As the previous chapters have shown, the real relationship between Reavis and Peralta-Reavis was not so harmonious. In Fuller's own words, "The real Reavis lived out his final years in a shack, penniless and abandoned," and Peralta-Reavis eventually filed for divorce on the grounds of nonsupport.[44] In his other films, Fuller gravitates to exactly this sort of antipayoff, probing the depths of the lonely, depressed, and directionless. Yet in *The Baron of Arizona* he chooses "an upbeat ending to the picture, even though it wasn't historically factual."[45] It seems strange that a movie so pervaded by disappointment, abandonment, and unfulfilled promises would end with such unwavering devotion. The only explanation Fuller offers for such an uncharacteristic choice is that, "in the movie business, a good ending must sometimes hold sway over the truth."[46] This explanation, however, sounds odd coming from someone like Fuller who was never defined or deterred by the demands of the movie business. The unbelievable romance rings untrue, unable to gloss over the real-life complexities that make the Peralta Land Grant case so interesting and alarming.

The final scene of *The Baron of Arizona* begins with a close-up of a sign that reads Santa Fe Prison, illuminated by a solitary light and moistened by falling rain. The camera pans to the left to reveal the backlit vertical bars of a locked gate. A man wearing a cowboy hat moves to unlock the gate as his figure and the bars make a shadow on the ground. The sound of rain falling is accompanied by sweeping strings playing a romantically tinged version of the film score's theme. A tall man wearing a black hat and cape follows the man with the keys and passes through the now-unlocked gate. Pulling his collar up around his neck to shield himself from the rain, the man slowly makes his way toward the foreground, where the viewer sees that it is Reavis. The long camera shot follows Reavis walking alone in the rain against a black background, then suddenly opens into the street outside the prison, where a carriage awaits. As the strings grow louder, Reavis approaches the carriage, where Peralta-Reavis occupies the front passenger seat, waiting. The camera cuts to a close-up of Reavis, now fully soaked from the rain, with a perplexed look on his face, as he musters the words, "I thought I told you to leave me." The camera cuts to a close-up of Peralta-Reavis, whose smile erupts into the words, "Get in." The camera returns to a close-up of Reavis, a smile now growing across his face, as the scene fades and "THE END" appears across the screen.

The Baron of Arizona is full of romance, both real and forged. Reavis is a relentless womanizer throughout the film, using his charm to convince a gypsy woman to help him break into a Spanish nobleman's home so that Reavis can forge one of his books, then seducing the nobleman's wife in order to gain access to the book once inside the home, and finally, convincing Peralta-Reavis to marry him so that he can connect himself directly to the Peralta claim. To each of these women, Reavis repeats the line, "I've been with many women before, but with you . . . I'm afraid." The melodramatic line is the sort of thing viewers expect to hear in a B movie like *The Baron of Arizona*. Reavis's false vulnerability helps develop his villainous nature as the kind of man who not only steals from unsuspecting victims but takes advantage of innocent women to do so.

According to the film, Peralta-Reavis's unrelenting love for Reavis is what ultimately redeems him. When he confesses to Peralta-Reavis that he forged the Peralta Land Grant and her identity and that he only married her to realize his scheme, she does not respond in anger but rather tells him, "I don't want you to go." Her unwavering devotion to Reavis is not surprising given the lack of character development of Peralta-Reavis, who is simply a devoted wife who adores her husband no matter what he does throughout the film. Her role as the moral compass of the couple becomes clear when Reavis proposes that they have enough money to run away to Europe together and evade the law. Horrified at his suggestion, Peralta-Reavis insists that they are guilty and must give the money back to the people they extorted. In a tearful speech, she tells Reavis, "I am Mrs. James Reavis, and one of us must have the dignity to accept punishment. One of us must have the dignity to recognize love. I'll always love you. Nothing can change that. . . . I'll want you until the day I die. It is not death, it is dying that alarms me. It is not your crime, it's your weakness that alarms me." In her speech, Peralta-Reavis collapses her relationship with Reavis with the Peralta Land Grant scheme. The scheme is what brought them together, and now it is what threatens to tear them apart. In a miraculous change for a character who has up to this point been entirely duplicitous, Reavis is convinced by her sincerity to own up to his crime and face punishment. Moved by his wife's speech, Reavis responds, "Arizona seems so small. You suddenly seem so great. Now I know what I was looking for—a woman who would love me for what I am. No man can live without that. No man can ask for more." In the melodramatic exchange, in an instant, true love transforms Reavis from a womanizing con man into a repentant husband. He realizes that he was wrong to pursue riches when it is love and companionship that are the true treasures in life.

Reavis's response, "Arizona seems so small. You suddenly seem so great," brings together the two forgeries at the heart of his scheme. Up until this point, Reavis has been so focused on Arizona that Peralta-Reavis appeared to him as nothing more than a pawn in his plan. In this pivotal moment, redeemed by the purity of her true love for him, Reavis realizes that he has had his priorities wrong all along. It is not the land but the lady that he has truly been searching for all this time.

Happy Endings

Fuller's happy ending, however, cannot fully resolve the conflicts that characterize the preceding scenes. Peralta-Reavis's contested racial identity is a troubling window into the racial hierarchies that defined property ownership in the late nineteenth-century Southwest. The settlers' racialized hostility toward the Peralta Land Grant is an alarming picture of interethnic relations in territorial Arizona, culminating in the disturbing violence of a lynch mob. Though the film attempts to smooth over these clashes in the final scene of romantic fulfillment, the hostilities of the previous scenes haunt this sudden shift toward peaceful reconciliation.

In the end, the audience is left wondering what to make of this melodramatic Western noir romance that concludes in an unbelievable happy ending. The only explanation for such an incongruous ending is that it reflects the conflicts at the heart of the Peralta Land Grant case, which remain unresolved to this day. The racialization of non-Anglo people and the rights they enjoy continues to plague not only the past but also the future of the United States, as nativist resentment has arguably only increased since Reavis's day. Ultimately, the frustration that *The Baron of Arizona*'s overly simple ending generates points to the way that the case continues to unsettle our understanding of the history of the settlement of the West, eluding easy answers about the content of that history and how it continues to impact the region today.

Epilogue

FORGETTING THE PERALTA LAND GRANT

Whatever the decision of the court may be the name Peralta will be a familiar one in the southwest for generations to come.
—*Santa Fe Weekly New Mexican and Livestock Journal,* March 22, 1894

In 1894 it was impossible for the staff at the *Santa Fe Weekly New Mexican and Livestock Journal* to imagine the name Peralta, which had so dominated its headlines, disappearing from the southwestern landscape. A little more than sixty years after the paper's declaration, in the foreword to his comprehensive study of the history of the Peralta Land Grant, Donald M. Powell begins by stating that "nearly everyone in the Southwest has heard of the Peralta Grant and of the Baron of Arizona, James Addison Reavis, but very few have any accurate knowledge of the story."[1] Both the paper's staff and Powell would be surprised to learn that the same cannot be said today. Few have ever heard, much less know the details, of the Peralta Land Grant, the Baron of Arizona, and the rest of the counterfeit narrative that James Addison Reavis created. What happened in between the publication of the 1894 article, Powell's 1960 study, and today? Why have we forgotten the Peralta Land Grant?

Just as Powell set out in his book to correct the misinformation surrounding the Peralta Land Grant case, I have set out in this book to contextualize the many iterations of the Peralta Land Grant, from the original forgeries to fictional reimaginings, in order to investigate not so much what is true and what is not but rather why the story has been told in particular ways at particular times. Reavis's original forgeries preyed on the prevailing misconceptions created by the doctrine of Manifest Destiny and the war with Mexico that it justified. At the trial, the racial uncertainties the war fomented came to life in the opposing characterizations of Sofia Loreto Peralta-Reavis. In the newspaper coverage, these opposing characterizations were brought to the court of public opinion. In William Atherton DuPuy's novel, the Peralta Land Grant became a vehicle for consolidating a counterfeit nostalgia about an invented history of the Old West that was tied to the United States' rise as a global superpower. In Samuel Fuller's film, the unresolved questions that Reavis's counterfeit narrative provoked about national identity haunt a story infused with Cold War anxieties. With this long and winding genealogy in mind, I ask, What prevents this history, no matter what iteration it may take, from being told today?

Put another way, what would the impact of telling the story of the Peralta Land Grant now be? To begin to answer this question, I return to how I came to this project in the first place. In 2008 I moved from Arizona, where I had lived my entire life, to join the PhD program in literature at the University of California, San Diego. In my second year in the program, Arizona passed its now-infamous Senate Bill 1070 and House Bill 2281 and the state suddenly found itself in the national spotlight for the controversial anti-immigrant and anti-ethnic studies stances of the respective laws. I, too, suddenly found myself in the spotlight, called on by my California colleagues to answer for the behavior of the state where I had been born and raised. In the endless conversations that followed, both in my own life and on the national level, I quickly noticed a pattern. Regardless of the viewpoint, there was a general dismissal of the complexities of Arizona. Whether people were in favor of or against the laws, they painted Arizona as universally xenophobic. Being an Arizonan who is not, I knew that such was not the case, but I could not explain why this distorted depiction of the state had so much currency across the political spectrum.

I shifted my research to investigate how Arizona had gained such a reputation and why it was so widely accepted. Though my initial question was inspired by the contemporary political landscape, it eventually led me to Arizona's territorial period and its tortured road to statehood. I quickly discovered that there was much less scholarship on territorial Arizona than on neighboring New Mexico, California, and Texas, so I turned to the archives. There, despite the anticipated gaps and silences, I nevertheless found a wealth of underexplored documents that painted a different, more complex picture of Arizona.

One of these complex stories was the history of the Peralta Land Grant. I came across the trial transcript by accident at the Bancroft Library at the University of California, Berkeley, and was instantly intrigued by the details of a case I had never heard of previously. In the limited horizon of graduate school, I lacked sufficient time to delve into the details of the case much further, dedicating one dissertation chapter to a topic to which I knew I would return. Years later, I found myself back in my home state, this time as an assistant professor at the University of Arizona. I delved back into my notes and resumed my research, excavating the history of the Peralta Land Grant and its afterlives. As I worked, I began to ask coworkers, community members, and librarians what they knew of the case. I began to screen Fuller's *Baron of Arizona* (1950) for my undergraduate students, most of whom had lived in Arizona their entire lives but had never heard of Reavis or the Peralta Land Grant. With the exception of a handful of very knowledgeable archivists, hardly anyone I approached was familiar with Reavis's spectacular fraud or its later fictionalizations.

As I began writing the book, I started to realize that Reavis's counterfeit narrative not only was forgotten but in fact *could not be remembered*. Though distant in time, Reavis's invented history of a fake land grant and its claimant seemed more relevant than ever. In a politically charged climate filled with "fake news" and "alternative facts," Reavis's counterfeit narrative uncovered a long genealogy of deliberately manipulating and distorting the truth in order to consolidate power. Moreover, the specific contents of the counterfeit narrative he created pointed to the still unresolved questions about the relationship among narrative, racial identity, and belonging in the United States in general and Arizona in particular.

As I conclude this book, the urgency of investigating the contours of this relationship is all too palpable. A large number of Central Americans who have been alternately termed refugees, asylum seekers, a migrant caravan, and an invading horde, are currently making their way toward the U.S.-Mexico border. To prepare for their arrival, President Donald Trump is deploying a minimum of 5,200 U.S. troops to the border to block their entry, including the entry of those who intend to seek asylum in the United States.[2] The competing narratives describing the impending collision of the two groups are highly polarized, an utterly unsurprising reality given that the 2018 midterm elections are but one week away. By the time this book is published, we will know the result of these elections and perhaps will already be seeing their effects in the intensification or repudiation of current policies.

But in this moment of unease and anticipation, I am prompted to reflect on how the underlying dynamics that define the Peralta Land Grant saga are palpable within this twenty-first century border crisis. Though the exact destination of those in route is still unknown, it might well be Arizona. This potential spatial convergence brings to mind Natalia Molina's theorization of what she calls *racial scripts*, or "the ways in which the lives of racialized groups are linked across time and space and thereby affect one another, even when they do not directly cross paths."[3] Though the Central Americans moving toward the U.S.-Mexico border will not cross paths with Sofia Peralta-Reavis, they are linked by centuries of borderlands racial scripts that have been the focus of this book. Though the specific contours of the counterfeit narratives that exclude them from the nation differ, they are joined together by common elements. Both rely on a rewriting or total erasure of U.S. history, whether with regard to U.S. territorial expansion in the mid-nineteenth century or U.S. foreign policy in Central America in the late twentieth century. Both also depend on racialized constructions of U.S. citizenship that foreclose certain populations from becoming part of the citizenry. Those racialized constructions are necessarily connected to gender and class, making poor women of color like Sofia Peralta-Reavis and many of the migrants moving toward the border today particularly vulnerable. The complexity of their stories is largely unacknowledged and rarely remembered. In all likelihood, this current crisis, though currently dominating the headlines, will like the Peralta Land Grant soon fade from memory.

If it is important to remember the Peralta Land Grant now, it is because it reminds us to look for and analyze the narratives that determine who belongs within the borders of the nation—and to be ready to denounce counterfeits. In *Forging Arizona*, I have recovered some of the temporal and generic translations and transformations of Reavis's counterfeit narrative in order to reveal the counterfeit content of the dominant narratives that were fundamental to the forging of Arizona and the West. The doctrine of Manifest Destiny mapped a historical and racial reality onto the West that did not match its actual reality. That doctrine was then used to marginalize the territory's non-Anglo inhabitants, who, as the current political climate has proved, still find themselves on the outskirts of a national identity that was founded on their exclusion. In recovering not only Reavis's counterfeit narrative but also the dominant narratives that it imitated, in *Forging Arizona* I have recovered the mechanisms by which narratives, both real and imaginary, forge borders.

Acknowledgments

This book is only possible because of the support of many individuals and institutions. The earliest support of this project came from my dissertation committee at the University of California, San Diego: Sara Johnson, Curtis Márez, Rosaura Sánchez, Shelley Streeby, and Nicole Tonkovich. Thank you to my editor, Leslie Mitchner, who supported me and encouraged me to continue developing my ideas for many, many years, as well as Nicole Solano and the rest of the staff at Rutgers University Press. Thank you also to the anonymous reviewers for their thoughtful feedback. An excerpt from chapter 2 appeared in *English Language Notes* and is republished here by permission of the publisher, Duke University Press. Thank you to the special issue editors, Maria A. Windell and Jesse Alemán, as well as the anonymous reviewers, for their careful and constructive feedback.

Archival research is costly in both time and money, and I am grateful to the Bancroft Library, the University of Arizona Department of Spanish and Portuguese and College of Humanities, and the University of New Mexico Center for Regional Studies for their financial support of this project. I would especially like to thank Gabriel Meléndez, director of the University of New Mexico Center for Regional Studies, whose enthusiastic support of this project enabled me to spend a semester in the archives in New Mexico revising the manuscript. Thank you also to Alisha Fitzgerald for making my transition to Albuquerque so seamless.

Archivists in many different locations helped me gather the materials necessary to complete this book. Thank you to those at the Bancroft Library, University of Arizona Special Collections, Arizona Historical Society, University of New Mexico Center for Southwest Research and Special Collections, New Mexico State Records Center and Archives, Arizona State University Archives, and the Mexican Archivo General de la Nación. Thank you especially to those who have gone above and beyond to support me and my work: Laura Hoff, Caitlin Lampman, Verónica Reyes-Escudero, and Lizeth Zepeda.

I am fortunate to have been surrounded by wonderful colleagues at every stop along the way. At the University of California, San Diego, I benefited from conversations, collaborations, and friendships across campus. Thank you to those from whom I learned so much, all of whom I admire very deeply: Jennie Daniels, Josen Díaz, Andrea Domínguez, Jodi Eisenberg, Ana Grinberg, Lauren Heintz, Bernadine Hernández, Joo Ok Kim, Ashvin Kini, Ryan Lepic, Chien-ting Lin, Stephanie Gomez Menzies, Jacqueline Munguía, Yumi Pak, Chris Perreira, Morelia Rivas, Violeta Sánchez, Thea Quiray Tagle, and Lisa Thomas, along with many others.

As I was revising the manuscript at the University of New Mexico, I benefited from the generous support of many colleagues. In the Department of Spanish and Portuguese, I am grateful to Enrique Lamadrid, Anna Nogar, and Santiago Vaquera-Vásquez, who were generous in sharing their considerable expertise with me. In the Department of English, I am grateful to Jesse Alemán for including me in an archives symposium that he organized, which helped me clarify some of the central ideas of this book. At the Center for Southwest Research, I am grateful to Suzanne Schadl and Samuel Sisneros for their invaluable help navigating the archives. Thank you also to the National Hispanic Cultural Center for inviting me to share my work as part of the La Canoa Legacy Talks series.

My colleagues at the University of Arizona have been an invaluable network of support. I am grateful to Malcolm Compitello and the Department of Spanish and Portuguese as well as Alain-Philippe Durand and the College of Humanities for the many ways they have supported this project. Thank you especially to those who read drafts of this manuscript at varying stages: Bram Acosta, Sony Coráñez Bolton, Steph Brown, Faith Harden, Jamie Lee, Anne Garland Mahler, and Kaitlin M. Murphy. Thank you also to those whose expertise and friendship I value so dearly: Kevin Byrne, Maritza Cardenas, Ana Carvalho, Javier Durán, Leah Durán, Lillian Gorman, Adela Licona, Mauricio Magaña, Jen Martin, Ana Martínez, Antxon Olarrea, Miquel Simonet, Michelle Téllez, Beatriz Urrea, and Desiree Vega.

To my *comadres* Marci McMahon and Aïda Valenzuela, who so graciously read endless drafts of this manuscript and cheered me on from start to finish.

To my students, who remind me daily why this work matters.

To my chosen family, who are too numerous to name. So many of you work tirelessly each day to make Arizona a better place. You all inspire me.

To the many others whom I am inevitably overlooking here, please know that I am grateful and forgive me for my memory lapse. Writing a book will do that to you.

And last, to my family. I am grateful to have the most incredible *suegros*, who are a constant source of joy and encouragement. I am forever thankful to my parents, whose unwavering support has made this book possible in innumerable ways, large and small. And to Joaquín. You are, in so many ways, the reason for all of this.

Notes

INTRODUCTION

1. Donald M. Powell, *The Peralta Grant: James Addison Reavis and the Barony of Arizona* (Norman: University of Oklahoma Press, 1960), 12.

2. Powell.

3. E. H. Cockridge, *The Baron of Arizona* (New York: John Day, 1967).

4. See María E. Montoya, *Translating Property: The Maxwell Land Grant and the Conflict over Land in the American West, 1840–1900* (Berkeley: University of California Press, 2002); and David Correia, *Properties of Violence: Law and Land Grant Struggle in Northern New Mexico* (Athens: University of Georgia Press, 2013).

5. I use the term *Anglo* throughout this book to refer to the people whom the U.S. Census today classifies as "non-Hispanic white." I employ *Anglo* instead of *white* because of its geographic specificity to the U.S. Southwest, although its use here is somewhat anachronistic. As Katherine Benton-Cohen clarifies, while "it is a term that appeared in the records only in the 1930s . . . 'Anglo' developed as a synonym for 'white' that avoided the problem that Mexicans were legally white. In the Southwest, Mexicans are never 'Anglo'; but people of Jewish, Slavic, and Italian descent can be." Katherine Benton-Cohen, *Borderline Americans: Racial Division and Labor War in the Arizona Borderlands* (Cambridge, Mass.: Harvard University Press, 2009), 15. For further discussion of how the category of whiteness has developed in the United States, see David Roediger, *The Wages of Whiteness: Race and the Making of the American Working Class* (New York: Verso, 1991) and *Working Toward Whiteness: How America's Immigrants Became White, The Strange Journey from Ellis Island to the Suburbs* (New York: Basic Books, 2005); Ian Haney López, *White by Law: The Legal Construction of Race* (New York: New York University Press, 1996); Reginald Horsman, *Race and Manifest Destiny: The Origins of American Racial Anglo-Saxonism* (Cambridge, Mass.: Harvard University Press, 1986); George Lipsitz, *The Possessive Investment in Whiteness: How White People Profit from Identity Politics* (Philadelphia: Temple University Press, 2006); and Matthew Frye Jacobson, *Whiteness of a Different Color: European Immigrants and the Alchemy of Race* (Cambridge, Mass.: Harvard University Press, 1999).

6. Throughout this book I use the term Southwest to refer to the land that Mexico ceded to the United States at the close of the U.S.-Mexican War. Though this term is U.S.-centric—that is, Southwest only makes sense as a directional indication if one presumes the United States as a starting point—it underscores the distorted and often damaging consequences that emerge from a U.S.-centered perspective, which are a central concern of this book.

7. This body of scholarship is immense, but of particular interest here are those studies that specifically engage the history of U.S. westward expansion and its relationship to racial discrimination. See, for example, Shelley Streeby, *American Sensations: Class, Empire, and the Production of Popular Culture* (Berkeley: University of California Press, 2002); Deena J. González, *Refusing the Favor: The Spanish-Mexican Women of Santa Fe, 1820–1880* (Oxford: Oxford University Press, 2001); Montoya, *Translating Property*; Miroslava Chávez-García, *Negotiating Conquest: Gender and Power in California, 1770s to 1880s* (Tucson: University of Arizona Press, 2004); María Raquél Casas, *Married to a Daughter of the Land: Spanish-Mexican Women and Interethnic Marriage in California, 1820–1880* (Reno: University of Nevada Press, 2007); Raúl A. Ramos, *Beyond the Alamo: Forging Mexican Ethnicity in San Antonio, 1821–1861* (Chapel Hill: University of North Carolina Press, 2008); Anthony Mora, *Border Dilemmas: Racial and National Uncertainties in New Mexico, 1848–1912* (Durham, N.C.: Duke University Press, 2011); Omar S. Valerio-Jiménez, *River of Hope: Forging Identity and Nation in the Rio Grande Borderlands* (Durham, N.C.: Duke University Press, 2013); and Karen R. Roybal, *Archives of Dispossession: Recovering the Testimonios of Mexican American Herederas, 1848–1960* (Chapel Hill: University of North Carolina Press, 2017).

8. Rodrigo Lazo, "Introduction: Historical Latinidades and Archival Encounters," in *The Latino Nineteenth Century: Archival Encounters in American Literary History*, ed. Rodrigo Lazo and Jesse Alemán (New York: New York University Press, 2016), 10–11.

9. Here I invoke the term *unsettlement* as used by scholars in early and nineteenth-century American studies in order to challenge the inevitability and extensiveness of U.S. settlement within the borders of what today composes the nation. See Kirsten Silva Gruesz, "Unsettlers and Spectators," *PMLA* 131, no. 3 (2016): 743–751.

10. See "Recovering the U.S. Hispanic Literary Heritage," Arte Público Press, accessed April 19, 2017, https://artepublicopress.com/recovery-project/.

11. See, for example, Ann Laura Stoler's discussion of this interdisciplinary turn in *Along the Archival Grain: Epistemic Anxieties and Colonial Common Sense* (Princeton, N.J.: Princeton University Press, 2009), 44–46.

12. Stoler, 44; Jacques Derrida, *Archive Fever: A Freudian Impression* (Chicago: University of Chicago Press, 1996). For the relationship between history and power, see Michel-Rolph Trouillot, *Silencing the Past: Power and the Production of History* (Boston: Beacon, 1995).

13. Michelle Caswell, "'The Archive' Is Not an Archives: Acknowledging the Intellectual Contributions of Archival Studies," *Reconstruction: Studies in Contemporary Culture* 16, no. 1 (2016), https://escholarship.org/uc/item/7bn4v1fk.

14. See, for example, Francis X. Blouin Jr. "Archivists, Mediation, and Constructs of Social Memory," *Archival Issues* 24, no. 2 (1999): 101–112; Verne Harris, "The Archival Sliver: Power, Memory, and Archives in South Africa," *Archival Science* 2 (2002): 63–86; Rodney G. S. Carter, "Of Things Said and Unsaid: Power, Archival Silences, and Power in Silence," *Archivaria* 61 (2006): 215–233; Jeannette Bastian, "'Play Mas': Carnival in the

Archives and the Archives in Carnival: Records and Community Identity in the US Virgin Islands," *Archival Science* 9 (2009): 113-125; and Jamie A. Lee, "Archives," in *The Routledge History of American Sexuality*, ed. Kevin P. Murphy, Jason Ruiz, and David Serlin (New York: Routledge, expected 2019).

15. Stoler, *Along the Archival Grain*; Emma Pérez, *The Decolonial Imaginary: Writing Chicanas into History* (Bloomington: Indiana University Press, 1999); Maylei Blackwell, *Chicana Power! Contested Histories of Feminism in the Chicano Movement* (Austin: University of Texas Press, 2011).

16. See, for example, Brien Brothman, "Afterglow: Conceptions of Record and Evidence in Archival Discourse," *Archival Science* 2 (2002): 311-342; Elizabeth Shepherd, "Culture and Evidence: Or What Good Are the Archives? Archives and Archivists in Twentieth Century England," *Archival Science* 9 (December 2009): 173-185; Kimberly Anderson, "The Footprint and the Stepping Foot: Archival Records, Evidence, and Time," *Archival Science* 12 (2012): 349-371; and Terry Cook, "Evidence, Memory, Identity, and Community: Four Shifting Archival Paradigms," *Archival Science* 13 (2013): 95-120.

17. Anna Brickhouse, *The Unsettlement of America: Translation, Interpretation, and the Story of Don Luis de Velasco, 1560-1945* (Oxford: Oxford University Press, 2015), 2.

18. Raúl Coronado, *A World Not to Come: A History of Latino Writing and Print Culture* (Cambridge, Mass.: Harvard University Press, 2013), 34.

19. For a detailed discussion and critique of the doctrine of Manifest Destiny, see Stephanie LeMenager, *Manifest and Other Destinies: Territorial Fictions of the Nineteenth-Century United States* (Lincoln: University of Nebraska Press, 2004); Horsman, *Race and Manifest Destiny*; and Amy S. Greenberg, *Manifest Destiny and American Territorial Expansion: A Brief History with Documents* (Boston: Bedford/St. Martin's, 2012).

20. This territory includes what became part or all of what are today the states of California, New Mexico, Nevada, Utah, Wyoming, Colorado, Kansas, Oklahoma, and Arizona. See David J. Weber, *Foreigners in Their Native Land: Historical Roots of the Mexican Americans* (Albuquerque: University of New Mexico Press, 1996), 140.

21. The treaty did not explicitly grant citizenship rights to Native Americans living in the formerly Mexican land. As Martha Menchaca explains, it did not grant citizenship to "Mexican Indians" and gave Congress the power "to validate or extinguish all land grant agreements that Spain and Mexico had made with Mexican Indians, including the mission Indians." Menchaca, *Recovering History, Constructing Race: The Indian, Black, and White Roots of Mexican Americans* (Austin: University of Texas Press, 2001), 234.

22. The history of discrimination against Mexican American people has been well documented by many scholars. See David Montejano, *Anglos and Mexicans in the Making of Texas, 1836-1986* (Austin: University of Texas Press, 1987); George J. Sánchez, *Becoming Mexican American: Ethnicity, Culture, and Identity in Chicano Los Angeles, 1900-1945* (Oxford: Oxford University Press, 1993); David Gutiérrez, *Walls and Mirrors: Mexican Americans, Mexican Immigrants, and the Politics of Ethnicity* (Berkeley: University of California Press, 1995); Weber, *Foreigners*; and Neil Foley, *Mexicans in the Making of America* (Cambridge, Mass.: Harvard University Press, 2014).

23. Richard Griswold del Castillo, *The Treaty of Guadalupe Hidalgo: A Legacy of Conflict* (Norman: University of Oklahoma Press, 1990).

24. Rosaura Sánchez, *Telling Identities: The Californio Testimonios* (Minneapolis: University of Minnesota Press, 1995).

25. María Montoya discusses how dominant understandings of the U.S. West as unsettled territory impacted land grant cases and approaches to property rights. See *Translating Property*.

26. Laura E. Gómez, *Manifest Destinies: The Making of the Mexican American Race* (New York: New York University Press, 2007).

27. For a comprehensive history of U.S. racial regimes, see Michael Omi and Howard Winant, *Racial Formation in the United States*, 3rd ed. (New York: Routledge, 2015).

28. For a history of the Spanish racial hierarchy, or casta system, in Mexico, see María Elena Martínez, *Genealogical Fictions: Limpieza de Sangre, Religion, and Gender in Colonial Mexico* (Stanford, Calif.: Stanford University Press, 2008).

29. Natalia Molina, *How Race Is Made in America: Immigration, Citizenship, and the Historical Power of Racial Scripts* (Berkeley: University of California Press, 2014), 24.

30. Carey McWilliams, *North from Mexico: The Spanish-Speaking People of the United States* (New York: Greenwood, 1968), 36; Raymund Paredes, "The Evolution of Chicano Literature," in *Three American Literatures: Essays in Chicano, Native American, and Asian American Literature for Teachers of American Literature*, ed. Houston A. Baker Jr. (New York: Modern Language Association, 1982), 52.

31. Martha Menchaca, "Chicano Indianism: A Historical Account of Racial Repression in the United States," *American Ethnologist* 20, no. 3 (1993): 587.

32. Benton-Cohen, *Borderline Americans*, 21; Eric V. Meeks, *Border Citizens: The Making of Indians, Mexicans, and Anglos in Arizona* (Austin: University of Texas Press, 2007), 82–83.

33. For a study focused specifically on how this dominant narrative evolved in Arizona, see Geraldo L. Cadava, *Standing on Common Ground: The Making of a Sunbelt Borderland* (Cambridge, Mass.: Harvard University Press, 2013).

34. Mark E. Pry, "Statehood Politics and Territorial Development: The Arizona Constitution of 1891," *Journal of Arizona History* 35, no. 4 (1994): 399–400.

35. See Pry, "Statehood Politics"; Mark E. Pry, "Arizona and the Politics of Statehood, 1889–1912" (PhD diss., Arizona State University, 1995); and Linda C. Noel, *Debating American Identity: Southwestern Statehood and Mexican Immigration* (Tucson: University of Arizona Press, 2014).

36. I am here using Doris Sommer's conceptualization of the term *foundational fictions* as elaborated in her book *Foundational Fictions: The National Romances of Latin America* (Berkeley: University of California Press, 1991).

37. Meeks, *Border Citizens*, 37.

38. See Anita Huizar-Hernández, "The Specter of Statehood: Inventing Arizona" in Charles D. Poston's *Building a State in Apache Land* and Marie Clara Zander's 'The Life of an Arizona Pioneer.'" *MELUS: Multi-ethnic Literature of the U.S.* 42, no. 2 (2017): 53–78.

39. S. 1070, 49th Leg., 2d Reg. Sess. (Ariz. 2010), https://www.azleg.gov/legtext/49leg /2r/bills/sb1070s.pdf.

40. Mark B. Evans, "Text of Governor Brewer's Speech after Signing SB 1070," *Tucson Citizen*, April 23, 2010, http://tucsoncitizen.com/mark-evans/2010/04/23/text-of-gov -brewers-speech-after-signing-sb-1070/.

41. S. 1070.

42. S. 1070.

43. H.R. 2281, 49th Leg., 2d Reg. Sess. (Ariz. 2010), https://www.azleg.gov/legtext/49leg /2r/bills/hb2281s.pdf.

44. Emily Gersema, "Tucson Ethnic Studies Program Not Illegal, Audit Says," *Arizona Republic*, June 16, 2011, http://archive.azcentral.com/news/election/azelections /articles/2011/06/16/20110616tucson-ethnic-studies-audit0616.html.

45. Julie Depenbrock, "Federal Judge Finds Racism behind Arizona Law Banning Ethnic Studies," *All Things Considered*, August 22, 2017, podcast, 3:44, http://www.npr.org /sections/ed/2017/08/22/545402866/federal-judge-finds-racism-behind-arizona-law -banning-ethnic-studies.

46. Royal A. Johnson, *Adverse Report of the Surveyor General of Arizona, Royal A. Johnson, upon the "Alleged Peralta Grant": A Complete Expose of Its Fraudulent Character* ([Phoenix]: Arizona Gazette Book and Job Office, 1890).

CHAPTER 1 — COUNTERFEIT NARRATIVES

1. Reavis actually made two separate and somewhat contradictory claims to the Peralta Land Grant. In the first, he claimed that his business partner, a man named George Willing, had purchased the grant from the direct descendant of Miguel Peralta himself. After the death of Willing, foreseeing problems with the solidity of this claim, Reavis then claimed a new connection to the grant, this time through his wife, who he affirmed was the long-lost orphaned heiress to the Peralta fortune. As my purpose in this book is not to carefully reconstruct Reavis's con but rather to read his larger project as a window into the political, economic, and cultural shifts of the late nineteenth-century U.S. Southwest, I do not go into the history of both claims and focus only on the second, which eventually went to trial in Santa Fe, New Mexico. For an excellent and exhaustive step-by-step re-creation of Reavis's scheme, see Donald M. Powell, *The Peralta Grant: James Addison Reavis and the Barony of Arizona* (Norman: University of Oklahoma Press, 1960).

2. Powell explains that an 1854 act of Congress established a process in which "the grantee, or his descendants or assigns, had first to file a claim with the United States surveyor general of the proper area. It was the duty of the surveyor to study the supporting documents, investigate the claim, and then make his report and recommendations to the secretary of the interior. The secretary, in turn, laid the report before the Congress, with any further recommendations he cared to make. Congress, by special legislation, validated or invalidated the claim" (85).

3. Powell, 50–51.

4. Powell, 50–51.

5. Powell, 86.

6. According to Powell, "Land Commissioner Sparks ordered [Johnson] to cease work in May, 1885 . . . and since Johnson was a Republican, he was shortly thereafter replaced under the Democratic regime of Cleveland by John Hise" (88). Johnson was then reappointed in 1889 following Harrison's defeat of Cleveland in the 1888 presidential election (Powell, 90).

7. Royal A. Johnson, *Adverse Report of the Surveyor General of Arizona, Royal A. Johnson, upon the Alleged "Peralta Grant": A Complete Expose of Its Fraudulent Character* ([Phoenix]: Arizona Gazette Book and Job Office, 1890).

8. Powell, *Peralta Grant*, 76.

9. Powell, 80 (emphasis mine).

10. Reavis did not wait for the Peralta Land Grant to be confirmed to begin profiting off it. He signed agreements with the Southern Pacific Railroad, the Silver King Mining Company, and individuals to allow them to continue living or working on "his" land. See Powell, *Peralta Grant*, 76–79.

11. See Linda C. Noel, *Debating American Identity: Southwestern Statehood and Mexican Immigration* (Tucson: University of Arizona Press, 2014).

12. See Raúl Coronado, *A World Not to Come: A History of Latino Writing and Print Culture* (Cambridge, Mass.: Harvard University Press, 2013); Kirsten Silva Gruesz, "Unsettlers and Speculators," *PMLA* 131, no. 3 (2016): 743–751; Anna Brickhouse, *The Unsettlement of America: Translation, Interpretation, and the Story of Don Luis de Velasco, 1560–1945* (Oxford: Oxford University Press, 2015); and Dana Luciano and Ivy G. Wilson, eds., *Unsettled States: Nineteenth-Century American Literary Studies* (New York: New York University Press, 2014).

13. Brickhouse, *Unsettlement of America*, 2.

14. Johnson, *Adverse Report*, 8–9.

15. Johnson writes,

The front of the sheet is printed in Spanish and reads as follows: "Book which only serves to note therein the deposits that may be delivered to me by order of the Royal Holy Inquisition for the proofs of petitioners that may be as a depository of the same, June 23rd, 1768." Now this frontispiece to this remarkable production of alleged antiquity would indicate that it was a cover to a book of records of the acts of the Inquisition, and certainly leads me to suspect that it was copied from some such book. In this particular instance it seems much out of place, as what follows this original sheet under consideration is not such records as are kept by such officials as the reading on the page would indicate, the reading on the page would make the man in whose possession it is, a recorder of papers of the Holy Inquisition, and should appear on the cover of a general record book of such papers; instead of which it is filed here as a frontispiece of half a dozen pages of matter, all of which pages appertain to the alleged grant of Peralta, and in no way, shape, or form go to make up several acts of the Royal Inquisition, as the page referred to indicates. (*Adverse Report*, 11–12)

16. Johnson, 12.

17. Johnson, 12.

18. Johnson, 14.

19. Johnson, 13.

20. Johnson, 13.

21. Johnson, 16.

22. Johnson, 16.

23. Johnson, 17.

24. Johnson, 12–13.

25. Johnson, 62.

26. Johnson, 11–12, 17–19.

27. French theorists Michel Foucault and Jacques Derrida both theorize the relationship between the archive and knowledge production, though they define the archive very differently. For Foucault, the archive is the discursive possibility of what can be said, whereas Derrida discusses actual archives as institutions that collect and preserve

documents. See Michel Foucault, *The Archaeology of Knowledge* (New York: Vintage Books, 2010); and Jacques Derrida, *Archive Fever: A Freudian Impression* (Chicago: University of Chicago Press, 1996). A few notable examples of case studies that examine particular archives include Diana Taylor, *The Archive and the Repertoire* (Durham, N.C.: Duke University Press, 2003); Carolyn Steedman, *Dust: The Archive and Cultural History* (New Brunswick, N.J.: Rutgers University Press, 2002); Ann Cvetkovich, *An Archive of Feelings: Trauma, Sexuality, and Lesbian Public Cultures* (Durham, N.C.: Duke University Press, 2003); Ann Laura Stoler, *Along the Archival Grain: Epistemic Anxieties and Colonial Common Sense* (Princeton, N.J.: Princeton University Press, 2009); Antoinette M. Burton, ed., *Archive Stories: Facts, Fictions, and the Writing of History* (Durham, N.C.: Duke University Press, 2005); and Anjali Arondekar, *For the Record: On Sexuality and the Colonial Archive in India* (Durham, N.C.: Duke University Press, 2009), though the list continues far beyond these.

28. See Michelle Caswell, "'The Archive' Is Not an Archives: Acknowledging the Intellectual Contributions of Archival Studies," *Reconstruction: Studies in Contemporary Culture* 16, no. 1 (2016), http://reconstruction.eserver.org/Issues/161/Caswell .shtml#_edn1.

29. Derrida, *Archive Fever*, 90.

30. Rodrigo Lazo, "The Invention of American Again: On the Impossibility of an Archive," *American Literary History* 25, no. 4 (2013): 753.

31. Lazo, 753.

32. S. Muller, J. A. Feith, and R. Fruin, *Manual for the Arrangement and Description of Archives*, trans. of 2nd ed. by Arthur H. Leavitt (New York: H. W. Wilson, 1940).

33. Jamie A. Lee, "Archives," in *The Routledge History of American Sexuality*, ed. Kevin P. Murphy, Jason Ruiz, and David Serlin (New York: Routledge, expected 2019), 2.

34. Lee, 2.

35. Hilary Jenkinson, *A Manual of Archive Administration* (London: Percy Lund, Humphries, 1937).

36. Terry Cook, "What Is Past Is Prologue: A History of Archival Ideas since 1898, and the Future Paradigm Shift," *Archivaria* 43 (1996): 24.

37. Cook, 27.

38. Theodore Schellenberg, "The Appraisal of Modern Public Records," *Bulletins of the National Archives* 8 (1956): 1–46.

39. Cook, "What Is Past," 27.

40. Tom Nesmith, "Still Fuzzy, but More Accurate: Some Thoughts on the 'Ghosts' of Archival Theory," *Archivaria* 47 (1999): 146. For other reinterpretations of provenance, see also Laura Millar, "The Death of the Fonds and the Resurrection of Provenance: Archival Context in Space and Time," *Archivaria* 53, no. 1 (2002): 1–15; Joel Wurl, "Ethnicity as Provenance: In Search of Values and Principles for Documenting the Immigrant Experience," *Archival Issues* 29, no. 1 (2005): 65–76; Chris Hurley, "Parallel Provenance (If These Are Your Records, Where Are Your Stories?)," *Archives and Manuscripts* 33, nos. 1, 2 (2005): 1–43; and Jennifer Douglas, "Origin: Evolving Ideas about the Principle of Provenance," in *Currents of Archival Thinking*, ed. Terry Eastwood and Heather MacNeil (Santa Barbara, Calif.: Libraries Unlimited, 2010), 23–43.

41. Cook, "What Is Past," 48.

42. Cook, 48.

43. Wai Chee Dimock, *Empire for Liberty: Melville and the Poetics of Individualism* (Princeton, N.J.: Princeton University Press, 1989), 133.

44. Daniel Cooper Alarcón, *The Aztec Palimpsest* (Tucson: University of Arizona Press, 1997), xvi, 4.

45. María Josefina Saldaña-Portillo, *Indian Given: Racial Geographies across Mexico and the Unites States* (Durham, N.C.: Duke University Press, 2016), 24.

46. John L. O'Sullivan, "The Great Nation of Futurity," *United States Magazine and Democratic Review* 6, no. 23 (1839): 429.

47. Thomas Allen, *A Republic in Time: Temporality and Social Imagination in Nineteenth-Century America* (Chapel Hill: University of North Carolina Press, 2008), 23.

48. O'Sullivan, "Great Nation of Futurity," 427.

49. Allen, *Republic in Time*, 20, 23.

50. O'Sullivan, "Great Nation of Futurity," 430.

51. John L. O'Sullivan, "Annexation," *United States Magazine and Democratic Review* 17, no. 85 (1845): 5.

52. O'Sullivan, 9.

53. David J. Weber, *Foreigners in Their Native Land: Historical Roots of the Mexican Americans* (Albuquerque: University of New Mexico Press, 1996), 140.

54. "Treaty of Guadalupe Hidalgo," Library of Congress, accessed Mar. 18, 2017, articles VIII and IX, http://memory.loc.gov/cgi-bin/ampage?collId=llsl&fileName =009/llsl009.db&recNum=983.

55. Richard Griswold del Castillo, *The Treaty of Guadalupe Hidalgo: A Legacy of Conflict* (Norman: University of Oklahoma Press, 1990), 63.

56. Griswold del Castillo, 73–74, 86.

57. Fredrick Jackson Turner, *The Frontier in American History* (New York: Henry Holt, 1921), 1.

58. Turner, 2.

59. María E. Montoya, *Translating Property: The Maxwell Land Grant and the Conflict over Land in the American West, 1840–1900* (Berkeley: University of California Press, 2002), 5–6.

60. See María DeGuzmán, *Spain's Long Shadow: The Black Legend, Off-Whiteness, and Anglo-American Empire* (Minneapolis: University of Minnesota Press, 2005).

61. Brickhouse, *Unsettlement of America*, 2.

62. Dana Luciano, "Introduction: On Moving Ground," in Luciano and Wilson, *Unsettled States*, 5.

63. Ian Haywood, *Faking It: Art and the Politics of Forgery* (New York: St. Martin's, 1987), 2.

64. S. 1070, 49th Leg., 2d Reg. Sess. (Ariz. 2010), https://www.azleg.gov/legtext/49leg /2r/bills/sb1070s.pdf.

65. H.R. 2281, 49th Leg., 2d Reg. Sess. (Ariz. 2010), https://www.azleg.gov/legtext/49leg /2r/bills/hb2281s.pdf.

66. Luciano, "Introduction," 11.

CHAPTER 2 — SEARCHING FOR SOFIA

1. Amended Answer and Cross-Petition of the United States, June 1, 1895, Rolls 62–63, Coll. 1972-007, Spanish Archives of New Mexico I, New Mexico State Archives.

2. Transcript of Testimony Taken on Trial of the Case before the Court of Private Land Claims at Santa Fe, New Mexico, June 1–17, 1895, Rolls 62-63, Coll. 1972-007, Spanish Archives of New Mexico I, New Mexico State Archives, June 17, 1895, 940–941.

3. Transcript of Testimony, 941.

4. Transcript of Testimony, 941.

5. Transcript of Testimony, 941.

6. Transcript of Testimony, 941.

7. Transcript of Testimony, 942.

8. Transcript of Testimony, 942.

9. Transcript of Testimony, 942.

10. Transcript of Testimony, 942.

11. María E. Montoya, *Translating Property: The Maxwell Land Grant and the Conflict over Land in the American West, 1840–1900* (Berkeley: University of California Press, 2002), 4.

12. Here Reavis meant to say Treadway, a reference to John A. Treadway, the Anglo man with whom Peralta-Reavis lived as a child. According to Reavis, Treadway was merely her caretaker. During the trial, however, witnesses who knew Peralta-Reavis as a child testified that Treadway was in fact her father. See Donald M. Powell, *The Peralta Grant: James Addison Reavis and the Barony of Arizona* (Norman: University of Oklahoma Press, 1960), 66, 126–127.

13. Transcript of Testimony, June 12, 1895, 624–625.

14. Jesse Alemán, "Crossing the Mason-Dixon Line in Drag: The Narrative of Loreta Janeta Velazquez, Cuban Woman and Confederate Soldier," in *Look Away! The U.S. South in New World Studies*, ed. Jon Smith and Deborah Cohn (Durham, N.C.: Duke University Press, 2004), 122.

15. The palpable instability of racial and national categories at the 1895 Peralta Land Grant trial stemmed from the geopolitical upheavals that had occurred earlier in the century and the impact they had on citizenship and its accordant rights, including the property rights at stake in the Peralta trial. For an in-depth discussion of the relationship among racial identity, citizenship, and property rights in the early and mid-nineteenth century, see Grace Hong, *The Ruptures of American Capital: Women of Color, Feminism, and the Culture of Immigrant Labor* (Minneapolis: University of Minnesota Press, 2006); and Cheryl I. Harris, "Whiteness as Property," *Harvard Law Review* 106, no. 8 (1993): 1707–1791.

16. Powell, *Peralta Grant*, 130, 50–51.

17. Powell, 131.

18. Transcript of Testimony, June 15, 1895, 868.

19. Somewhat paradoxically, though this strategic portrayal of Peralta-Reavis as Spanish was a direct response to U.S. westward expansion and its linking of racial identity with full citizenship rights, it was also embedded within the racial logics of the preceding Spanish conquest, in particular the *limpieza de sangre* doctrine. For further discussion of the *limpieza de sangre* doctrine and its circulation in colonial Mexico, see María Elena Martínez, *Genealogical Fictions: Limpieza de Sangre, Religion, and Gender in Colonial Mexico* (Stanford, Calif.: Stanford University Press, 2008).

20. "Treaty of Guadalupe Hidalgo," articles 8 and 9.

21. John Nieto-Phillips notes that when the United States expanded into the Southwest, "federal and territorial officials reinstated the legal distinction between 'Indians'

and non-Indians, a distinction that had formed the basis of Spanish colonial society and that [had] been legally abolished in 1821 by the Plan de Iguala." John Nieto-Phillips, *The Language of Blood: The Making of Spanish-American Identity in New Mexico, 1880s–1930s* (Albuquerque: University of New Mexico Press, 2004), 54.

22. John-Michael Rivera defines the "Mexican Question" as "a European American inquiry into the very constitution of Mexican peoplehood that found its rhetorical dimensions within the perimeters of democratic expansion and racialization of the Mexican peoples who lived in the 'frontier.'" That is to say, "the Mexican Question found its roots in the period of expansion into the western and southwestern lands of Mexicans and Native Americans, the period when both the promise of terra incognita and the savage other emerged in the consciousness of the American public." John-Michael Rivera, *The Emergence of Mexican America: Recovering Stories of Mexican Peoplehood in U.S. Culture* (New York: New York University Press, 2006), 54.

23. Martha Menchaca explains that the Treaty of Guadalupe Hidalgo did not grant citizenship to "Mexican Indians" and gave Congress the power "to validate or extinguish all land grant agreements that Spain and Mexico had made with Mexican Indians, including the mission Indians." Martha Menchaca, *Recovering History, Constructing Race: The Indian, Black, and White Roots of Mexican Americans* (Austin: University of Texas Press, 2001), 234.

24. Laura E. Gómez, *Manifest Destinies: The Making of the Mexican American Race* (New York: New York University Press, 2007), 3.

25. Carey McWilliams, *North from Mexico: The Spanish-Speaking People of the United States* (New York: Greenwood, 1968), 36; Raymund Paredes, "The Evolution of Chicano Literature," in *Three American Literatures: Essays in Chicano, Native American, and Asian American Literature for Teachers of American Literature*, ed. Houston A. Baker Jr. (New York: Modern Language Association, 1982), 52.

26. Martha Menchaca, "Chicano Indianism: A Historical Account of Racial Repression in the United States," *American Ethnologist* 20, no. 3 (1993): 587.

27. Significantly, only wealthy and phenotypically lighter-skinned Mexican Americans could employ this strategy effectively, resisting their individual disenfranchisement at the cost of affirming a U.S. racial hierarchy that was based on the marginalization of poor, nonwhite people. See Jesse Alemán, "Historical Amnesia and the Vanishing Mestiza: The Problem of Race in *The Squatter and the Don* and *Ramona*," *Aztlán* 27, no. 1 (2002): 59–93.

28. Anthony Mora, *Border Dilemmas: Racial and National Uncertainties in New Mexico, 1848–1912* (Durham, N.C.: Duke University Press, 2011), 187.

29. Transcript of Testimony, June 15, 1895, 868.

30. See also Maria Josefina Saldaña-Portillo, *Indian Given: Racial Geographies across Mexico and the United States* (Durham, N.C.: Duke University Press, 2016), 171.

31. Deposition of Jennie Mack, Dec. 18, 1894, Spanish Archives of New Mexico I.

32. Deposition of Jennie Mack.

33. Martínez, *Genealogical Fictions*, 158.

34. Martínez, 158.

35. Miroslava Chávez-García, *Negotiating Conquest: Gender and Power in California, 1770s to 1880s* (Tucson: University of Arizona Press, 2004), 156.

36. Chávez-García, 155–156.

37. Chávez-García, 160.

38. Chávez-García, 172–173.

39. Deposition of Jennie Mack.

40. Deposition of Jennie Mack.

41. Deposition of Jennie Mack.

42. Mora, *Border Dilemmas*, 4–5.

43. Transcript of Testimony, June 12, 1895, 660–661.

44. María Raquél Casas, *Married to a Daughter of the Land: Spanish-Mexican Women and Interethnic Marriage in California, 1820–1880* (Reno: University of Nevada Press, 2007), 14.

45. Casas, 14.

46. Casas, 15.

47. Casas, 15.

48. Casas, 9.

49. Casas, 9–10.

50. The story of this loss became the plot of María Amparo Ruíz de Burton's well-known California-based novel, *The Squatter and the Don*, and Jovita González and Eve Raleigh's Texas-based tale, *Caballero: A Historical Novel*. See María Amparo Ruíz de Burton, *The Squatter and the Don* (Houston: Arte Público, 1997); and Jovita González and Eve Raleigh, *Caballero: A Historical Novel* (College Station: Texas A&M University Press, 1996).

51. Deena J. González, *Refusing the Favor: The Spanish-Mexican Women of Santa Fe, 1820–1880* (Oxford: Oxford University Press, 2001), 113.

52. Katherine Benton-Cohen, *Borderline Americans: Racial Division and Labor War in the Arizona Borderlands* (Cambridge, Mass.: Harvard University Press, 2009), 21; Eric V. Meeks, *Border Citizens: The Making of Indians, Mexicans, and Anglos in Arizona* (Austin: University of Texas Press, 2007), 82–83.

53. Sal Acosta, *Sanctioning Matrimony: Western Expansion and Interethnic Marriage in the Arizona Borderlands* (Tucson: University of Arizona Press, 2016), 92–93.

54. Casas, *Married to a Daughter*, 80.

55. Casas, 80.

56. Casas, 80.

57. Casas, 108–110.

58. See chapters 3, 4, and 5 of this book.

59. Elaine Ginsberg, *Passing and the Fictions of Identity* (Durham, N.C.: Duke University Press, 1996), 2.

60. Ginsberg, 2.

61. Transcript of Testimony, June 12, 1895, 625 (emphasis mine).

62. Transcript of Testimony, June 15, 1895, 868 (emphasis mine).

63. According to Carolyn Dean and Dana Leibsohn, these paintings were usually "composed of 16 scenes—and thus 16 admixtures—which register, through the presentation of family groups, the progressive dilution of 'pure' Spanish, Indian, and African blood. Inscriptions set within or near to each painted panel identify the names assigned to each new 'racial' combination." Carolyn Dean and Dana Leibsohn, "Hybridity and Its Discontents: Considering Visual Culture in Colonial Spanish America," *Colonial Latin American Review* 12, no. 1 (2003): 9.

64. Dean and Leibsohn, 9–10.

65. Ramón Gutiérrez, *When Jesus Came, the Corn Mothers Went Away: Marriage, Sexuality, and Power in New Mexico, 1500–1846* (Stanford, Calif.: Stanford University Press, 1991), 198.

66. Alejandro Lipschütz, *El indoamericanismo y el problema racial en las Américas* (Santiago: Chile Nascimiento, 1944).

67. Menchaca, "Chicano Indianism," 599.

68. Menchaca, *Recovering History, Constructing Race*, 217.

69. For further reading on the relationship between phenotype and cultural citizenship among Mexican Americans after U.S. expansion, see also Tomás Almaguer, *Racial Fault Lines: The Historical Origins of White Supremacy in California* (Berkeley: University of California Press, 1994); and Omar S. Valerio-Jiménez, *River of Hope: Forging Identity and Nation in the Rio Grande Borderlands* (Durham, N.C.: Duke University Press, 2013).

70. According to Powell, Valencia later "confessed to perjury" and "produced a contract executed by Miguel Noe, Sr., at the request of James Addison Reavis, in which it was agreed that he should receive $20,000 for his testimony in the event that the grant was confirmed. Valencia then stated that he knew nothing at all of the facts and that he had been coached by Noe." *Peralta Grant*, 174.

71. Deposition of Jose Ramon Valencia, May 10, 1893, Spanish Archives of New Mexico I, 88.

72. Casas, *Married to a Daughter*, 80.

73. Deposition of Jose Ramon Valencia, 96.

74. Deposition of Jose Ramon Valencia, 96–97.

75. Chávez-García, *Negotiating Conquest*, 154.

76. Amy Robinson, "It Takes One to Know One: Passing and Communities of Common Interest," *Critical Inquiry* 20, no. 4 (1994): 716.

77. Ginsberg, *Passing*, 6.

78. Jennifer Leeman, for example, notes that in 1890 the U.S. Census began asking questions about language, marking "a shift in US language ideologies towards an increased importance of language in the national imaginary." Jennifer Leeman, "Categorizing Latinos in the History of the US Census: The Official Racialization of Spanish," in *A Political History of Spanish: The Making of a Language*, ed. José del Valle (Cambridge: Cambridge University Press, 2013), 310. For further discussion on the relationship between language and nationality more broadly, see S. Gal, "Language and Political Economy," *Annual Review of Anthropology* 18 (1989): 345–367.

79. Elise DuBord, "Language Policy and the Drawing of Social Boundaries: Public and Private Schools in Territorial Tucson," *Spanish in Context* 7, no. 1 (2010): 30.

80. DuBord, 40.

81. José del Valle and Ofelia García, "Introduction to the Making of Spanish: US Perspectives," in del Valle, *Political History of Spanish*, 257.

82. Transcript of Testimony, June 12, 1895, 671.

83. Transcript of Testimony, 671.

84. Transcript of Testimony, June 17, 1895, 928.

85. DuBord, "Language Policy," 40.

86. Ann Laura Stoler, *Along the Archival Grain: Epistemic Anxieties and Colonial Common Sense* (Princeton, N.J.: Princeton University Press, 2009), 20.

87. Deena J. González, *Refusing the Favor*, 105.

88. Karen R. Roybal, *Archives of Dispossession: Recovering the Testimonios of Mexican American Herederas, 1848–1960* (Chapel Hill: University of North Carolina Press, 2017), 25.

89. Transcript of Testimony, June 17, 1895, 942.

90. Deena J. González, *Refusing the Favor*, 24.

CHAPTER 3 — SOUTHWEST SPECULATION

1. See Donald M. Powell, *The Peralta Grant: James Addison Reavis and the Barony of Arizona* (Norman: University of Oklahoma Press, 1960), 80–83.

2. "A Strange Story. A Company Organized to Improve the Peralta Land Grant in Arizona," *Daily Inter Ocean* (Chicago), July 28, 1887.

3. "The Great Peralta Grant: Sensational Developments in Regard to the Old Spanish Grant," *Salt Lake Weekly Tribune* (Salt Lake City, Utah), July 28, 1887.

4. "Claiming an Estate: A Girl Who Says She Is Heiress to 5,000,000 Acres of Land," *New York Times*, July 29, 1887, and *Macon (Ga.) Daily Telegraph*, Aug. 2, 1887.

5. "Great Peralta Grant."

6. Gerald J. Baldasty, *The Commercialization of News in the Nineteenth Century* (Madison: University of Wisconsin Press, 1992).

7. For a detailed discussion of the emergence of the term *yellow journalism*, see W. Joseph Campbell, *Yellow Journalism: Puncturing the Myths, Defining the Legacies* (Westport, Conn.: Praeger, 2001), 25–49.

8. Quoted in Karen Roggenkamp, *Narrating the News: New Journalism and Literary Genre in Late Nineteenth-Century American Newspapers and Fiction* (Kent, Ohio: Kent State University Press, 2005), xii.

9. Baldasty, *Commercialization of News*, 4.

10. Roggenkamp, *Narrating the News*, xiv. Though yellow journalism has often been characterized as appealing to poor and uneducated readers, it was in fact read by a much broader part of the populace. See Campbell, *Yellow Journalism*, 63.

11. "About Land Grants. A Curious One Now Pending. Heritage of the 'Last of the Aztecs' Bequeathed by the 'Baron of the Colorados'—Unsettled Land Titles," *Oregonian* (Portland, Ore.), May 15, 1892.

12. "Impostor Now a Herder. Once Famous He Is Now Living a Recluse Life in New Mexico," *Kansas Semi-weekly Capital* (Topeka), Oct. 5, 1900.

13. Barbara Cloud, *The Business of Newspapers on the Western Frontier* (Reno: University of Nevada Press, 1992), 4.

14. Cloud, 5.

15. Ben Procter, *William Randolph Hearst: The Early Years, 1863–1910* (Oxford: Oxford University Press, 1998), 41.

16. Procter, 43, 46–47.

17. Procter, 41.

18. Procter, 53–61.

19. Procter, 69.

20. "The Peralta Claim. Array of Public Men Who Are Interested in the Scheme. Opinions That It Is Bolstered Up by Manufactured Testimony," *Tombstone (Ariz.) Epitaph*, Aug. 6, 1887.

21. Cloud, *Business of Newspapers*, 122.

22. The Peralta Land Grant was a hot-button issue in Arizona's territorial politics. Territorial delegate to the U.S. Congress Mark A. Smith, for example, came under fire for his inability to squelch Reavis's claim. See "Open Letter to M. A. Smith," *Tombstone (Ariz.) Epitaph*, Oct. 19, 1890.

23. Cloud, *Business of Newspapers*, 123.

24. Katherine Ellinghaus discusses colonial ideologies that framed race as something that was inherited and carried with it specific traits. See Katherine Ellinghaus, *Blood Will Tell: Native Americans and Assimilation Policy* (Lincoln: University of Nebraska Press, 2017), xiv.

25. For more on the racialization of Mexican Americans and the rise of scientific racism in the U.S. Southwest, see Katherine Benton-Cohen, *Borderline Americans: Racial Division and Labor War in the Arizona Borderlands* (Cambridge, Mass.: Harvard University Press, 2009), 88.

26. "Peralta Claim."

27. "Peralta Claim."

28. Lauren Basson, *White Enough to Be American? Race Mixing, Indigenous People, and the Boundaries of State and Nation* (Chapel Hill: University of North Carolina Press, 2008), 31.

29. "Peralta Claim."

30. "Peralta Claim."

31. "Peralta Claim."

32. Thomas Ingersoll, *To Intermix with Our White Brothers: Indian Mixed Bloods in the United States from Earliest Times to the Indian Removals* (Albuquerque: University of New Mexico Press, 2005), xxi.

33. As Ellinghaus explains, "People of mixed descent were depicted as cunning, exploitative, and undeserving of the benefits and rights that came with Indian ancestry" (*Blood Will Tell*, xiii). Condemnations of Peralta-Reavis's attempted land grab easily fit into the narrative that people of mixed descent were attempting to cheat the system and take what did not belong to them, as they were neither white enough to enjoy full citizenship nor Indian enough to be entitled to certain federal rights, such as allotment. See Ellinghaus, xiii–xxvi.

34. Martha Menchaca, *Recovering History, Constructing Race: The Indian, Black, and White Roots of Mexican Americans* (Austin: University of Texas Press, 2001), 217.

35. Ingersoll, *To Intermix*, xiv.

36. "Peralta-Reavis Grant Case. Wonderful Structure Founded on Fraud, Perjury and Forgery About to Fall. Baron Peralta a Myth—The Alleged Grant a Fraud—Pretended Baroness a Half-Breed Indian," *Daily New Mexican* (Santa Fe), June 3, 1895.

37. "Peralta-Reavis Grant Case."

38. "La merced Peralta-Reavis. Esta por caer una magnífica estructura fundada en fraude y perjurio. El baron de Peralta un mito—la pretendida merced un fraude—la supuesta baronesa no pasa de ser una Coyota," in *El nuevo mexicano* (Santa Fe), June 8, 1895, and "Historia de la Merced de Peralta," *El fronterizo* (Tucson), June 15, 1895.

39. "La merced Peralta-Reavis"; "Historia de la merced de Peralta."

40. "Peralta-Reavis Grant Case"; "La merced Peralta-Reavis."

41. Magali Carrera, *Imagining Identity in New Spain: Race, Lineage, and the Colonial Body in Portraiture and Casta* (Austin: University of Texas Press, 2003), 93. Though Carrera cites various Spanish *casta* paintings that use this definition, James Officer notes

that in Sonora in the eighteenth century, *coyote* also functioned as a synonym for *mestizo*, or the offspring of a European and an *indio*. See James Officer, *Hispanic Arizona, 1536–1856* (Tucson: University of Arizona Press, 1989), 41.

42. Mary Dashnaw, "An Unframeable Icon: Coyote, *Casta*, and the *Mestizaje* in Colonial New Spanish Art" (master's thesis, Arizona State University, 2014), i. Ramón Gutiérrez attributes the term to Native American folklore, in which coyotes function as a trickster figure, "an animal that constantly crosses borders, surviving at the margins." Ramón Gutiérrez, "New Mexico, Mestizaje, and the Transnations of North America," in *Mexico and Mexicans in the Making of the United States*, ed. John Tutino (Austin: University of Texas Press, 2012), 280.

43. "Peralta-Reavis Case. Hearing Concluded and Case Submitted without Argument—Decision May Be Expected Soon—Fraudulent Character of Grant Clearly Established," *Daily New Mexican* (Santa Fe), June 19, 1895.

44. "Grant Cases Dismissed. Peralta-Reavis Grant Pronounced Purely Fictitious by the U.S. Land Court. Reavis Arrested by the United States Marshal—Juan Gid Grant Declared Void," *Daily New Mexican* (Santa Fe), June 25, 1895.

45. "Grant Cases Dismissed."

46. Basson, *White Enough to Be American*, 18.

47. Mark E. Pry, "Statehood Politics and Territorial Development: The Arizona Constitution of 1891," *Journal of Arizona History* 35, no. 4 (1994): 422.

48. Linda C. Noel, *Debating American Identity: Southwestern Statehood and Mexican Immigration* (Tucson: University of Arizona Press, 2014), 5.

49. Basson, *White Enough to Be American*, 58.

50. "Reavis Written Up," *Weekly Phoenix Herald*, January 27, 1898.

51. "Reavis Written Up."

52. Powell, *Peralta Grant*, 122.

53. Martin Padget, "Travel, Exoticism, and the Writing of the Region: Charles Fletcher Lummis and the 'Creation' of the Southwest," *Journal of the Southwest* 37, no. 3 (1995): 422.

54. Charles Fletcher Lummis, "In the Lion's Den," *Land of Sunshine* 4, no. 2 (January 1896): 89.

55. Padget, "Travel, Exoticism," 422.

56. Padget, 422.

57. Padget, 448–449.

58. Jennifer Watts, "Photography in the Land of Sunshine: Charles Fletcher Lummis and the Regional Ideal," *Southern California Quarterly* 87, no. 4 (2005–2006): 347.

59. Watts, 345.

60. William M. Tipton, "The Prince of Impostors," *Land of Sunshine* 8, no. 3 (1898): 109.

61. Tipton, 111.

62. Tipton, 111.

63. Tipton, 110.

64. "Clarence Budington Kelland, Prolific Author, Is Dead at 82," *New York Times*, Feb. 19, 1964.

65. Geraldo L. Cadava, *Standing on Common Ground: The Making of a Sunbelt Borderland* (Cambridge, Mass.: Harvard University Press, 2013), 1–2.

66. Cadava, 3.

67. Clarence Budington Kelland, "The Red Baron of Arizona," *Saturday Evening Post*, October 1947, 22.

68. Kelland, 22.

69. Kelland, 84.

70. Kelland, 89.

71. Powell, *Peralta Grant*, 177.

72. Kelland, "Red Baron of Arizona," 90.

73. Soroush Vosoughi, Deb Roy, and Sinan Aral, "The Spread of True and False News Online," *Science* 359, no. 6380 (2018): 1146, http://science.sciencemag.org/content /359/6380/1146/tab-pdf.

74. Vosoughi, Roy, and Aral, 1146.

75. Vosoughi, Roy, and Aral, 1146.

76. See Hunt Allcott and Matthew Gentzkow, "Social Media and Fake News in the 2016 Election," *Journal of Economic Perspectives* 31, no. 2 (2017): 211–236.

CHAPTER 4 — COUNTERFEIT NOSTALGIA

1. "Following the Frontier Line, 1790 to 1890," U.S. Census Bureau, September 6, 2012, https://www.census.gov/dataviz/visualizations/001/.

2. For a discussion of wars against Native Americans in the mid- to late nineteenth-century western United States, see Robert Utley, *The Indian Frontier, 1846–1890* (Albuquerque: University of New Mexico Press, 2003). For a discussion of the causes and consequences of the U.S.-Mexican War, see Amy S. Greenberg, *A Wicked War: Polk, Clay, Lincoln, and the 1846 U.S. Invasion of Mexico* (New York: Vintage Books, 2012).

3. For a general introduction to this history, see Brad K. Berner, ed., *The Spanish-American War: A Documentary History with Commentaries* (Madison, Wis.: Farleigh Dickinson University Press, 2014).

4. See Linda C. Noel, *Debating American Identity: Southwestern Statehood and Mexican Immigration* (Tucson: University of Arizona Press, 2014); and Anita Huizar-Hernández, "The Specter of Statehood: Inventing Arizona in Charles D. Poston's *Building a State in Apache Land* and Marie Clara Zander's 'The Life of an Arizona Pioneer,'" *MELUS: Multi-ethnic Literature of the U.S.* 42, no. 2 (2017): 53–78.

5. Geraldo L. Cadava, *Standing on Common Ground: The Making of a Sunbelt Borderland* (Cambridge, Mass.: Harvard University Press, 2013), 11.

6. Cadava, 3, 31.

7. Houston Baker Jr., "Critical Memory and the Black Public Sphere," in *Cultural Memory and the Construction of Identity*, ed. Dan Ben-Amos and Liliane Weissberg (Detroit: Wayne State University Press, 1999), 264.

8. In this way, counterfeit nostalgia is similar to Renato Rosaldo's "imperialist nostalgia," when colonizers nostalgically remember, and even yearn for, the cultures they destroyed through their act of colonization. Rosaldo notes that appealing to a nostalgic impulse portrays the colonizers as "innocent bystanders" as opposed to agents of "brutal domination." See Renato Rosaldo, *Culture and Truth: The Remaking of Social Analysis* (Boston: Beacon, 1989), 69–70.

9. "William Atherton DuPuy," Find a Grave, March 5, 2010, https://www.findagrave .com/cgi-bin/fg.cgi?page=gr&GRid=49176446&ref=acom.

10. "William Atherton DuPuy: United States Passport Applications," FamilySearch, March 18, 2014, https://familysearch.org/ark:/61903/1:1:QV5B-3DZZ.

11. William Atherton DuPuy, *The Baron of the Colorados* (San Antonio, Tex.: Naylor, 1940), ix.

12. DuPuy, x.

13. DuPuy, x.

14. "William Atherton DuPuy," March 5, 2010.

15. "William A. DuPuy: United States Census, 1920," FamilySearch, March 18, 2014, https://familysearch.org/ark:/61903/1:1:MNLT-X19.

16. DuPuy, *Baron of the Colorados*, x.

17. DuPuy, x.

18. Thomas McCormick has argued that U.S. expansion in the nineteenth and twentieth centuries are two phases of the same imperial growth. In the case of the former, across the continent, and in the case of the latter, overseas. See Thomas McCormick, "From Old Empire to New: The Changing Dynamics and Tactics of American Empire," in *The Colonial Crucible: Empire in the Making of the Modern American State*, ed. Alfred W. McCoy and Francisco A. Scarano (Madison: University of Wisconsin Press, 2009), 64.

19. In his introduction to DuPuy's report, Secretary Ray Lyman Wilbur writes that an incident "in the autumn of 1931" "led newspapers, reacting as a result of known strife elsewhere, to conclude that a delicate race situation existed in Hawaii." The secretary then decided to investigate the situation, and in the summer of 1931, he sent DuPuy, "executive assistant to the Secretary, an experienced investigator and a quite disinterested witness . . . to Hawaii with instructions to observe the facts and report his findings" to "tell us of the new Americans that are resulting from the unprecedented situation that exists in the islands; how they get along, one with the other, and how they are fitting into that scheme of self-government bond to blue-eyed peoples on the other side of the world and previously experienced by few of those who contributed to these strange intermixtures of blood." See Ray Lyman Wilbur, introduction to *Hawaii and Its Race Problem*, by William Atherton DuPuy (Washington, D.C.: Government Printing Office, 1932), ix.

20. DuPuy, *Hawaii and Its Race Problem*, 1.

21. DuPuy, *Baron of the Colorados*, ix.

22. Nathaniel Lewis argues that establishing authenticity and authority are both common tropes of Westerns. See Nathaniel Lewis, "Truth or Consequences: Projecting Authenticity in the 1830s," in *True West: Authenticity and the American West*, ed. William Handley and Nathaniel Lewis (Lincoln: University of Nebraska Press, 2004), 22–24, 27.

23. DuPuy, *Baron of the Colorados*, xi.

24. DuPuy, 23.

25. DeGuzmán writes, "The construction of Anglo-American identity as 'American' has been dependent on figures of Spain. Figures of Spain have been central to the dominant fictions of 'American' exceptionalism, revolution, manifest destiny, and birth/rebirth; to Anglo-America's articulation of its empire as anti empire (the 'good' empire that is not one); and to its fears of racial contamination and hybridity. Figures of Spain have been indispensable to the constitution, elaboration, and even interrogation of these dominant fictions." María DeGuzmán, *Spain's Long Shadow: The Black Legend, Off-Whiteness, and Anglo-American Empire* (Minneapolis: University of Minnesota Press, 2005), xii.

26. Many scholars of U.S. empire have pointed out the inaccuracy of these dominant fictions. See Amy Kaplan, *The Anarchy of Empire in the Making of U.S. Culture* (Cambridge, Mass.: Harvard University Press, 2002); Donald E. Pease, *National Identities and Post-Americanist Narratives* (Durham, N.C.: Duke University Press, 1994) and *The New American Exceptionalism* (Minneapolis: University of Minnesota Press, 2009); and Amy Kaplan and Donald E. Pease, eds., *Cultures of United States Imperialism* (Durham, N.C.: Duke University Press, 1993).

27. DuPuy, *Baron of the Colorados*, x.

28. DuPuy, 3.

29. DeGuzmán, *Spain's Long Shadow*, xvii. See also Alfred W. McCoy, Francisco A. Scarano, and Courtney Johnson, "On the Tropic of Cancer: Transitions and Transformations in the U.S. Imperial State," in McCoy and Scarano, *Colonial Crucible*, 11–12.

30. Shelley Streeby, *American Sensations: Class, Empire, and the Production of Popular Culture* (Berkeley: University of California Press, 2002), 58–66.

31. DeGuzmán, *Spain's Long Shadow*, 139–185.

32. William Atherton DuPuy, *Uncle Sam's Modern Miracles: His Gigantic Tasks That Benefit Humanity* (New York: Frederick A. Stokes, 1914), 16.

33. DuPuy, 16–17.

34. DuPuy, 110–111, 117.

35. For studies that show the long genealogy of these fears, see Lee Bebout, *Whiteness on the Border: Mapping the U.S. Racial Imagination in Brown and White* (New York: New York University Press, 2016); William Anthony Nericcio, *Tex{t}-Mex: Seductive Hallucinations of the "Mexican" in America* (Austin: University of Texas Press, 2007); and Arnoldo De León, *They Called Them Greasers: Anglo Attitudes toward Mexicans in Texas, 1821–1900* (Austin: University of Texas Press, 1983).

36. DuPuy, *Baron of the Colorados*, 1.

37. David H. DeJong, *Stealing the Gila: The Pima Agricultural Economy and Water Deprivation, 1848–1921* (Tucson: University of Arizona Press, 2016).

38. Donald M. Powell, *The Peralta Grant: James Addison Reavis and the Barony of Arizona* (Norman: University of Oklahoma Press, 1960), 122.

39. Powell, 161–162.

40. William M. Tipton, "The Prince of Impostors," *Land of Sunshine* 8, no. 3 (1898): 107–118; William M. Tipton, "The Prince of Impostors (Concluded)," *Land of Sunshine* 8, no. 4 (1898): 161–170.

41. DuPuy, *Baron of the Colorados*, title page.

42. DuPuy, 16.

43. DuPuy, 16–17.

44. Cadava, *Standing on Common Ground*, 21, 24–25.

45. DuPuy, *Baron of the Colorados*, 15.

46. Cadava, *Standing on Common Ground*, 29, 39–41.

47. DuPuy, *Baron of the Colorados*, 118.

48. DuPuy, 120.

49. See, for example, June Namias, *White Captives: Gender and Ethnicity on the American Frontier* (Chapel Hill: University of North Carolina Press, 1993); and Audra Simpson, "From White into Red: Captivity Narratives as Alchemies of Race and Citizenship," *American Quarterly* 60, no. 2 (2008): 251–257.

50. DuPuy, *Baron of the Colorados*, 125.

51. For a history of Cochise, see Edwin R. Sweeney, *Cochise: Chiricahua Apache Chief* (Norman: University of Oklahoma Press, 1991).

52. For a discussion of the Apache Wars and their relationship to U.S. national identity, see William M. Clements, *Imagining Geronimo: An Apache Icon in Popular Culture* (Albuquerque: University of New Mexico Press, 2013); and Karl Jacoby, *Shadows at Dawn: An Apache Massacre and the Violence of History* (New York: Penguin, 2008).

53. DuPuy, *Baron of the Colorados*, 65–66.

54. For a discussion of how the discourse of noble savagery functioned in the United States, see Philip J. Deloria, *Playing Indian* (New Haven, Conn.: Yale University Press, 1998), 4.

55. As Andrea Smith affirms, "Colonial relationships are themselves gendered and sexualized." Andrea Smith, *Conquest: Sexual Violence and American Indian Genocide* (Cambridge, Mass.: South End, 2005), 1.

56. Shari M. Huhndorf, *Mapping the Americas: The Transnational Politics of Contemporary Native Culture* (Ithaca, N.Y.: Cornell University Press, 2009), 106.

57. Huhndorf, 107.

58. DuPuy, *Baron of the Colorados*, 175.

59. Gerald Vizenor, *Manifest Manners: Postindian Warriors of Survivance* (Hanover, N.H.: University Press of New England, 1994).

60. Thomas Sheridan notes that much of this confusion was the result of the Apaches' tribal structure. The Apaches were not a monolithic or even unified group of people, composed instead of smaller bands held together by dynamic, shifting alliances. This meant that when Europeans made an agreement with one band, it did not hold true for the others. See Thomas Sheridan, *Arizona: A History* (Tucson: University of Arizona Press, 2012), 44.

61. The United States quickly realized this was impossible and the article was overturned only six years later in the Treaty of Mesilla, also known as the Gadsden Purchase. See Sheridan, 65–66.

62. Sheridan, 44.

63. Philip J. Deloria affirms, "If you had to pick a single person to stand for *Indianness*, you could do worse than Geronimo, the iconic Apache leader who stands in American popular memory for resistant warriors everywhere and the defeated prisoners we imagine they became." Philip J. Deloria, *Indians in Unexpected Places* (Lawrence: University Press of Kansas, 2004), 136.

64. Clements, *Imagining Geronimo*, 5–8.

65. Clements, 8–9.

66. Clements, 9.

67. Edwin R. Sweeney affirms that Cochise was "the most powerful chief of the Chiricahua Apaches in recorded times" and his reputation had mythic proportions. Sweeney, *Cochise*, xiii–xx.

68. DuPuy, *Baron of the Colorados*, 165–166.

69. This is actually true. Reavis and Peralta-Reavis did travel to Spain, where the Spanish nobility accepted them as one of their own. Their twin sons even purportedly played with the Spanish prince. See Clarence Budington Kelland, "The Red Baron of Arizona," *Saturday Evening Post*, October 1947, 93.

70. Vizenor, *Manifest Manners*, vii.

71. Deloria, *Indians in Unexpected Places*, 231.

72. Henry Nash Smith, *Virgin Land: The American West as Symbol and Myth* (Cambridge, Mass.: Harvard University Press, 1970), 125-129.

73. Smith, 128.

74. Smith, 128.

75. "The Homestead Act of 1862," National Archives, last updated October 3, 2016, https://www.archives.gov/education/lessons/homestead-act.

76. DuPuy, *Baron of the Colorados*, 4.

77. DuPuy, 4.

78. Henry Nash Smith, *Virgin Land*, 169.

79. Patrick Wolfe, "Settler Colonialism and the Elimination of the Native," *Journal of Genocide Research* 8, no. 4 (2006): 396.

80. Cadava, *Standing on Common Ground*, 3.

81. DuPuy, *Baron of the Colorados*, 178.

82. See Doris Sommer, *Foundational Fictions: The National Romances of Latin America* (Berkeley: University of California Press, 1991).

83. Kaplan, *Anarchy of Empire*, 1.

84. Kaplan, 23-50.

85. Kaplan, 14.

CHAPTER 5 — THE BARON IS LIKE A BATTLEGROUND

1. Samuel Fuller, dir., *The Baron of Arizona* (1950; New York: Eclipse Criterion Collection, 2007), DVD.

2. Charles Renshaw Jr., "The Baron of Arizona," *American Weekly* (New York), January 9, 1949.

3. Samuel Fuller, *A Third Face: My Tale of Writing, Fighting, and Filmmaking* (New York: Applause Theater and Cinema Books, 2002), 255.

4. In his study of early Westerns, *Shooting Cowboys and Indians*, Andrew Brodie Smith defines the Western as a film "referred to as such by producers, exhibitors, or moviegoers" that portrayed "either cowboy or Indian characters or both and sometimes ethnic Mexicans" and explored "conditions associated with the frontier or with the consequences of U.S. territorial expansion—including, but not limited to, conflict between whites and nonwhites, migration, ranching, mining, and banditry." Westerns were popular with U.S. filmmakers because they allowed the filmmakers to distinguish themselves on the international market, were inexpensive to produce, and easily captivated moviegoing audiences. Andrew Brodie Smith, *Shooting Cowboys and Indians: Silent Western Films, American Culture, and the Birth of Hollywood* (Boulder: University Press of Colorado, 2003), 6, 37-38.

5. Chon Noriega, "Introduction: Chicanos and Film," in *Chicanos and Film: Essays on Chicano Representation and Resistance*, ed. Chon Noriega (New York: Garland, 1992), xiv.

6. See Gary Keller, *Chicano Cinema: Research, Reviews, and Resources* (Binghamton, N.Y.: Bilingual Review/Press, 1985); William Anthony Nericcio, *Tex{t}-Mex: Seductive Hallucinations of the "Mexican" in America* (Austin: University of Texas Press, 2007); Rosa Linda Fregoso, *The Bronze Screen* (Minneapolis: University of Minnesota Press, 1993); A. Gabriel Meléndez, *Hidden Chicano Cinema: Film Dramas in the Borderlands* (New Brunswick, N.J.: Rutgers University Press, 2013); and Camilla Fojas, *Border Bandits: Hollywood on the Southern Frontier* (Austin: University of Texas Press, 2008).

7. Scott Simmon, *The Invention of the Western Film: A Cultural History of the Genre's First Half-Century* (Cambridge: Cambridge University Press, 2003), 100.

8. Simmon, 100.

9. George Sherman, dir., *The Night Riders* (Republic Pictures, 1939).

10. Simmon, *Invention of the Western Film*, 161.

11. See George J. Sánchez, *Becoming Mexican American; Ethnicity, Culture, and Identity in Chicano Los Angeles, 1900–1945* (Oxford: Oxford University Press, 1993); David Gutiérrez, *Walls and Mirrors: Mexican Americans, Mexican Immigrants, and the Politics of Ethnicity* (Berkeley: University of California Press, 1995); Abraham Hoffman, *Unwanted Mexican Americans in the Great Depression: Repatriation Pressures, 1929–1939* (Tucson: University of Arizona Press, 1974); Camille Guerin-Gonzales, *Mexican Workers and American Dreams: Immigration, Repatriation, and California Farm Labor, 1900–1939* (New Brunswick, N.J.: Rutgers University Press, 1994); Douglas Monroy, *Rebirth: Mexican Los Angeles from the Great Migration to the Great Depression* (Berkeley: University of California Press, 1999); and Francisco E. Balderrama and Raymond Rodríguez, *Decade of Betrayal: Mexican Repatriation in the 1930s* (Albuquerque: University of New Mexico Press, 2006).

12. Richard Slotkin, *Gunfighter Nation: The Myth of the Frontier in Twentieth-Century America* (New York: Atheneum, 1992), 334.

13. Imogen Sara Smith, *In Lonely Places: Film Noir beyond the City* (Jefferson, N.C.: McFarland, 2011), 179.

14. Simmon, *Invention of the Western Film*, 204.

15. Slotkin, *Gunfighter Nation*, 334.

16. Jean-Luc Godard, dir., *Pierrot le Fou* (Films Georges de Beauregard, 1965).

17. Lisa Dombrowski, *The Films of Samuel Fuller: If You Die, I'll Kill You!* (Middletown, Conn.: Wesleyan University Press, 2008), 12.

18. Despite Fuller's own insistence that he was born in the United States and decades of scholarship affirming this, Marsha Gordon has recently shown that he was born in Russia as Michal Filler. His family later changed his first name and Americanized their last name from Filler to Fuller. About this heritage, Gordon states,

> Why he chose not to disclose his immigration (presuming he was aware of it) is unclear, but he expressed precisely the kind of enthusiasm for being an American, for American history, and for American freedoms that is not unusual for an immigrant eager to demonstrate his connection to his country, rather than a citizen resting comfortably on an entitled-by-birth identity. While Fuller could not have predicted the political climate of Hollywood in the 1940s and 1950s, it is also likely that this disassociation with his national origin saved him from having to defend his patriotism before HUAC as well as from being blacklisted. Being Russian-born, however young at the time of emigration, would have been a serious liability in an era of such paranoid, anti-communist fervor, especially for someone who was already being scrutinized for his political leanings. (Marsha Gordon, *Film Is like a Battleground: Sam Fuller's War Movies* [New York: Oxford University Press, 2017], 26)

19. Gordon, 4.

20. Gordon, 6, 14.

21. Gordon, 1.

22. Gordon, 1. Gordon cites as examples "Manny Farber's mixed assessment in 'The Films of Sam Fuller and Don Siegel'" (*December* 12 [1970]: 170–175), and "Andrew Sarris's dismissal of Fuller's films as 'too broad and oversimplified for any serious analysis'" (quoting Andrew Sarris, "Samuel Fuller," in *Directors and Directions* [New York: Octagon, 1982], 94). She continues, "In his review of David Will and Peter Wollen's 1969 edited collection about Fuller, Paul Joannides calls Fuller 'crude, clumsy and prejudiced,' while also acknowledging 'an extremist visual courage and dynamism which few other directors ever approach'" (quoting Paul Joannides, review of *Samuel Fuller*, edited by David Will and Peter Wollen, *Cinema* 5 [February 1970]: 9). Gordon, *Film Is like a Battleground*, 32n1. See also Peter Stanfield, *Maximum Movies Pulp Fictions: Film Culture and the Worlds of Samuel Fuller, Mickey Spillane, and Jim Thompson* (New Brunswick, N.J.: Rutgers University Press, 2011).

23. See Stanfield, *Maximum Movies Pulp Fictions*, 115.

24. Fuller eventually secured a hybrid contract from Twentieth Century Fox that required him to work half of the year for Fox as a screenwriter and director on their projects but left him the remaining half of the year to work on other, independent projects. See Gordon, *Film Is like a Battleground*, 16.

25. Gordon, 15.

26. "*The Baron of Arizona* (1950)," American Film Institute Catalog, Los Angeles: American Film Institute. Accessed June 6, 2017. http://ezproxy.library.arizona.edu /login?url=https://search.proquest.com/docview/1746500197?accountid=8360. While *The Baron of Arizona* did not have the production budget of a large studio feature, it nevertheless did have a substantial budget for an independent film. A September 17, 1949, article in *Boxoffice* classifies the film as being in Lippert's high-budget category, and an article in *Variety* from February 15, 1950, affirms that "Lippert ha[d] supplied producer Carl K. Hittleman and director-scripter Samuel Fuller with considerable [*sic*]more production coin than usually allotted indie features." An article from February 18, 1950, in *Feature Reviews* calls it "far and away [Lippert's] most ambitious and expensive effort." "33 Features, 6 Shorts on Lippert Lineup," *Boxoffice* (New York), September 17, 1949; "The Baron of Arizona," *Variety* (New York), February 15, 1950; "The Baron of Arizona," *Feature Reviews* (New York), February 18, 1950.

27. "*Baron of Arizona* (1950)."

28. A December 16, 1950, *Coming Your Way* review asserted that "the far-fetched tale is helped out by good performances from Vincent Price and Reed Hadley, and well directed crowd scenes," and the February 18, 1950, *Feature Reviews* article proposed that the film would garner a large audience thanks to its "impressive cast [and] . . . opulent mountings, and its historical genesis," as well as "the spectacle, aura and locale of the always-reliable western" and "generally good" performances. The review in *Variety* from February 15, 1950, was not so generous. The reviewer writes that "Fuller misses in scripting and direction" by trying "to be too erudite, losing the fast action needed to put this one over with the general ticketbuyer." The *New York Times* likewise declared the film to be "short of sensational." See "The Baron of Arizona," *Coming Your Way* (London), December 16, 1950; "Baron of Arizona," *Feature Reviews*; "Baron of Arizona," *Variety*; and "Skulduggery in Arizona Land Office," *New York Times*, June 23, 1950. See also Dombrowski, *Films of Samuel Fuller*, 39.

29. Arnoldo De León, *They Called Them Greasers: Anglo Attitudes toward Mexicans in Texas, 1821–1900* (Austin: University of Texas Press, 1983), 16. Ken Gonzales-Day

notes that the term was closely associated with *mongrel* and *half-breed* and was a clear reaction to the Mexicans' mestizo identity. Ken Gonzales-Day, *Lynching in the West, 1850–1935* (Durham, N.C.: Duke University Press, 2006), 30.

30. De León, *They Called Them Greasers*, 21.

31. See Shelley Streeby, *American Sensations: Class, Empire, and the Production of Popular Culture* (Berkeley: University of California Press, 2002).

32. Nericcio, *Tex{t}-Mex*, 25.

33. Charles Ramírez Berg, *Latino Images in Film: Stereotypes, Subversion, and Resistance* (Austin: University of Texas Press, 2002), 89–90.

34. Marci McMahon, *Domestic Negotiations: Gender, Nation, and Self-Fashioning in US Mexicana and Chicana Literature and Art* (New Brunswick, N.J.: Rutgers University Press, 2013), 159.

35. Drew's real name was Esther Loretta Ray. See "Ellen Drew, 89, Film Star of 30's and 40's, Dies," *New York Times*, December 9, 2003.

36. Jane Tompkins, *West of Everything: The Inner Life of Westerns* (Oxford: Oxford University Press, 1992), 73.

37. Stanley Corkin, *Cowboys as Cold Warriors: The Western and U.S. History* (Philadelphia: Temple University Press, 2004), 1–3.

38. Corkin, 5.

39. Jonathan Auerbach, *Dark Borders: Film Noir and American Citizenship* (Durham, N.C.: Duke University Press, 2011), 3.

40. Dombrowski, *Films of Samuel Fuller*, 38.

41. Manfred Berg, *Popular Justice: A History of Lynching in America* (Chicago: Ivan R. Dee, 2011), 46.

42. Berg, 48.

43. Gonzales-Day, *Lynching in the West*, 3.

44. Fuller, *Third Face*, 254.

45. Fuller, 254.

46. Fuller, 254.

EPILOGUE

1. Donald M. Powell, *The Peralta Grant: James Addison Reavis and the Barony of Arizona* (Norman: University of Oklahoma Press, 1960), vii.

2. Michael D. Shear and Thomas Gibbons-Neff, "Trump Sending 5,200 Troops to the Border in an Election-Season Response to Migrants," *New York Times*, October 29, 2018.

3. Natalia Molina, *How Race Is Made in America* (Berkeley: University of California Press, 2014), 6.

Bibliography

"About Land Grants. A Curious One Now Pending. Heritage of the 'Last of the Aztecs' Bequeathed by the 'Baron of the Colorados'—Unsettled Land Titles." *Oregonian* (Portland, Ore.), May 15, 1892.

Acosta, Sal. *Sanctioning Matrimony: Western Expansion and Interethnic Marriage in the Arizona Borderlands.* Tucson: University of Arizona Press, 2016.

Alemán, Jesse. "Crossing the Mason-Dixon Line in Drag: The Narrative of Loreta Janeta Velazquez, Cuban Woman and Confederate Soldier." In *Look Away! The U.S. South in New World Studies,* edited by Jon Smith and Deborah Cohn, 110–129. Durham, N.C.: Duke University Press, 2004.

———. "Historical Amnesia and the Vanishing Mestiza: The Problem of Race in *The Squatter and the Don* and *Ramona.*" *Aztlán* 27, no. 1 (2002): 59–93.

Allcott, Hunt, and Matthew Gentzkow. "Social Media and Fake News in the 2016 Election." *Journal of Economic Perspectives* 31, no. 2 (2017): 211–236.

Allen, Thomas. *A Republic in Time: Temporality and Social Imagination in Nineteenth-Century America.* Chapel Hill: University of North Carolina Press, 2008.

Almaguer, Tomás. *Racial Fault Lines: The Historical Origins of White Supremacy in California.* Berkeley: University of California Press, 1994.

Amended Answer and Cross-Petition of the United States, June 1, 1895. Rolls 62–63, Coll. 1972 007. Spanish Archives of New Mexico I. New Mexico State Archives (Santa Fe).

Anderson, Kimberly. "The Footprint and the Stepping Foot: Archival Records, Evidence, and Time." *Archival Science* 12 (2012): 349–371.

Arondekar, Anjali. *For the Record: On Sexuality and the Colonial Archive in India.* Durham, N.C.: Duke University Press, 2009.

Auerbach, Jonathan. *Dark Borders: Film Noir and American Citizenship.* Durham, N.C.: Duke University Press, 2011.

Baker, Houston, Jr. "Critical Memory and the Black Public Sphere." In *Cultural Memory and the Construction of Identity,* edited by Dan Ben-Amos and Liliane Weissberg, 264–296. Detroit: Wayne State University Press, 1999.

Baldasty, Gerald J. *The Commercialization of News in the Nineteenth Century.* Madison: University of Wisconsin Press, 1992.

Balderrama, Francisco E., and Raymond Rodríguez. *Decade of Betrayal: Mexican Repatriation in the 1930s.* Albuquerque: University of New Mexico Press, 2006.

"The Baron of Arizona." *Coming Your Way* (London), December 16, 1950.

"The Baron of Arizona." *Feature Reviews* (New York), February 18, 1950.

"The Baron of Arizona." *Variety* (New York), February 15, 1950.

"*The Baron of Arizona* (1950)." American Film Institute Catalog. Los Angeles: American Film Institute. Accessed June 6, 2017. http://ezproxy.library.arizona.edu/login?url =https://search.proquest.com/docview/1746500197?accountid=8360.

Basson, Lauren. *White Enough to Be American? Race Mixing, Indigenous People, and the Boundaries of State and Nation.* Chapel Hill: University of North Carolina Press, 2008.

Bastian, Jeannette. "'Play Mas': Carnival in the Archives and the Archives in Carnival: Records and Community Identity in the US Virgin Islands." *Archival Science* 9 (2009): 113–125.

Bebout, Lee. *Whiteness on the Border: Mapping the U.S. Racial Imagination in Brown and White.* New York: New York University Press, 2016.

Benton-Cohen, Katherine. *Borderline Americans: Racial Division and Labor War in the Arizona Borderlands.* Cambridge, Mass.: Harvard University Press, 2009.

Berg, Manfred. *Popular Justice: A History of Lynching in America.* Chicago: Ivan R. Dee, 2011.

Berner, Brad K., ed. *The Spanish-American War: A Documentary History with Commentaries.* Madison, Wis.: Farleigh Dickinson University Press, 2014.

Blackwell, Maylei. *Chicana Power! Contested Histories of Feminism in the Chicano Movement.* Austin: University of Texas Press, 2011.

Blouin, Francis X., Jr. "Archivists, Mediation, and Constructs of Social Memory." *Archival Issues* 24, no. 2 (1999): 101–112.

Brickhouse, Anna. *The Unsettlement of America: Translation, Interpretation, and the Story of Don Luis de Velasco, 1560–1945.* Oxford: Oxford University Press, 2014.

Brothman, Brien. "Afterglow: Conceptions of Record and Evidence in Archival Discourse." *Archival Science* 2 (2002): 311–342.

Burton, Antoinette M., ed. *Archive Stories: Facts, Fictions, and the Writing of History.* Durham, N.C.: Duke University Press, 2005.

Cadava, Geraldo L. *Standing on Common Ground: The Making of a Sunbelt Borderland.* Cambridge, Mass.: Harvard University Press, 2013.

Campbell, W. Joseph. *Yellow Journalism: Puncturing the Myths, Defining the Legacies.* Westport, Conn.: Praeger, 2001.

Carrera, Magali. *Imagining Identity in New Spain: Race, Lineage, and the Colonial Body in Portraiture and Casta.* Austin: University of Texas Press, 2003.

Carter, Rodney G. S. "Of Things Said and Unsaid: Power, Archival Silences, and Power in Silence." *Archivaria* 61 (2006): 215–233.

Casas, María Raquél. *Married to a Daughter of the Land: Spanish-Mexican Women and Interethnic Marriage in California, 1820–1880.* Reno: University of Nevada Press, 2007.

Caswell, Michelle. "'The Archive' Is Not an Archives: Acknowledging the Intellectual Contributions of Archival Studies." *Reconstruction: Studies in Contemporary Culture* 16, no. 1 (2016). https://escholarship.org/uc/item/7bn4v1fk.

Chávez-García, Miroslava. *Negotiating Conquest: Gender and Power in California, 1770s to 1880s*. Tucson: University of Arizona Press, 2004.

"Claiming an Estate: A Girl Who Says She Is Heiress to 5,000,000 Acres of Land." *New York Times*, July 29, 1887.

"Claiming an Estate: A Girl Who Says She Is Heiress to 5,000,000 Acres of Land." *Macon (Ga.) Daily Telegraph*, August 2, 1887.

"Clarence Budington Kelland, Prolific Author, Is Dead at 82." *New York Times*, February 19, 1964.

Clements, William M. *Imagining Geronimo: An Apache Icon in Popular Culture*. Albuquerque: University of New Mexico Press, 2013.

Cloud, Barbara. *The Business of Newspapers on the Western Frontier*. Reno: University of Nevada Press, 1992.

Cockridge, E. H. *The Baron of Arizona*. New York: John Day, 1967.

Cook, Terry. "Evidence, Memory, Identity, and Community: Four Shifting Archival Paradigms." *Archival Science* 13 (2013): 95–120.

———. "What Is Past Is Prologue: A History of Archival Ideas since 1898, and the Future Paradigm Shift." *Archivaria* 43 (1996): 17–63.

Cooper Alarcón, Daniel. *The Aztec Palimpsest*. Tucson: University of Arizona Press, 1997.

Corkin, Stanley. *Cowboys as Cold Warriors: The Western and U.S. History*. Philadelphia: Temple University Press, 2004.

Coronado, Raúl. *A World Not to Come: A History of Latino Writing and Print Culture*. Cambridge, Mass.: Harvard University Press, 2013.

Correia, David. *Properties of Violence: Law and Land Grant Struggle in Northern New Mexico*. Athens: University of Georgia Press, 2013.

Cvetkovich, Ann. *An Archive of Feelings: Trauma, Sexuality, and Lesbian Public Cultures*. Durham, N.C.: Duke University Press, 2003.

Dashnaw, Mary. "An Unframeable Icon: Coyote, *Casta*, and the *Mestizaje* in Colonial New Spanish Art." Master's thesis, Arizona State University, 2014.

Dean, Carolyn, and Dana Leibsohn. "Hybridity and Its Discontents: Considering Visual Culture in Colonial Spanish America." *Colonial Latin American Review* 12, no. 1 (2003): 5–35.

DeGuzmán, María. *Spain's Long Shadow: The Black Legend, Off-Whiteness, and Anglo-American Empire*. Minneapolis: University of Minnesota Press, 2005.

DeJong, David H. *Stealing the Gila: The Pima Agricultural Economy and Water Deprivation, 1848–1921*. Tucson: University of Arizona Press, 2016.

De León, Arnoldo. *They Called Them Greasers: Anglo Attitudes toward Mexicans in Texas, 1821–1900*. Austin: University of Texas Press, 1983.

Deloria, Philip J. *Indians in Unexpected Places*. Lawrence: University Press of Kansas, 2004.

———. *Playing Indian*. New Haven, Conn.: Yale University Press, 1998.

Del Valle, José, and Ofelia García. "Introduction to the Making of Spanish: US Perspectives." In *A Political History of Spanish: The Making of a Language*, edited by José del Valle, 249–259. Cambridge: Cambridge University Press, 2013.

Depenbrock, Julie. "Federal Judge Finds Racism behind Arizona Law Banning Ethnic Studies." *All Things Considered*, August 22, 2017. Podcast, 3:44. http://www.npr.org

/sections/ed/2017/08/22/545402866/federal-judge-finds-racism-behind-arizona-law
-banning-ethnic-studies.

Deposition of Jennie Mack. December 18, 1894. Spanish Archives of New Mexico I
(Santa Fe).

Deposition of Jose Ramon Valencia. May 10, 1893. Spanish Archives of New Mexico I
(Santa Fe).

Derrida, Jacques. *Archive Fever: A Freudian Impression*. Chicago: University of Chicago
Press, 1996.

Dimock, Wai Chee. *Empire for Liberty: Melville and the Poetics of Individualism*.
Princeton, N.J.: Princeton University Press, 1989.

Dombrowski, Lisa. *The Films of Samuel Fuller: If You Die, I'll Kill You!* Middletown,
Conn.: Wesleyan University Press, 2008.

Douglas, Jennifer. "Origin: Evolving Ideas about the Principle of Provenance." In *Currents of Archival Thinking*, edited by Terry Eastwood and Heather MacNeil, 23–43.
Santa Barbara, Calif.: Libraries Unlimited, 2010.

DuBord, Elise. "Language Policy and the Drawing of Social Boundaries: Public and
Private Schools in Territorial Tucson." *Spanish in Context* 7, no. 1 (2010): 25–45.

DuPuy, William Atherton. *The Baron of the Colorados*. San Antonio, Tex.: Naylor, 1940.

———. *Hawaii and Its Race Problem*. Washington, D.C.: Government Printing Office,
1932.

———. *Uncle Sam's Modern Miracles*. New York: Frederick A. Stokes, 1914.

"Ellen Drew, 89, Film Star of 30's and 40's, Dies." *New York Times*, December 9, 2003.

Ellinghaus, Katherine. *Blood Will Tell: Native Americans and Assimilation Policy*. Lincoln: University of Nebraska Press, 2017.

Evans, Mark B. "Text of Governor Brewer's Speech after Signing SB 1070." *Tucson Citizen*, April 23, 2010. http://tucsoncitizen.com/mark-evans/2010/04/23/text-of-gov
-brewers-speech-after-signing-sb-1070/.

Fojas, Camilla. *Border Bandits: Hollywood on the Southern Frontier*. Austin: University
of Texas Press, 2008.

Foley, Neil. *Mexicans in the Making of America*. Cambridge, Mass.: Harvard University
Press, 2014.

"Following the Frontier Line, 1790 to 1890." U.S. Census Bureau, September 6, 2012.
https://www.census.gov/dataviz/visualizations/001/.

Foucault, Michel. *The Archaeology of Knowledge*. New York: Vintage Books, 2010.

Fregoso, Rosa Linda. *The Bronze Screen*. Minneapolis: University of Minnesota Press,
1993.

Fuller, Samuel, dir. *The Baron of Arizona*. 1950. New York: Eclipse Criterion Collection,
2007. DVD.

———. *A Third Face: My Tale of Writing, Fighting, and Filmmaking*. New York: Applause
Theater and Cinema Books, 2002.

Gal, S. "Language and Political Economy." *Annual Review of Anthropology* 18 (1989):
345–367.

Gersema, Emily. "Tucson Ethnic Studies Program Not Illegal, Audit Says." *Arizona
Republic*, June 16, 2011. http://archive.azcentral.com/news/election/azelections/articles
/2011/06/16/20110616tucson-ethnic-studies-audit0616.html.

Ginsberg, Elaine. *Passing and the Fictions of Identity*. Durham, N.C.: Duke University
Press, 1996.

Godard, Jean-Luc, dir. *Pierrot le Fou*. Films Georges de Beauregard, 1965.

Gómez, Laura E. *Manifest Destinies: The Making of the Mexican American Race*. New York: New York University Press, 2007.

González, Deena J. *Refusing the Favor: The Spanish-Mexican Women of Santa Fe, 1820–1880*. Oxford: Oxford University Press, 1999.

González, Jovita, and Eve Raleigh. *Caballero: A Historical Novel*. College Station: Texas A&M University Press, 1996.

Gonzales-Day, Ken. *Lynching in the West, 1850–1935*. Durham, N.C.: Duke University Press, 2006.

Gordon, Marsha. *Film Is like a Battleground: Sam Fuller's War Movies*. New York: Oxford University Press, 2017.

"Grant Cases Dismissed. Peralta-Reavis Grant Pronounced Purely Fictitious by the U.S. Land Court. Reavis Arrested by the United States Marshal—Juan Gid Grant Declared Void." *Daily New Mexican* (Santa Fe), June 25, 1895.

"The Great Peralta Grant: Sensational Developments in Regard to the Old Spanish Grant." *Salt Lake Weekly Tribune* (Salt Lake City, Utah), July 28, 1887.

Greenberg, Amy S. *Manifest Destiny and American Territorial Expansion: A Brief History with Documents*. Boston: Bedford/St. Martin's, 2012.

———. *A Wicked War: Polk, Clay, Lincoln, and the 1846 U.S. Invasion of Mexico*. New York: Vintage Books, 2012.

Griswold del Castillo, Richard. *The Treaty of Guadalupe Hidalgo: A Legacy of Conflict*. Norman: University of Oklahoma Press, 1990.

Guerin-Gonzales, Camille. *Mexican Workers and American Dreams: Immigration, Repatriation, and California Farm Labor, 1900–1939*. New Brunswick, N.J.: Rutgers University Press, 1994.

Gutiérrez, David. *Walls and Mirrors: Mexican Americans, Mexican Immigrants, and the Politics of Ethnicity*. Berkeley: University of California Press, 1995.

Gutiérrez, Ramón. "New Mexico, Mestizaje, and the Transnations of North America." In *Mexico and Mexicans in the Making of the United States*, edited by John Tutino, 257–284. Austin: University of Texas Press, 2012.

———. *When Jesus Came, the Corn Mothers Went Away: Marriage, Sexuality, and Power in New Mexico, 1500–1846*. Stanford, Calif.: Stanford University Press, 1991.

Haney López, Ian. *White by Law: The Legal Construction of Race*. New York: New York University Press, 1996.

Harris, Cheryl I. "Whiteness as Property." *Harvard Law Review* 106, no. 8 (1993): 1707–1791.

Harris, Verne. "The Archival Sliver: Power, Memory, and Archives in South Africa." *Archival Science* 2 (2002): 63–86.

Haywood, Ian. *Faking It: Art and the Politics of Forgery*. New York: St. Martin's, 1987.

"Historia de la Merced de Peralta." *El fronterizo* (Tucson), June 15, 1895.

"The Homestead Act of 1862." National Archives. Last updated Oct. 3, 2016. https://www.archives.gov/education/lessons/homestead-act.

Hoffman, Abraham. *Unwanted Mexican Americans in the Great Depression: Repatriation Pressures, 1929–1939*. Tucson: University of Arizona Press, 1974.

Hong, Grace. *The Ruptures of American Capital: Women of Color, Feminism, and the Culture of Immigrant Labor*. Minneapolis: University of Minnesota Press, 2006.

Horsman, Reginald. *Race and Manifest Destiny: The Origins of American Racial Anglo-Saxonism*. Cambridge, Mass.: Harvard University Press, 1986.

H.R. 2281, 49th Leg., 2d Reg. Sess. (Ariz. 2010). https://www.azleg.gov/legtext/49leg/2r/bills/hb2281s.pdf.

Huhndorf, Shari M. *Mapping the Americas: The Transnational Politics of Contemporary Native Culture*. Ithaca, N.Y.: Cornell University Press, 2009.

Huizar-Hernández, Anita. "The Specter of Statehood: Inventing Arizona in Charles D. Poston's *Building a State in Apache Land* and Marie Clara Zander's 'The Life of an Arizona Pioneer.'" *MELUS: Multi-ethnic Literature of the U.S.* 42, no. 2 (2017): 53–78.

Hurley, Chris. "Parallel Provenance (If These Are Your Records, Where Are Your Stories?)." *Archives and Manuscripts* 33, nos. 1, 2 (2005): 1–43.

"Impostor Now a Herder. Once Famous He Is Now Living a Recluse Life in New Mexico." *Kansas Semi-weekly Capital* (Topeka), October 5, 1900.

Ingersoll, Thomas. *To Intermix with Our White Brothers: Indian Mixed Bloods in the United States from Earliest Times to the Indian Removals*. Albuquerque: University of New Mexico Press, 2005.

Jacobson, Matthew Frye. *Whiteness of a Different Color: European Immigrants and the Alchemy of Race*. Cambridge, Mass.: Harvard University Press, 1999.

Jacoby, Karl. *Shadows at Dawn: An Apache Massacre and the Violence of History*. New York: Penguin, 2008.

Jenkinson, Hilary. *A Manual of Archive Administration*. London: Percy Lund, Humphries, 1937.

Johnson, Royal A. *Adverse Report of the Surveyor General of Arizona, Royal A. Johnson, upon the Alleged "Peralta Grant": A Complete Expose of Its Fraudulent Character*. [Phoenix]: Arizona Gazette Book and Job Office, 1890.

Kaplan, Amy. *The Anarchy of Empire in the Making of U.S. Culture*. Cambridge, Mass.: Harvard University Press, 2002.

Kaplan, Amy, and Donald E. Pease, eds. *Cultures of United States Imperialism*. Durham, N.C.: Duke University Press, 1993.

Kelland, Clarence Budington. "The Red Baron of Arizona." *Saturday Evening Post*, October 1947, 22–23, 76, 78, 81, 83–84, 89–90.

Keller, Gary. *Chicano Cinema: Research, Reviews, and Resources*. Binghamton, N.Y.: Bilingual Review/Press, 1985.

"La merced Peralta-Reavis. Esta por caer una magnífica estructura fundada en fraude y perjurio. El baron de Peralta un mito—la pretendida merced un fraude—la supuesta baronesa no pasa de ser una coyota." *El nuevo mexicano* (Santa Fe, N. Mex.), June 8, 1895.

Lazo, Rodrigo. "Introduction: Historical Latinidades and Archival Encounters." In *The Latino Nineteenth Century: Archival Encounters in American Literary History*, edited by Rodrigo Lazo and Jesse Alemán, 1–19. New York: New York University Press, 2016.

———. "The Invention of American Again: On the Impossibility of an Archive." *American Literary History* 25, no. 4 (2013): 751–771.

Lee, Jamie A. "Archives." In *The Routledge History of American Sexuality*, edited by Kevin P. Murphy, Jason Ruiz, and David Serlin. New York: Routledge, expected 2019.

Leeman, Jennifer. "Categorizing Latinos in the History of the US Census: The Official Racialization of Spanish." In *A Political History of Spanish: The Making of a Language*, edited by José del Valle, 305–323. Cambridge: Cambridge University Press, 2013.

LeMenager, Stephanie. *Manifest and Other Destinies: Territorial Fictions of the Nineteenth Century United States*. Lincoln: University of Nebraska Press, 2004.

Lewis, Nathaniel. "Truth or Consequences: Projecting Authenticity in the 1830s." In *True West: Authenticity and the American West*, edited by William Handley and Nathaniel Lewis, 21–37. Lincoln: University of Nebraska Press, 2004.

Lipschütz, Alejandro. *El indoamericanismo y el problema racial en las Américas*. Santiago: Chile Nascimiento, 1944.

Lipsitz, George. *The Possessive Investment in Whiteness: How White People Profit from Identity Politics*. Philadelphia: Temple University Press, 2006.

Luciano, Dana. "Introduction: On Moving Ground." In *Unsettled States: Nineteenth-Century American Literary Studies*, edited by Dana Luciano and Ivy G. Wilson, 1–28. New York: New York University Press, 2014.

Lummis, Charles Fletcher. "In the Lion's Den." *Land of Sunshine* 4, no. 2 (January 1896): 87–89.

Martínez, María Elena. *Genealogical Fictions: Limpieza de Sangre, Religion, and Gender in Colonial Mexico*. Stanford, Calif.: Stanford University Press, 2008.

McCormick, Thomas. "From Old Empire to New: The Changing Dynamics and Tactics of American Empire." In *The Colonial Crucible: Empire in the Making of the Modern American State*, edited by Alfred W. McCoy and Francisco A. Scarano, 63–80. Madison: University of Wisconsin Press, 2009.

McCoy, Alfred W., Francisco A. Scarano, and Courtney Johnson. "On the Tropic of Cancer: Transitions and Transformations in the U.S. Imperial State." In *The Colonial Crucible: Empire in the Making of the Modern American State*, edited by Alfred W. McCoy and Francisco A. Scarano, 3–33. Madison: University of Wisconsin Press, 2009.

McMahon, Marci. *Domestic Negotiations: Gender, Nation, and Self-Fashioning in US Mexicana and Chicana Literature and Art*. New Brunswick, N.J.: Rutgers University Press, 2013.

McWilliams, Carey. *North from Mexico: The Spanish-Speaking People of the United States*. New York: Greenwood, 1968.

Meeks, Eric V. *Border Citizens: The Making of Indians, Mexicans, and Anglos in Arizona*. Austin: University of Texas Press, 2007.

Meléndez, A. Gabriel. *Hidden Chicano Cinema: Film Dramas in the Borderlands*. New Brunswick, N.J.: Rutgers University Press, 2013.

Menchaca, Martha. "Chicano Indianism: A Historical Account of Racial Repression in the United States." *American Ethnologist* 20, no. 3 (1993): 583–603.

———. *Recovering History, Constructing Race: The Indian, Black, and White Roots of Mexican Americans*. Austin: University of Texas Press, 2001.

Millar, Laura. "The Death of the Fonds and the Resurrection of Provenance: Archival Context in Space and Time." *Archivaria* 53, no. 1 (2002): 1–15.

Molina, Natalia. *How Race Is Made in America: Immigration, Citizenship, and the Historical Power of Racial Scripts*. Berkeley: University of California Press, 2014.

Monroy, Douglas. *Rebirth: Mexican Los Angeles from the Great Migration to the Great Depression*. Berkeley: University of California Press, 1999.

Montejano, David. *Anglos and Mexicans in the Making of Texas, 1836–1986*. Austin: University of Texas Press, 1987.

Montoya, María E. *Translating Property: The Maxwell Land Grant and the Conflict over Land in the American West, 1840–1900*. Berkeley: University of California Press, 2002.

Mora, Anthony. *Border Dilemmas: Racial and National Uncertainties in New Mexico, 1848–1912*. Durham, N.C.: Duke University Press, 2011.

Muller, S., J. A. Feith, and R. Fruin. *Manual for the Arrangement and Description of Archives.* Translation of the 2nd ed. by Arthur H. Leavitt. New York: H. W. Wilson, 1940.

Namias, June. *White Captives: Gender and Ethnicity on the American Frontier.* Chapel Hill: University of North Carolina Press, 1993.

Nericcio, William Anthony. *Tex{t}-Mex: Seductive Hallucinations of the "Mexican" in America.* Austin: University of Texas Press, 2007.

Nesmith, Tom. "Still Fuzzy, but More Accurate: Some Thoughts on the 'Ghosts' of Archival Theory." *Archivaria* 47 (1999): 136–150.

Nieto-Phillips, John. *The Language of Blood: The Making of Spanish-American Identity in New Mexico, 1880s–1930s.* Albuquerque: University of New Mexico Press, 2004.

Noel, Linda C. *Debating American Identity: Southwestern Statehood and Mexican Immigration.* Tucson: University of Arizona Press, 2014.

Noriega, Chon. "Introduction: Chicanos and Film." In *Chicanos and Film: Essays on Chicano Representation and Resistance,* edited by Chon Noriega, xi–xxv. New York: Garland, 1992.

Officer, James. *Hispanic Arizona, 1536–1856.* Tucson: University of Arizona Press, 1989.

Omi, Michael, and Howard Winant. *Racial Formation in the United States.* 3rd ed. New York: Routledge, 2015.

"Open Letter to M. A. Smith." *Tombstone (Ariz.) Epitaph,* Oct. 19, 1890.

O'Sullivan, John L. "Annexation." *United States Magazine and Democratic Review* 17, no. 85 (1845): 5–10.

———. "The Great Nation of Futurity." *United States Magazine and Democratic Review* 6, no. 23 (1839): 426–430.

Padget, Martin. "Travel, Exoticism, and the Writing of the Region: Charles Fletcher Lummis and the 'Creation' of the Southwest." *Journal of the Southwest* 37, no. 3 (1995): 421–449.

Paredes, Raymund. "The Evolution of Chicano Literature." In *Three American Literatures: Essays in Chicano, Native American, and Asian American Literature for Teachers of American Literature,* edited by Houston A. Baker Jr., 33–79. New York: Modern Language Association, 1982.

Pease, Donald E. *National Identities and Post-Americanist Narratives.* Durham, N.C.: Duke University Press, 1994.

———. *The New American Exceptionalism.* Minneapolis: University of Minnesota Press, 2009.

"The Peralta Claim. Array of Public Men Who Are Interested in the Scheme. Opinions That It Is Bolstered Up by Manufactured Testimony." *Tombstone (Ariz.) Epitaph,* August 6, 1887.

"Peralta-Reavis Case. Hearing Concluded and Case Submitted without Argument—Decision May Be Expected Soon—Fraudulent Character of Grant Clearly Established." *Daily New Mexican* (Santa Fe), June 19, 1895.

"Peralta-Reavis Grant Case. Wonderful Structure Founded on Fraud, Perjury and Forgery About to Fall. Baron Peralta a Myth—The Alleged Grant a Fraud—Pretended Baroness a Half-Breed Indian." *Daily New Mexican* (Santa Fe), June 3, 1895.

Pérez, Emma. *The Decolonial Imaginary: Writing Chicanas into History.* Bloomington: Indiana University Press, 1999.

Powell, Donald M. *The Peralta Grant: James Addison Reavis and the Barony of Arizona.* Norman: University of Oklahoma Press, 1960.

Procter, Ben. *William Randolph Hearst: The Early Years, 1863–1910.* Oxford: Oxford University Press, 1998.

Pry, Mark E. "Arizona and the Politics of Statehood, 1889–1912." PhD diss., Arizona State University, 1995.

———. "Statehood Politics and Territorial Development: The Arizona Constitution of 1891." *Journal of Arizona History* 35, no. 4 (1994): 397–426.

Ramírez Berg, Charles. *Latino Images in Film: Stereotypes, Subversion, and Resistance.* Austin: University of Texas Press, 2002.

Ramos, Raúl A. *Beyond the Alamo: Forging Mexican Ethnicity in San Antonio, 1821–1861.* Chapel Hill: University of North Carolina Press, 2008.

"Reavis Written Up." *Weekly Phoenix Herald,* January 27, 1898.

"Recovering the U.S. Hispanic Literary Heritage." Arte Público Press. Accessed April 19, 2017. https://artepublicopress.com/recovery-project/.

Renshaw, Charles, Jr. "The Baron of Arizona." *American Weekly* (New York), January 9, 1949.

Rivera, John-Michael. *The Emergence of Mexican America: Recovering Stories of Mexican Peoplehood in U.S. Culture.* New York: New York University Press, 2006.

Robinson, Amy. "It Takes One to Know One: Passing and Communities of Common Interest." *Critical Inquiry* 20, no. 4 (1994): 715–736.

Roediger, David. *The Wages of Whiteness: Race and the Making of the American Working Class.* New York: Verso, 1991.

———. *Working Toward Whiteness: How America's Immigrants Became White, The Strange Journey from Ellis Island to the Suburbs.* New York: Basic Books, 2005.

Roggenkamp, Karen. *Narrating the News: New Journalism and Literary Genre in Late Nineteenth-Century American Newspapers and Fiction.* Kent: Kent State University Press, 2005.

Rosaldo, Renato. *Culture and Truth: The Remaking of Social Analysis.* Boston: Beacon, 1989.

Roybal, Karen R. *Archives of Dispossession: Recovering the Testimonios of Mexican American Herederas, 1848–1960.* Chapel Hill: University of North Carolina Press, 2017.

Ruíz de Burton, María Amparo. *The Squatter and the Don.* Houston: Arte Público, 1997.

S. 1070, 49th Leg., 2d Reg. Sess. (Ariz. 2010). https://www.azleg.gov/legtext/49leg/2r/bills/sb1070s.pdf.

Saldaña-Portillo, María Josefina. *Indian Given: Racial Geographies across Mexico and the United States.* Durham, N.C.: Duke University Press, 2016.

Sánchez, George J. *Becoming Mexican American: Ethnicity, Culture, and Identity in Chicano Los Angeles, 1900–1945.* Oxford: Oxford University Press, 1993.

Sánchez, Rosaura. *Telling Identities: The Californio Testimonios.* Minneapolis: University of Minnesota Press, 1995.

Schellenberg, Theodore. "The Appraisal of Modern Public Records." *Bulletins of the National Archives* 8 (1956): 1–46.

Shear, Michael D., and Thomas Gibbons-Neff. "Trump Sending 5,200 Troops to the Border in an Election-Season Response to Migrants." *New York Times,* October 29, 2018.

Shepherd, Elizabeth. "Culture and Evidence: Or What Good Are the Archives? Archives and Archivists in Twentieth Century England." *Archival Science* 9 (December 2009): 173–185.

Sheridan, Thomas. *Arizona: A History*. Tucson: University of Arizona Press, 2012.

Sherman, George, dir. *The Night Riders*. Republic Pictures, 1939.

Silva Gruesz, Kirsten. "Unsettlers and Speculators." *PMLA* 131, no. 3 (2016): 743–751.

Simmon, Scott. *The Invention of the Western Film: A Cultural History of the Genre's First Half-Century*. Cambridge: Cambridge University Press, 2003.

Simpson, Audra. "From White into Red: Captivity Narratives as Alchemies of Race and Citizenship." *American Quarterly* 60, no. 2 (2008): 251–257.

"Skulduggery in Arizona Land Office." *New York Times*, June 23, 1950.

Slotkin, Richard. *Gunfighter Nation: The Myth of the Frontier in Twentieth-Century America*. New York: Atheneum, 1992.

Smith, Andrea. *Conquest: Sexual Violence and American Indian Genocide*. Cambridge, Mass.: South End, 2005.

Smith, Andrew Brodie. *Shooting Cowboys and Indians: Silent Western Films, American Culture, and the Birth of Hollywood*. Boulder: University Press of Colorado, 2003.

Smith, Henry Nash. *Virgin Land: The American West as Symbol and Myth*. Cambridge, Mass.: Harvard University Press, 1970.

Smith, Imogen Sara. *In Lonely Places: Film Noir beyond the City*. Jefferson, N.C.: McFarland, 2011.

Sommer, Doris. *Foundational Fictions: The National Romances of Latin America*. Berkeley: University of California Press, 1991.

Stanfield, Peter. *Maximum Movies Pulp Fictions: Film Culture and the Worlds of Samuel Fuller, Mickey Spillane, and Jim Thompson*. New Brunswick, N.J.: Rutgers University Press, 2011.

Steedman, Carolyn. *Dust: The Archive and Cultural History*. New Brunswick, N.J.: Rutgers University Press, 2002.

Stoler, Ann Laura. *Along the Archival Grain: Epistemic Anxieties and Colonial Common Sense*. Princeton, N.J.: Princeton University Press, 2009.

"A Strange Story. A Company Organized to Improve the Peralta Land Grant in Arizona." *Daily Inter Ocean* (Chicago), July 28, 1887.

Streeby, Shelley. *American Sensations: Class, Empire, and the Production of Popular Culture*. Berkeley: University of California Press, 2002.

Sweeney, Edwin R. *Cochise: Chiricahua Apache Chief*. Norman: University of Oklahoma Press, 1991.

Taylor, Diana. *The Archive and the Repertoire*. Durham, N.C.: Duke University Press, 2003.

"33 Features, 6 Shorts on Lippert Lineup." *Boxoffice* (New York), September 17, 1949.

Tipton, William M. "The Prince of Impostors." *Land of Sunshine* 8, no. 3 (1898): 107–118.

———. "The Prince of Impostors (Concluded)." *Land of Sunshine* 8, no. 4 (1898): 161–170.

Tompkins, Jane. *West of Everything: The Inner Life of Westerns*. Oxford: Oxford University Press, 1992.

Transcript of Testimony Taken on Trial of the Case before the Court of Private Land Claims at Santa Fe, New Mexico, June 1–17, 1895. Rolls 62–63, Coll. 1972-007. Spanish Archives of New Mexico I, New Mexico State Archives (Santa Fe).

"Treaty of Guadalupe Hidalgo." Library of Congress. Accessed March 18, 2017. http://memory.loc.gov/cgi-bin/ampage?collId=llsl&fileName=009/llsl009.db&recNum=983.

Trouillot, Michel-Rolph. *Silencing the Past: Power and the Production of History*. Boston: Beacon, 1995.

Turner, Fredrick Jackson. *The Frontier in American History*. New York: Henry Holt, 1921.

Utley, Robert. *The Indian Frontier, 1846–1890*. Albuquerque: University of New Mexico Press, 2003.

Valerio-Jiménez, Omar S. *River of Hope: Forging Identity and Nation in the Rio Grande Borderlands*. Durham, N.C.: Duke University Press, 2013.

Vizenor, Gerald. *Manifest Manners: Postindian Warriors of Survivance*. Hanover, N.H.: University Press of New England, 1994.

Vosoughi, Soroush, Deb Roy, and Sinan Aral. "The Spread of True and False News Online." *Science* 359, no. 6380 (2018): 1146–1151. http://science.sciencemag.org/content/359/6380/1146/tab-pdf.

Watts, Jennifer. "Photography in the Land of Sunshine: Charles Fletcher Lummis and the Regional Ideal." *Southern California Quarterly* 87, no. 4 (2005–2006): 339–376.

Weber, David J. *Foreigners in Their Native Land: Historical Roots of the Mexican Americans*. Albuquerque: University of New Mexico Press, 1996.

Wilbur, Ray Lyman. Introduction to *Hawaii and Its Race Problem*, by William Atherton DuPuy. Washington: Government Printing Office, 1932.

"William A. DuPuy: United States Census, 1920." FamilySearch, March 18, 2014. https://familysearch.org/ark:/61903/1:1:MNLT-X19.

"William Atherton DuPuy." Find a Grave, March 5, 2010. https://www.findagrave.com/cgi-bin/fg.cgi?page=gr&GRid=49176446&ref=acom.

"William Atherton DuPuy: United States Passport Applications." FamilySearch, March 18, 2014. https://familysearch.org/ark:/61903/1:1:QV5B-3DZZ.

Wolfe, Patrick. "Settler Colonialism and the Elimination of the Native." *Journal of Genocide Research* 8, no. 4 (2006): 387–409.

Wurl, Joel. "Ethnicity as Provenance: In Search of Values and Principles for Documenting the Immigrant Experience." *Archival Issues* 29, no. 1 (2005): 65–76.

Index

Note: Figures are identified by *f* following the page reference.

About the Author

Anita Huizar-Hernández is an assistant professor of border studies in the Department of Spanish and Portuguese at the University of Arizona. She holds a PhD in literature (cultural studies) from the University of California, San Diego, where she specialized in literatures and cultures of the U.S.-Mexico borderlands. Her research examines how narratives, both real and imagined, have shaped the political, economic, and cultural landscape of the Southwest. Her work has appeared in *MELUS, SAIL, Aztlán*, and *English Language Notes*.

Desirée A. Martín, *Borderlands Saints: Secular Sanctity in Chicano/a and Mexican Culture*

Marci R. McMahon, *Domestic Negotiations: Gender, Nation, and Self-Fashioning in US Mexicana and Chicana Literature and Art*

A. Gabriel Meléndez, *Hidden Chicano Cinema: Film Dramas in the Borderlands*

Priscilla Peña Ovalle, *Dance and the Hollywood Latina: Race, Sex, and Stardom*

Amalia Pallares, *Family Activism: Immigrant Struggles and the Politics of Noncitizenship*

Luis F. B. Plascencia, *Disenchanting Citizenship: Mexican Migrants and the Boundaries of Belonging*

Cecilia M. Rivas, *Salvadoran Imaginaries: Mediated Identities and Cultures of Consumption*

Jayson Gonzales Sae-Saue, *Southwest Asia: The Transpacific Geographies of Chicana/o Literature*

Mario Jimenez Sifuentez, *Of Forest and Fields: Mexican Labor in the Pacific Northwest*

Maya Socolovsky, *Troubling Nationhood in U.S. Latina Literature: Explorations of Place and Belonging*

Susan Thananopavarn, *LatinAsian Cartographies*